Understanding the CDM 2007
Regulations

Understanding the CDM 2007 Regulations

2nd Edition

Owen V. Griffiths and
Alun V. Griffiths

Spon Press
an imprint of Taylor & Francis
LONDON AND NEW YORK

First edition published 2007
by Spon Press

This second edition published 2011
by Spon Press
2 Park Square, Milton Park, Abingdon, Oxon OX14 4RN

Simultaneously published in the USA and Canada
by Spon Press
270 Madison Avenue, New York, NY 10016, USA

*Spon Press is an imprint of the Taylor & Francis Group,
an informa business*

© 2011 Owen V. Griffiths and Alun V. Griffiths

Typeset in Sabon by Pindar NZ, Auckland, New Zealand
Printed and bound in Great Britain by
CPI Antony Rowe, Chippenham, Wiltshire

British Library Cataloguing in Publication Data
A catalogue record for this book is available from the British Library

Library of Congress Cataloging-in-Publication Data
Griffiths, Owen V.
   Understanding the CDM 2007 regulations / Owen V. Griffiths and
   Alun V. Griffiths. — 2nd ed.
      p. cm.
   Originally published: Understanding the CDM regulations. 2006.
   1. Great Britain. Construction (Design and Management)
Regulations 1994. 2. Construction industry—Safety
regulations—Great Britain. I. Griffiths, Alun V. II. Title. III. Title:
Understanding the CDM regulations.
   KD3172.C6G75 2011

   343.41'078624—dc22   2010028613

ISBN13: 978-0-415-55653-8 (pbk)
ISBN13: 978-0-203-86930-7 (ebk)

Contents

Illustrations

Acknowledgements

This book references indirectly *Managing Health and Safety in Construction: Construction (Design and Management) Regulations 2007*, Approved Code of Practice L144, 2007, HSE Books

Crown Copyright material is reproduced with the permission of the Controller of HMSO and the Queen's Printer for Scotland.

Introduction

This book has been written to provide construction students, CDM duty holders, health and safety consultants and construction professionals with practical advice on the Construction (Design and Management) Regulations 2007 (CDM) and their intended objectives. It also appreciates that organisations and individual project duty holders need clear arrangements and tools to facilitate practical application. The book also aims to provide guidance on designing appropriate and succinct management systems to facilitate compliance.

The theme of the book is that if CDM is to work it must be an integrated, indeed embedded, element of all the planning, design, management and construction functions. It is understood that professionals in the construction industry have many elements to manage at various stages throughout a project. The CDM Regulations provide additional impetus for one more manageable element – namely, the 'hazard'.

The benefits of an effective CDM strategy at a project level will also be covered and the additional added value of such a policy will be illustrated with case studies throughout.

The book consists of eight chapters plus appendices. The first chapter contains an overview of health and safety in the construction industry, legislation and the fundamental principles of the CDM Regulations themselves. As we develop this holistic picture of health and safety in the construction industry we shall prove the case for the necessity of appropriate project hazard management arrangements. This will allow us to provide more detail in the subsequent chapters.

Chapter 2 covers the role of the CDM client. One could argue that without their commitment to risk management, and without the client establishing clearly defined CDM project arrangements, the effective management of health and safety is significantly weakened. We will also attempt to establish how the regulations aim to cater for the diversity of client types, the wide disparity of client knowledge and the respective procurement routes.

Chapter 3 looks at the role of and issues pertaining to the CDM co-ordinator. This duty holder was established fundamentally to assist the client with their duties. They need the necessary skill set to fully integrate their functions into the project, facilitate design risk management and continually monitor the effectiveness of the arrangements for safety management to be able to advise the client. This requires sufficient knowledge of the design process, construction processes *and* considerable understanding of occupational health and safety legislation. As well as addressing their statutory responsibilities, we will debate their respective effectiveness since the introduction of the regulations and ask who is best placed to undertake this role on a project.

Chapter 4 covers the role of designers. They have the ability and potential to initially impact on the health and safety of a project by virtue of their duty to inform the client of their CDM duties. Also, arguably their greatest contribution comes from their duty to design with adequate regard to health and safety. Early and ongoing intervention by a designer in designing to avoid or reduce the impact of environmental and social issues, and hazards associated with certain materials and construction activities, has significant benefits on the health and safety risk profile of a project. There is, however, certain evidence to suggest that this potential is not being fully realised and the design fraternity is failing to make a demonstrable contribution to the risk management process. The CDM Regulations also define a designer as more than the traditional architect or engineer and this far-reaching definition will be explored.

Chapter 5 explores the duties of the principal contractor and the responsibility they have to manage all aspects of health and safety during the construction phase of a project. The principal contractor is usually, but not always, the main contractor on a construction project. We shall explore their statutory responsibilities and, by means of case studies, look at examples of good practice that exist to communicate and co-ordinate health and safety where it matters most – on site.

Chapter 6 looks at the role of the contractor and their working relationship with the principal contractor as a part of the site team. Contractors have been facilitating health and safety legislation long before the introduction of CDM and it is interesting to see how they have integrated their CDM duties into their risk management procedures.

Chapter 7 looks at the CDM duties that apply specifically to health and safety on construction sites. This includes statutory requirements for such issues and activities as site security, demolition, temporary works, excavations, cofferdams, caissons, reports of inspections, traffic routes, fire safety, emergency routes and exits, fresh air, temperature and weather protection and lighting. It will also be beneficial at this point to look at the requirements of the Work at Height Regulations 2005, as falls from height remain the single highest cause of fatalities in the construction industry.

Chapter 8 provides a complete CDM system of all duty holders, including a useful project checklist. This will make the book more practically useful and set you on your way to actively applying the learning outcomes from the text.

As you read through the book, it is very important to develop your own thoughts on the CDM Regulations and their potential effectiveness in reducing fatalities, injuries and incidents of ill health. According to the Health and Safety Executive, in the past 25 years more than 2,800 people have died from injuries they received as a result of construction work, and many more have been seriously injured or made ill. It is only by wrestling with our social responsibilities, through individual opinions and debate, that improvements are made in legislation.

1 Overview of the CDM Regulations

What are the CDM Regulations?

History of the CDM Regulations

As a member state of the European Union the UK is subject to legal directives, which it must interpret and implement. Such directives impose a duty on each member state to:

- make regulations to conform with any directive
- enforce those regulations.

The Construction (Design and Management) Regulations are, therefore, the UK's response to EU Directive 92/57 EEC 'The Management of Health and Safety Requirements at Temporary or Mobile Construction Sites'. Although, arguably, existing health and safety legislation was already in place to cover many of the areas it was hoped CDM would address, such as the Health and Safety at Work etc. Act 1974 and the Management of Health and Safety at Work Regulations 1992 (now 1999), it was deemed necessary to provide additional impetus for construction safety. The regulations became effective on 31 March 1995 and marked a new era in construction health and safety management.

Then, following a thorough and lengthy consultation process involving the Health and Safety Commission (since merged with Health and Safety Executive) and the construction industry itself, the CDM Regulations were revised in an attempt to further engage the project team and improve clarity, and were reintroduced with several significant modifications on 6 April 2007 as the Construction (Design and Management) Regulations 2007.

An Approved Code of Practice to support the regulations was then published which attempted to offer advice and guidance on practical implementation of the regulations. The construction industry also initially produced a series of guidance documents on specific areas of CDM to assist those having to implement the new legislation. The legal status of the Approved Code of Practice and the industry guidance documents will be clarified elsewhere in this chapter.

The current regulations place a heavy emphasis on the general principles of competence, co-operation and co-ordination across the team and the principles of risk management. They also provide the respective duty holder with the confidence to apply an appropriate health and safety management approach and avoid an overly bureaucratic strategy. The Approved Code of Practice offers the following comfort:

> The effort devoted to planning and managing health and safety should be in proportion to the risks and complexity associated with the project. When deciding what you need to do to comply with these Regulations, your focus should always be on action necessary to reduce and manage

risks. Any paperwork produced should help with communication and risk management. Paperwork which adds little to the management of risk is a waste of effort, and can be a dangerous distraction from the real business of risk reduction and management.

Health and safety in the construction industry

The construction industry is quite simply the largest industry in the UK and constitutes approximately 9 per cent of the UK's gross domestic product. It has been estimated that over 2 million people work in the construction industry.

Given the industry is so diverse and wide-ranging, it is generally regarded as a relatively high-risk industry to work in. For example, Health and Safety Executive statistics remind us that:

*   since 1985 2,800 people have died from injuries received as a result of construction work;
*   asbestos-related diseases cause an estimated 4,000 deaths each year;
*   an estimated 11.6 million working days a year are lost to work-related muscular skeletal disorders, many of which are in the construction industry (http://www.hse.gov.uk/statistics).

There has been a major move by the industry itself to improve the appalling levels of fatalities, major injuries and incidences of ill health over the last few years. The first construction summit was held in February 2001 where the industry decided to set targets for reducing the rate of fatal and major injury to workers by 66 per cent by 2009/10. The summit was seen as an

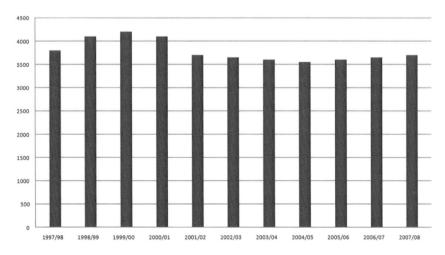

Figure 1.1 Number of major injuries in the construction industry, 1997–2007

opportunity to raise the profile of construction health and safety and the bold targets set there showed an impressive intent. Other important initiatives include, *Revitalising Health and Safety, Rethinking Construction* (the Egan Report), and *Achieving Excellence in Construction.*

The introduction of the CDM Regulations themselves must also be viewed as a major opportunity for the project team to further focus on the specific health and safety issues. The following quotation from John Egan is very much in line with the ideology that CDM is striving to achieve:

> I [. . .] passionately believe in the importance of tackling the industry's health and safety problems. Pre-planned, well designed projects, where inherently safe processes have been chosen, which are carried out by companies known to be competent, with trained work forces, will be safe: they will also be good, predictable projects. If we are to succeed in creating a modern, world class industry, the culture of the industry must change. It must value and respect its people, learn to work in integrated teams and deliver value for clients' money.
>
> Sir John Egan, *Accelerating Change*, 2002[1]

Health and safety legislation in the UK

In order to appreciate the significance of the CDM Regulations in legal terms we will now, albeit briefly, look at the legal framework in the United Kingdom as well as our obligations as a member state of the European Union.

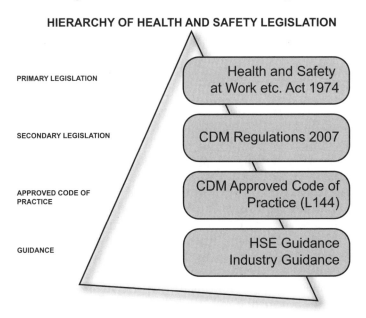

HIERARCHY OF HEALTH AND SAFETY LEGISLATION

PRIMARY LEGISLATION — Health and Safety at Work etc. Act 1974

SECONDARY LEGISLATION — CDM Regulations 2007

APPROVED CODE OF PRACTICE — CDM Approved Code of Practice (L144)

GUIDANCE — HSE Guidance Industry Guidance

Figure 1.2 Legal framework

The Health and Safety at Work etc. Act 1974 (HSWA)

This is the primary source of health and safety legislation in the United Kingdom. It was introduced to unify existing legislation and raise awareness of occupational health and safety. It aimed to move the focus on to 'people at work' in an attempt to reduce the general apathy that surrounded the subject of health and safety at the time.

The Act provided bold general duties for employers, the self-employed and even employees. For example:

> It shall be the duty of every employer to ensure, so far as is reasonably practicable, the health, safety and welfare at work of all his employees.
>
> HSWA section 2(1)

The Act also makes it necessary for employers to conduct their undertakings in such a way as to ensure, as far as is reasonably practicable, that persons not in their employment who may be affected thereby are not exposed to risk to their health and safety. The health and safety of the general public would be a good example of a cohort that an employer must consider.

Significantly, the Act also established both the Health and Safety Commission and the Health and Safety Executive (now merged into a single entity under the latter name). The former was established to primarily make arrangements to ensure the health and safety of people and work and those affected by that work. This is achieved through the proposal of new legislation and standards, instigating and conducting research and providing information and advice.

The Act also has the ability to make specific health and safety regulations, which serve to strengthen and support the principles of the primary legislation.

Regulations

The Health and Safety Executive (HSE) will, from time to time, propose additional legislation to facilitate its work. This is generally achieved through a regulation that would be brought into force under the Act. The proposal is made to, and introduced by, the appropriate government minister.

Regulations are seen as an appropriate means of setting new health and safety standards in a relatively quick timescale. A proposed regulation will automatically become law 21 days after submission to Parliament if no objections are made.

However, before the Executive proposes any new legislation it will consult with all interested parties, such as relevant industry bodies and trade unions.

Regulations are also used as a tool to implement the requirements of EU directives, as indeed was the case with the CDM Regulations.

There are numerous other health and safety regulations that are potentially relevant to the construction industry over and above CDM. Effectively, it could be argued that CDM sits above many of these other regulations as a management platform for their successful implementation and consequent risk reduction. It would be of value for a construction professional to have a general grounding in the most relevant regulations.

Examples of Health and Safety Regulations (that can be relevant to construction work) include:

- Management of Health and Safety at Work Regulations 1999
- Work at Height Regulations 2005
- Control of Substances Hazardous to Health Regulations 2002 (COSHH)
- Control of Asbestos Regulations 2006
- Lifting Operations and Lifting Equipment Regulations 1998 (LOLER)
- Provision and Use of Work Equipment Regulations 1998 (PUWER)
- Manual Handling Operations Regulations 1992
- Control of Noise at Work Regulations 2005
- Control of Vibration at Work Regulations 2005
- Health and Safety (First Aid) Regulations 1981
- Personal Protective Equipment Regulations 1992
- Reporting of Injuries, Diseases and Dangerous Occurrences Regulations 1995 (RIDDOR).

Approved Code of Practice

If it is felt that further clarity and practical guidance are necessary to facilitate compliance with a regulation, then it may be necessary to introduce an Approved Code of Practice (ACoP). It is important to understand the legal status of an ACoP. It is not a legal requirement to follow the information provided by any ACoP. However, failure to adopt the recommendations of the document in practice may be taken by a court in any criminal proceedings as evidence of failure to comply with the regulation to which it relates. Only if the defendant has demonstrated compliance by an alternative equally effective measure will this not count against them.

In terms of the CDM Regulations 2007, an ACoP was introduced immediately to assist with providing advice and guidance with the practical application of the regulations. This publication, *Managing Construction for Health and Safety* (L144), was well received by the industry with increased clarity and examples of good practice.

Guidance notes

One of the main reasons, therefore, for the relative success of the Approved Code of Practice was the fact that the document also contained a wealth of guidance and good practice for CDM duty holders to consider as they strived for compliance with the regulations.

A series of additional guidance documents has also been published by the Construction Industry Training Board with contributions from the industry itself. These are aimed at providing further practical advice and suggestions and can be more informative.

Guidance notes carry no legal standing but examples of case law do exist where the lack of adoption of guidance notes has been successfully used as evidence for the prosecution.

Enforcement of the CDM Regulations

The HSE has a specific statutory responsibility of its own for the enforcement of health and safety law, including, therefore, the CDM Regulations. The HSE has a number of inspectors whose primary objective is to encourage compliance with health and safety legislation. To this end the inspectors are awarded substantial powers to facilitate this aim and achieve improvements. These powers include the following:

1. Entering premises, at any reasonable time, if the inspector believes it is necessary to carry out any statutory provision, and taking a police constable along if deemed appropriate.
2. Providing advice or warnings.
3. Issuing an improvement notice. This will require any contravention to be remedied in a time that would be specified. Anyone who receives an improvement notice will be entered onto the notices database on the Health and Safety Executive website, which is for public consumption.
4. Issuing a prohibition notice. If an inspector believes there is, or is likely to be, a risk of serious personal injury they may issue a prohibition notice to cease an activity at any time unless or until the issue is resolved. Anyone who receives a prohibition notice will also be entered onto the notices database on the Health and Safety Executive website, which is for public consumption.
5. Prosecution in the criminal law courts.
6. Investigations of accidents or incidents. This includes being able to direct that any premises or area be left undisturbed, take photographs and measurements, and samples of any articles or substances including atmospheric samples.
7. Asking any person (the inspector has reasonable cause to believe to be able to provide information) to answer such questions the inspector may consider appropriate.

Any breach of the CDM Regulations is deemed a criminal offence under statute law and can bring about judicial proceedings through the criminal courts. This is generally at a magistrates' court or crown court depending on the nature and severity of the alleged breach.

Application of the CDM Regulations

We will next look at the CDM Regulations in terms of when and to what extent they are applicable. It will be necessary to define two key terms that are central to assessing application – namely, 'construction work' and 'structure'. These terms are clearly defined in Part 2 of the regulations themselves and are included below.

We shall also assess when the Health and Safety Executive needs to be informed of an intention to initiate a construction project. The term 'notification' is used to describe this requirement.

Quite simply the regulations apply to:

- all construction work in Great Britain (including its territorial sea)
- both employers and self-employed with no distinction.

Interpretation

Given the regulations apply to 'all construction work' we must clearly establish what actually constitutes 'construction' by definition.

"construction work" means the carrying out of any building, civil engineering or engineering construction work and includes—

(a) the construction, alteration, conversion, fitting out, commissioning, renovation, repair, upkeep, redecoration or other maintenance (including cleaning which involves the use of water or an abrasive at high pressure or the use of corrosive or toxic substances), decommissioning, demolition or dismantling of a structure;

(b) the preparation for an intended structure, including site clearance, exploration, investigation (but not site survey) and excavation, and the clearance or preparation of the site or structure for use or occupation at its conclusion;

(c) the assembly on site of prefabricated elements to form a structure or the disassembly on site of prefabricated elements which, immediately before such disassembly, formed a structure;

(d) the removal of a structure or of any product or waste resulting from demolition or dismantling of a structure or from disassembly of prefabricated elements which immediately before such disassembly formed such a structure; and

(e) the installation, commissioning, maintenance, repair or removal of mechanical, electrical, gas, compressed air, hydraulic, telecommunications, computer or similar services which are normally fixed within or to a structure.

Extract from CDM Regulation 2(1)

As the above definition of construction makes reference to a 'structure' or 'a part of a structure' a further definition is required.

"structure" means—

(a) any building, timber, masonry, metal or reinforced concrete structure, railway line or siding, tramway line, dock, harbour, inland navigation, tunnel, shaft, bridge, viaduct, waterworks, reservoir, pipe or pipe-line, cable, aqueduct, sewer, sewage works, gasholder, road, airfield, sea defence works, river works, drainage works, earthworks, lagoon, dam, wall, caisson, mast, tower, pylon, underground tank, earth retaining structure or structure designed to preserve or alter any natural feature, fixed plant and any structure similar to the foregoing; or

(b) any formwork, falsework, scaffold or other structure designed or used to provide support or means of access during construction work, and any reference to a structure includes a part of a structure.

Extract from CDM Regulation 2(1)

When notification is required

When considering the extent to which the regulations apply, there are basically two types of projects: 'notifiable projects' and 'non-notifiable projects'. Notification is a requirement to inform the Health and Safety Executive of certain particulars in relation to an intended project.

The following considerations determine whether the project is likely to require notification to the enforcement authority or is not notifiable (non-notifiable).

For the purposes of these Regulations, a project is notifiable if the construction phase is likely to involve more than—

(a) 30 days; or
(b) 500 person days,

of construction work.

CDM Regulation 2(3)

When estimating the number of days likely to be involved, consideration need only be given to days where construction work is due to take place. If no work is to take place – for example, at weekends or during holiday periods, then they would not count.

It is also necessary to appreciate that notification is not relevant to projects that have a domestic client. Domestic clients are further discussed in Chapter 2.

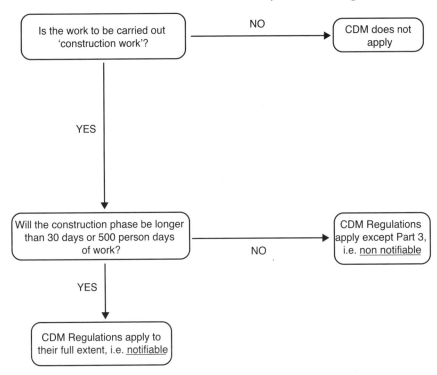

Figure 1.3 Application of CDM Regulations

CDM duty holders and their responsibilities

The principles of the CDM Regulations are simple in that they define responsibility and respective duties throughout all phases that make up a construction project. They have been designed to promote a proactive and integrated hazard management process that is addressed and communicated via defined means of communication and information flow.

There are five CDM duty holders:

- the client
- the CDM co-ordinator (notifiable projects only)
- the designer
- the principal contractor (notifiable projects only)
- the contractor.

As well as the specific requirements imposed on the above, there are general management duties imposed under Part 2 of the regulations on all CDM duty holders concerned in a project. These duties will be explored further once we have introduced the duty holders themselves.

The client

Without doubt the client holds the key to a project's success in terms of health and safety. They first have the opportunity to appoint the project team and, if all appointees are competent, cultured, work together and are resourced to address the issues likely to be involved, then health and safety management will truly become an integrated process of project management.

Second, the client has a major role to play in terms of providing relevant information to assist the team when making important design and planning decisions. Without information on the extent of existing services, ground contamination, asbestos and structural loadings, for example, it becomes unfair to expect designers and contractors to be expected to fulfil their respective roles effectively.

The degree of influence held by the client has not been lost by the regulations. So much so that the clients are charged under the regulations with ensuring that a project has robust and suitable arrangements throughout to facilitate the effective management of health and safety.

There are obviously varying degrees of client knowledge about health and safety legislation and management. Less experienced clients will depend on the designer or contractor to inform them of their duties as far as the CDM Regulations are concerned. On all but the smallest of projects the client will also engage a CDM co-ordinator to advise them of and assist them with their responsibilities in terms of health and safety management. Significantly, however, the client is unable to abdicate from their statutory CDM responsibilities as they are clearly seen as the key driver in delivering a successfully managed construction project.

The more experienced, professional construction clients are looking to establish good health and safety management procedures and protocols from the earliest opportunity. So-called 'smart clients' appreciate the valuable contribution they can make by setting high standards through appointments and through the provision of relevant information at the time it is needed.

There also exists a further opportunity for the client to contribute to the health and safety management process. They are charged (on notifiable projects) with ensuring that no construction work starts on site until a suitably developed construction phase plan has been produced by the principal contractor. This effectively acts as a procedural gateway to ensure that appropriate health and safety management arrangements exist on site.

Summary of client's duties

All projects

- Assess competence and resources of all appointees.
- Ensure there are suitable management arrangements for the project (including welfare facilities).
- Allow sufficient time and resources for all stages.
- Client to provide pre-construction information to designers and contractors.

Additional duties for a notifiable project

- Appoint a CDM co-ordinator and principal contractor.
- Ensure construction work does not begin until there is a suitably developed construction phase plan and adequate welfare facilities.
- Provide information relating to the health and safety file to the CDM co-ordinator.
- Make the health and safety file available.

Summarised from the CDM ACoP

The CDM co-ordinator

The EU directive on which CDM is based called for 'a co-ordinator of health and safety matters'. This duty holder was, therefore, created specifically as a result of the regulations themselves and, indeed, is often referred to as a 'creature of the regulations'. The CDM co-ordinator is essentially the facilitator of health and safety management throughout a project, and very much required to be the client's primary advisor on matters of construction health and safety management from the earliest design stages through to the conclusion of the construction phase.

The CDM co-ordinator also needs a close working relationship with the design team from an early stage as they are required to take all reasonable steps to ensure that designers fully consider all opportunities to manage hazards and minimise risk. This is because the CDM co-ordinator has a duty to ensure that the designers on a project actually comply with their CDM duties. Whether this function is limited to a CDM policeman or is undertaken as a more involved and helpful approach it is down to the level of risk involved and, equally, the competence of both duty holders.

The effectiveness of the CDM co-ordinator to perform a valuable and fully integrated part within a project team is reliant on several significant factors.

First, the timing of their appointment is critical. The late introduction of the CDM co-ordinator is seen as a lost opportunity to maximise hazard elimination and reduction from the outset of a project. If they are not involved in the initial design philosophy this sometimes can have negative consequences for those who must build, maintain, work in or even dismantle a structure. Be advised that the client has a legal duty to ensure this early appointment and, indeed, the designers also cannot legally move beyond initial design work until the CDM co-ordinator is in situ.

Second, and arguably essential to the holistic effectiveness of a project's health and safety strategy, is the competence and resources of the CDM co-ordinator. To appoint the right person, or indeed team of people, to be able to undertake the statutory duties is necessary. Clients and their advisors need to appreciate the skill set necessary to facilitate the role and also need to understand how they will achieve best value from their CDM co-ordinator.

Membership of certain organisations and inclusion on certain registers cannot be a guarantee of competence. Only when an appreciation of a project's health and safety risk profile requirements has been developed can a competent CDM co-ordinator be matched.

It has been suggested that the very need for a specific entity, a 'co-ordinator of health and safety matters' is a poor reflection on the significance tradition-ally afforded to health and safety management in construction design and management.

Summary of CDM co-ordinator's duties

- Advise and assist the client with his/her duties.
- Notify HSE.
- Co-ordinate health and safety aspects of design work.
- Co-operate with others involved with the project.
- Facilitate good communication between client, designers and contractors.
- Liaise with principal contractor regarding ongoing design.
- Identify, collect and pass on pre-construction information.
- Prepare/update health and safety file.

Summarised from the CDM ACoP

The designer

Anyone designing a structure or contributing towards the design of a structure has a duty to consider the health and safety implications of their choices in terms of avoiding risks to anyone carrying out construction work or cleaning work as well as anyone affected by this work.

Designers have immense power when it comes to avoiding or reducing the risks that arise day to day in construction and are legally bound to wield that power. Having said this, designers obviously have other influences to consider such as cost, aesthetics, building regulations, planning, environmental impact, party walls and so on.

Inevitably, designers assess the macro health and safety issues of structural form, loadings and materials, for example, but it has been suggested that they are not looking sufficiently at a systematic risk avoidance or reduction strategy for the people expected to construct and maintain their designs.

The term 'designer' in the CDM Regulations is far-reaching and the scope of the designer goes beyond that of the traditional architect or engineer. The full extent of who could be perceived as having designer duties will be clarified in Chapter 4. Suffice to say, when looking at who has designer duties under the regulations, that we need to consider the 'function' over the 'title'.

Summary of designer's duties

All projects

- Eliminate hazards and reduce risks during design.
- Provide information about remaining risks.

Additional duties for a notifiable project

- Check client is aware of duties and CDM co-ordinator has been appointed.
- Provide any information needed for the health and safety file.

Summarised from the CDM ACoP

The principal contractor

With the responsibility to manage health and safety throughout the construction phase, the principal contractor has numerous responsibilities under the CDM Regulations.

The principal contractor has emerged as a result of the CDM Regulations and it is important not to confuse the principal contractor with the main contractor or any other contractor. This duty holder is solely involved with the effective implementation of their responsibilities under the CDM Regulations.

Much of the work of the principal contractor relates to ensuring that the standards and rules set in the construction phase plan are adhered to on site. Their relationship with the contractors is pivotal to successful health and safety management during the construction period.

Summary of principal contractor's duties

- Plan, manage and monitor construction phase in liaison with contractor.
- Prepare, develop and implement a written plan and site rules.
- Give contractors relevant parts of the plan.

- Make sure suitable welfare facilities are provided from the start and maintained throughout the construction phase.
- Check competence of all appointees.
- Ensure all workers have site inductions and any further information and training needed for the work.
- Consult with the workers.
- Liaise with CDM co-ordinator regarding ongoing design.
- Secure the site.

Summarised from the CDM ACoP

The contractor

Contractors obviously have an important part to play in health and safety management as they are expected to carry out the actual construction work. Many are familiar with the principles of risk management as there is other legislation that requires employers, the self-employed and, indeed, employees to assess risks and adopt suitable control measures based on the principles of prevention.

As far as CDM in concerned, contractors need to co-operate and work closely with the principal contractor on notifiable projects in such a way as to consider and manage the health and safety implications of their work.

Also, whether the project is notifiable or non-notifiable, contractors must consider the requirements of Part 4 of the regulations, which refers specifically to duties relating to health and safety on construction sites.

Summary of contractor's duties

All projects

- Plan, manage and monitor own work and that of workers.
- Check competence of all their appointees and workers.
- Train own employees.
- Provide information to their workers.
- Comply with the specific requirements in Part 4 of the Regulations.
- Ensure there are adequate welfare facilities for their workers.

Additional duties for a notifiable project

- Check client is aware of duties and a CDM co-ordinator has been appointed and HSE notified before starting work.
- Co-operate with principal contractor in planning and managing work, including reasonable directions and site rules.
- Provide details to the principal contractor of any contractor whom he engages in connection with carrying out the work.
- Provide any information needed for the health and safety file.
- Inform principal contractor of problems with the plan.

> • **Inform principal contractor of reportable accidents, diseases and dangerous occurrences.**
>
> *Summarised from the CDM ACoP*

General management duties on all

Over and above the specific CDM duties placed on the client, CDM co-ordinator, designer, principal contractor and contractor, the regulations place a set of general duties on each of these in relation to competence, co-operation, co-ordination and a requirement to take account of the general principles of prevention.

Competence is a primary theme of the regulations. Any reference to 'competence' is to the competence of the respective duty holders in relation to their ability to undertake the requirements imposed on them by the regulations only. The regulations therefore offer that:

No person on whom these Regulations place a duty shall—

(a) appoint or engage a CDM co-ordinator, designer, principal contractor or contractor unless he has taken reasonable steps to ensure that the person to be appointed or engaged is competent;

(b) accept such an appointment or engagement unless he is competent;

(c) arrange for or instruct a worker to carry out or manage design or construction work unless the worker is;

    (i) competent, or

    (ii) under the supervision of a competent person.

CDM Regulation 4(1)

In an attempt to clarify what might define competence, in relation to one's ability to carry out one's CDM responsibilities, guidance has been provided following a research report undertaken by the Health and Safety Executive and included in the Approved Code of Practice.

We are advised that the focus when assessing the competence of any potential engagement should be proportionate to the risks, size and relative complexity of the project.

There is also a statutory requirement under these regulations for all duty holders to:

• seek the co-operation of any person involving construction work, either from within the same project or at an adjoining site; and
• co-operate with any person involving construction work, either from within the same project or at an adjoining site.

Also, every CDM duty holder has a duty to report any health and safety concerns they may have, with the regulations stating:

> Every person concerned in a project who is working under the control of another person shall report to that person anything which he is aware is likely to endanger the health or safety of himself or others.
>
> CDM Regulation 5(2)

A further general duty is placed on all those with responsibilities under these regulations to co-ordinate their activities to avoid harm. Again, this may appear to be very much a common-sense issue, but the law makers have felt it necessary to tell project teams to work together and co-ordinate actions to minimise risk. We are therefore told:

> All persons concerned in a project on whom a duty is placed by these Regulations shall co-ordinate their activities with one another in a manner which ensures, so far as is reasonably practicable, the health and safety of persons—
>
> (a) carrying out the construction work; and
> (b) affected by the construction work.
>
> CDM Regulation 6

All those with duties under the Construction (Design and Management) Regulations also have a requirement to consider what are called the 'general principles of prevention'. This terms refers to a requirement placed on employers and the self-employed by another piece of criminal legislation – namely, Regulation 4 of the Management of Health and Safety at Work Regulations 1999. It calls for the introduction of preventive and protective measures to control the risks identified by the risk assessment process.

Therefore, during the design, planning, preparation and construction phase of a project, all those with duties under the regulations need to consider the implementation of precautions that follow the principles listed below.

The general principles of prevention

(a) avoiding risks;
(b) evaluating the risks which cannot be avoided;
(c) combating the risks at source;
(d) adapting the work to the individual, especially as regards the design of workplaces, the choice of work equipment and the choice of working and production methods, with a view, in particular, to alleviating monotonous work and work at a predetermined work-rate and to reducing their effect on health;

(e) adapting to technical progress;
(f) replacing the dangerous by the non-dangerous or the less dangerous;
(g) developing a coherent overall prevention policy which covers technology, organisation of work, working conditions, social relationships and the influence of factors relating to the working environment;
(h) giving collective protective measures priority over individual protective measures; and
(i) giving appropriate instructions to employees.

Schedule 1 of the Management of Health and Safety at Work Regulations 1999

In summary, therefore, clients, designers, CDM co-ordinators, principal contractors and contractors, must, in relation to the design, planning, preparation and construction phase, ensure:

- competence has been considered in relation to the construction professionals being engaged, with regard to them being capable of complying with their respective duties within these regulations;
- sufficient co-operation exists among themselves as well as with any adjoining construction activities;
- there is a co-ordinated approach to undertaking their activities, as far as is reasonably practicable, to ensure the health and safety of those undertaking the construction work and also those affected by the construction work.

Project hazard management

If one of the primary objectives of the CDM Regulations is hazard management then the primary function of all duty holders to make their health and safety contribution at the appropriate stage of the project is fundamental.

Hazard management concepts

The definition of a hazard is 'something with the potential to cause harm'. The management of problems (or hazards) should be considered by all professionals as a part of the management function and not something that just health and safety people do. Most decisions in construction have an impact on design but also have financial, business risk, regulatory and health and safety implications. One could argue that most of the above are related and to make decisions independently is not prudent.

To simplify, hazards could be thought of as 'problems' and the undertaking to address these as 'actions'. Problems can be associated with the following categories on a project:

- Existing environment, which includes:
  - access to site, e.g. busy roads, shared access, low bridges, restricted by size, etc.

- access for materials to the workface, e.g. restricted by an adjacent building, overhead cables, etc.
- ground conditions, e.g. contamination, wet, slopes, unstable buried structures, etc.
- existing services, e.g. buried services, overhead services, etc.
- materials, e.g. asbestos, lead paint, existing chemical storage, etc.
- existing structures, e.g. unstable structures, existing temporary works, loose materials, etc.
- local weather, e.g. flooding, high winds, exposed, etc.
- existing activities, e.g. shops, operational use of the building, nearby school, hospital, etc.

- Design and construction, which include:

  - manual handling, e.g. laying 140 mm concrete blocks, 600 × 600 slabs, 86 kg kerbstones, etc.
  - vibration and noise, e.g. using pneumatic machinery
  - falls from height
  - falling objects, e.g. during lifting operations
  - site traffic, e.g. large plant and machinery
  - hazardous materials
  - uncontrolled collapse, e.g. excavations, structural instability
  - confined spaces, e.g. tanks, voids, basements
  - restricted access
  - lifting operations, e.g. use of cranes
  - existing services, e.g. buried services, overhead power lines
  - deep excavations.

- Future maintenance, which includes:

  - access for cleaning, e.g. working of ladders, tower scaffolding
  - component replacement, e.g. curtain walling, lights
  - access for maintenance, e.g. confined spaces, working at height.

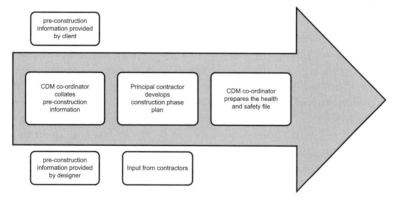

Figure 1.4 Flow of information for a notifiable project

When we consider hazard management, it is necessary to understand how valuable it is to communicate health and safety information through a construction project. Each CDM duty holder has a responsibility to provide and communicate information through a system of statutory protocols. We will now, albeit briefly, assess this holistic hazard management process. Figure 1.4 illustrates the process.

The client's hazard management contributions

A project, from a hazard management perspective, should start with the client identifying what information they need to provide to the CDM co-ordinator (for notifiable projects) and designers. This enables the team to consider the impact on the design and to take necessary actions to eliminate or reduce risk at the earliest stages if necessary. Therefore, providing the relevant information at the appropriate time to the right people is a significant contribution towards managing the hazard.

The information a client should provide is based on what is in the client's possession or 'reasonably obtainable' (examples are detailed in Chapter 2).

On many projects this work of information gathering is undertaken by the lead consultant, who is generally an architect or engineer. It is advisable to have a formal arrangement in place between the client and the person carrying out the work to define who is responsible for obtaining what information.

The designer's hazard management contributions

Potentially the designer is in the best position to manage significant hazards based on their early intervention on the project and by the relationship between all the aspects that define the design and hazards. Early decisions about the location of a structure, the materials and processes and the fundamental design of the structure affect buildability and health and safety throughout the life cycle of the structure. The management of these problems must be integrated within the design process, promote the identification of hazards at all stages of design and initiate a design response that is weighted according to the level of risk. This is termed the 'control hierarchy': it promotes a design to avoid or eliminate significant hazards; where this is not possible the design must reduce the level of risk to where it is not significant; and if this is not possible suitable control measures are required or the hazard will be transferred to the contractor. The most common process for achieving this is called 'design risk management', which is discussed in detail in Chapter 4.

The designer's duties are unique in that they apply to all projects irrespective of the size, risk profile, number of persons working on the project or even if the project is for a domestic client. On a project which is notifiable, the designer should communicate the outputs of their risk management process in terms of significant residual risks to the CDM co-ordinator.

The CDM co-ordinator's hazard management contributions (notifiable projects only)

One of the first contributions to be made by the CDM co-ordinator, in terms of hazard management, is the identification and collation of relevant information from the client on the site's environmental/inherent hazards. This can involve the CDM co-ordinator or another competent person undertaking a site visit and recommending relevant investigations.

The second and probably most important is the CDM co-ordinator's duty to ensure designers design with adequate regard to health and safety, and provide adequate information with their designs.

The significant residual risks from the site and the design are then collated as pre-construction information. This information alerts the principal contractor of the issues and allows them to plan and resource for health and safety management.

Finally, the CDM co-ordinator has a duty to prepare, or review and update, the health and safety file and provide it to the client. The health and safety file holds valuable health and safety information for all future projects, maintenance activities and operations throughout the life of the building or structure.

Of significance too, in terms of hazard management, is that the CDM co-ordinator needs to be in a position to advise the client throughout the scheme with the holistic arrangements for health and safety management. This requirement will be further discussed in Chapter 3.

The principal contractor's hazard management contributions

The principal contractor's appointment and position on the project as the manager of all aspects of health and safety during the construction phase places them in a pivotal position to contribute to health and safety management. The principal contractor should manage all aspects of safety through a project-specific set of arrangements called the 'construction phase plan'.

The standards and tools for the management of health and safety on site is delivered through the construction phase plan and includes risk assessments, method statements, fire, emergency, site traffic management and lifting plans, training, including induction, registers for inspections and permits to work.

The principal contractor and contractor's hazard management role is at the sharp end of construction and has direct links with fatalities and ill health, but as professionals their early contributions as site safety managers and as organisations with knowledge of constructability are invaluable.

Risk assessment and hazard management

Risk assessment is a discipline that all construction professionals must either legally or practically be confident in practising. From the earliest decisions on a project, the principles of risk assessment should be applied.

It is important to clarify that risk assessment is an integrated mindset that involves identification of problems and the development of solutions. The methodology, management of outputs and review should all be defined in either a health and safety policy or a safety plan before starting the process. The risk assessment pro forma should be considered as a report on one's findings that can be communicated for collaborative working, proof of compliance or action/implementation of safety or design standards, depending on the objective.

Regulation 3 of the Management of Health and Safety at Work Regulations 1999 requires employers to undertake risk assessments of their activities. However, the CDM Regulations do not specify the need for any risk assessment, but this is the most common process by which designers demonstrate they are designing with adequate regard to health and safety.

The fundamental elements of risk assessment involve the process or mechanism, which should be different for different objectives, and the competence of the person undertaking the process in knowing what outputs or standards to define.

The management of actions through a hazard identification process, for example, can be expanded to the use of a common risk register that provides a facility that is managed by controllers and contributed to by a defined user group. The controller or facilitator could be the lead designer or CDM co-ordinator for a design risk register or a project manager for an all-inclusive risk register, and the contributor could be the design team or the whole project team. Where appropriate, modern information technology provides opportunities for project teams to run live risk registers that not only record the problems and solutions but also project-manage the actions and provide all the associated information to whoever requires it.

To start the hazard management process, a hazard checklist can be beneficial. Examples of where such a checklist could be used on a project include:

- a developer making initial enquiries about a site;
- a client assessing the potential interface/impact of a project on existing operations, e.g. a highway, school/university, hospital, office, bridge, etc, and deciding what information to provide to potential designers and contractors;
- a designer undertaking a design review to check for significant hazards that could be designed out or reduced through design and what information to provide the contractors or CDM co-ordinator;
- a designer undertaking a post-construction activity assessment for large-component replacement and access for future maintenance including cleaning;
- a contractor undertaking an initial hazard identification process on a new project and allocating hazard ownership and actions to the contracting team.

The problems can be identified using the checklist as an aide-memoire or pro forma and recorded for action. Some of the hazards that could be considered on a checklist could include:

- asbestos
- falls from height
- falling objects
- fire risk
- manual handling
- noise and vibration
- site traffic
- highway traffic
- railways
- buried services
- overhead services
- confined spaces
- existing activities on site
- interface with public
- hazardous dust
- large difficult-to-manage components
- contaminated ground conditions
- buried structures
- condition of existing structure
- uncontrolled collapse
- access restriction (to site and workface)
- nearby/onsite water courses
- lifting operations.

Pre-construction information

As discussed in the previous section on project hazard management, relevant information is needed by the project team to consider the impact on any proposed project. The client must make available pre-construction information that is accurate, concise and to the level of detail commensurate to the issues and risk likely to be involved in the project. Architects and engineers, for example, require information on any contaminated land, topography, asbestos, existing services both buried and overhead, any existing structures and so on. This allows designers to make informed decisions that can eliminate and reduce risk during construction work.

Tendering contractors also need pre-construction information to allow them to consider the health and safety implications they must manage on site. They must assess their approach, necessary resources and costs for safety management based on the quality and relevance of the pre-construction information they receive.

The following headings are recommended in the Approved Code of Practice when considering the extent of pre-construction information that may be necessary, again reminding us that 'the level of detail in the information should be proportionate to the risks involved'.

1. Description of project
2. Client's considerations and management requirements
3. Environmental restrictions and existing on-site risks
4. Significant design and construction hazards
5. The health and safety file.

The above high-level headings for pre-construction information are expanded on in Chapter 8, where a full pre-construction information checklist is provided.

The construction phase plan

The construction phase plan is the master control document for site safety. Its development for work to start must be based on the first stages of the construction programme but also should have the infrastructure to demonstrate that health and safety will be managed throughout the project. To this end the development of the plan is critical as a hazard management tool.

A typical construction phase plan to be deemed suitably developed should contain the following:

- a description of the project, contact details and existing records and plans;
- arrangements for the communication and management of the work, including liaison between parties on site, consultation with the workforce, the exchange of design information, risk assessment and method statement production and approval, site rules and site emergency procedures;
- arrangements for controlling significant site health and safety risks, including temporary services, falls from height, lifting operations, traffic management, hazardous substances, removal of asbestos, contaminated land, reducing noise and vibration, manual handling, etc.;
- health and safety file layout and format, arrangements for collection of file information and storage arrangements.

The construction phase plan can be a stand-alone document and on more complex projects it can be an integrated element of the organisation's site safety management system.

The health and safety file

From a risk profile perspective, given that the majority of construction and maintenance operations will be undertaken post-construction, the health and safety file is considered to be an invaluable source of information. One of the initial concepts of the health and safety file is that any additional work, including demolition on the building or structure, will be supported by the file's information.

The health and safety file could be useful post-project completion for:

- designers and contractors on future refurbishment projects
- developing facilities maintenance or management contracts
- electrical maintenance and upgrades to the system
- mechanical maintenance and upgrades to the system
- cleaning contractors planning work
- the client or planning CDM co-ordinator in developing a tender
- an engineer tracing a fault on any system.

The file can be a stand-alone document or reference source but is often an integrated part of the operational and maintenance manual for the structure or building. Whatever approach is used, the contents should be relevant to the structure and readily available for use.

The biggest problem in developing a file is data management. The first stage is getting any data at all. The data then needs to be valuable; irrelevant information should be avoided. The file must also be kept up to date with any amendments. Version control is also important where multiple copies exist.

The format of the health and safety file should be based on the following information:

- a brief description of the work carried out
- residual risks and information to support their future management, e.g.

  - asbestos surveys and clearance certificates
  - existing buried services layout
  - contaminated land report

- key structural principles within the design, e.g.

  - substructural design, e.g. piles, foundations, etc.
  - structural frame / super structure elements, e.g. bracing, floor load-ings, roof loadings, energy-stored elements like pre-tensioned and post-tensioned beams, etc.

- hazardous materials used in the construction, e.g.

  - lead paint on reclaimed windows
  - low-level contaminated land during some landscaping
  - finishes used in which there is a risk when repairing or cleaning.

- future movement and dismantling of plant and equipment, e.g.

  - load weights and lifting arrangements

- decommissioning arrangements
- method statements for removal/installation of difficult-to-manage operations
- associated services information for removal/installation of difficult-to-manage operations.

- equipment provided and arrangements for cleaning, e.g.

  - access equipment training and safe operation
  - maintenance arrangements for equipment.

- detail on the nature, status and location of significant building, system or structure services, e.g.

  - fire-fighting mains
  - electrical supply
  - water supply
  - gas supply
  - telecommunications supply
  - sewage connections.

- as built and installed information on the structure and its equipment, e.g.

  - substructure
  - main superstructure
  - roofing system
  - external finish
  - windows and atria
  - internal finishes
  - mechanical and electrical (M&E) details
  - fire doors and compartmentation
  - interface with existing structures.

The development of the file is generally completed at the end of the project with the client and CDM co-ordinator defining the arrangements for its completion. However, many clients and contractors alike are seeing advantages in the ongoing development of the file from the start of the design stage, owing to the valuable nature of the information throughout the construction phase.

Note

1 Strategic Forum for Construction (chaired by Sir John Egan), 2002, *Accelerating Change,* Rethinking Construction c/o Construction Industry Council, London. Available online at: www.strategicforum.org.uk/pdf/report_sept02.pdf (ISBN 18986 71281).

2 The client and CDM

Introduction

It has long been argued that the client holds the key to the successful health and safety management of any construction project. In terms of the CDM Regulations this cannot be denied. Through the appointment of a competent, adequately resourced team, and by allocating sufficient time for the project to be properly planned, designed and constructed, the client can truly make the maximum contribution to health, safety and welfare on site. Indeed, the client is empowered by the regulations to ensure that effective arrangements for health and safety management are in fact implemented and also maintained throughout their project.

The cultured, well-advised client will also be aware of what information the team will require to be able to facilitate a proactively planned scheme. Designers and contractors need to be made aware of relevant health and safety information so they can then make the more considered choices based on the level of risk.

There is also the critical procedural gateway whereby the client must ensure that a suitably developed construction phase plan has been developed by the principal contractor. Once this is established, and the proposed onsite welfare arrangements deemed adequate, only then can the client allow construction work to begin.

The unprofessional or poorly advised client, who has not fully understood their role in terms of project health and safety management, can suffer potentially serious business risk issues by:

- enforcing unrealistic project timescales
- appointing incompetent and under-resourced designers, CDM co-ordinators and contractors
- not providing relevant health and safety information when it is needed
- not ensuring that arrangements for health and safety management are integrated in to the project's management
- allowing work to proceed without a suitably developed construction phase plan
- not making the health and safety file available post-construction.

It is understood that many clients may not be especially familiar with construction and the statutory requirements placed on them by the CDM regulations. The CDM Approved Code of Practice offers the following comfort for clients:

> Clients are not required or expected to plan or manage projects themselves. Nor do they have to develop substantial expertise in construction health and safety, unless this is central to their business. Clients must ensure that various things are done, but are not normally expected to do them themselves.

The regulations also require those they engage to alert them to their duties. Indeed, designers and contractors cannot legally commence their own work on a project until they are satisfied that the client is aware of their duties.

Finally, as if to underpin the importance of the client's opportunity to contribute to the safety management process throughout a construction project, the regulations introduce a further duty holder whose primary function is to help and advise the client on notifiable projects. This is the CDM co-ordinator whose role we will look at in more detail shortly.

Who is the client?

Before we take a detailed look at the respective statutory duties of the client, it is worth defining who the client actually is in terms of the regulations. Although it may appear obvious in many cases, it is important to establish who, on a particular project, fulfils the CDM functions of a client.

The interpretation offered by the regulations themselves states:

> "Client" means a person who in the course or furtherance of a business—
>
> (a) seeks or accepts the services of another which may be used in the carrying out of a project for him; or
> (b) carries out a project himself
>
> Extract from CDM Regulation 2(1)

Anyone initiating construction work for a business or other undertaking could, therefore, be considered a client by these regulations. Examples include local authorities, housing associations, charities, private developers, landlords, universities, power stations, utility services, insurance companies and even those instigating private finance initiative (PFI) schemes.

Noteworthy is that traditional domestic clients – that is, those undertaking construction work on their own home or perhaps family members' homes, not connected to a business – have no duties under these regulations.

It is valuable to ensure that there is clarity as to who is performing the duties of the client on a specific project. A CDM client representative is considered good practice. This brings clarity to the role and facilitates the arrangements for health and safety management. The lack of an appointed client contact with regard to CDM can only lead to ambiguity and uncertainty.

Certain projects for various reasons may have more than one client entity. Again, to bring clarity to the arrangements for health and safety management, the regulations make provision for such an eventuality. They provide the following:

> Where there is more than one client in relation to a project, if one or more of such clients elect in writing to be treated for the purposes of these Regulations as the only client or clients, no other client who has

agreed in writing to such election shall be subject after such election and consent to any duty owed by a client under these Regulations save the duties in regulations 5(l)(b), 10(1), 15 and 17(1) insofar as those duties relate to information in his possession.

CDM Regulation 8

In such circumstances, a written declaration is therefore necessary to clarify who is to undertake the client function on such project types. Those clients not elected must, however, comply with their statutory CDM duty to co-operate with others and to provide relevant information to assist those on the project designing and planning for safety.

The client's CDM duties explained

Appointing a competent team

Clearly, if the health and safety management of a project is to be in any way effective, then the appointed team must be both competent and adequately resourced to address the health and safety issues likely to be involved.

Competence has been identified as a fundamental requirement of the regulations. With the client generally making the key appointments, they need to ensure those they engage with duties under the regulations are able to make a demonstrable contribution to health and safety management. Note that when we discuss competence we are solely interested in this in terms of the ability to comply with those CDM obligations placed on the respective duty holder.

This duty, to ensure that appointees are competent, provides the client with an opportunity to make an immediate and valuable contribution to health and safety for the entire project from the very outset.

Where the project is notifiable then the client is challenged with appointing two significant duty holders in terms of health and safety management – both the CDM co-ordinator and the principal contractor.

Appointing the CDM co-ordinator

The CDM co-ordinator is the client's key advisor on matters of health, safety and welfare throughout the project. They will assist the client with their CDM duties and provide advice in the interest of health and safety management and compliance with these regulations.

Where a project is notifiable, the client shall appoint a person ("the CDM co-ordinator") to perform the duties specified in regulations 20 and 21 as soon as is practicable after initial design work or other preparation for construction work has begun.

CDM Regulation 14(1)

The competence of the CDM co-ordinator, based on the perceived project risk profile, and their relationship with the client are important to a successful project. The timing of the CDM co-ordinator's introduction to the project is also worthy of discussion as the regulations make reference to the appointment being made 'as soon as is practicable after initial design work or other preparation for construction work has begun'. This provides the client with an opportunity to assess the project needs, any restrictions, develop a financial profile and establish whether or not a scheme is viable prior to engaging a CDM co-ordinator. However, the Approved Code of Practice for the CDM Regulations suggests that the preparation of initial concept design and the implementation of any strategic brief would be considered significant detailed design work, beyond initial design, and, therefore, requires the appointment of a CDM co-ordinator.

To avoid any ambiguity as to the appointment of the CDM co-ordinator, the client needs to make a formal appointment in writing. This instruction should ideally include an agreed service level agreement articulating the full extent of the role and how the statutory undertakings are to be resourced.

The following chapter will look in detail at the CDM co-ordinator and their contributions to promoting a proactive approach to construction health, safety and welfare. To summarise, the importance of the early engagement of a competent CDM co-ordinator who can fully integrate and liaise with the team cannot be understated.

Appointing the principal contractor

When the project is notifiable the regulations call for the client to appoint a duty holder to be responsible for planning, co-ordinating and managing safety, health and welfare throughout the construction phase – namely, the principal contractor.

> After appointing a CDM co-ordinator under paragraph (1), the client shall appoint a person ("the principal contractor") to perform the duties specified in regulations 22 to 24 as soon as is practicable after the client knows enough about the project to be able to select a suitable person for such appointment.
>
> CDM Regulation 14(2)

The principal contractor appointment is interesting when considering the timing of their engagement. Again, as with the CDM co-ordinator, there are significant advantages in favour of an early appointment. Depending on the complexity of a proposed scheme, the early engagement of the experienced principal contractor can assist with the planning and preparation for health, safety and welfare on site. Some contractual arrangements also lend themselves to their early involvement and must be a consideration when forms of procurement are considered.

The CDM co-ordinator will be available to advise the client on the appointment of the principal contractor. Their involvement in any contractor interviews at the tender stage is recommended. This allows them to assess competence of the proposed principal contractors and advise accordingly.

Provision in the regulations for non-appointment of the CDM co-ordinator and the principal contractor

Many clients make late appointments of the CDM co-ordinator. For inexperienced clients, who need to depend on the advice given by the designers and contractors they engage, this may be understandable. However, for professional construction clients who introduce the CDM co-ordinator late into detailed design, or even at the production information/tender stages, a review is clearly needed as to how the requirements of the CDM Regulations are integrated into procurement policies and holistic project management arrangements.

The late or non-appointment of the CDM co-ordinator is considered a fundamental breakdown in project management by the regulations. To emphasise this point the regulations also require:

The client shall—

(a) be deemed for the purposes of these Regulations, . . . to have been appointed as the CDM co-ordinator or principal contractor, or both, for any period for which no person (including himself) has been so appointed; and
(b) accordingly be subject to the duties imposed by regulations 20 and 21 on a CDM co-ordinator or, as the case may be, the duties imposed by regulations 22 to 24 on a principal contractor, or both sets of duties.

CDM Regulations 14(4)

Therefore, on a notifiable project, the client must assume the statutory duties of the CDM co-ordinator and principal contractor until such time as they are appointed (in writing).

Arrangements for health and safety management

Again, as if to emphasise the influence held by the client in these regulations, they have a duty to ensure that health and safety is managed effectively throughout the project. Note that they are not expected to actually manage the process themselves, as many clients are not construction professionals; rather *ensure* that steps are taken towards a teamwide demonstrable approach to health and safety management. The regulations offer the following, highly significant, requirement:

(1) Every client shall take reasonable steps to ensure that the arrangements made for managing the project (including the allocation of sufficient time and other resources) by persons with a duty under these Regulations (including the client himself) are suitable to ensure that—

    (a) the construction work can be carried out so far as is reasonably practicable without risk to the health and safety of any person;

    (b) the requirements of Schedule 2 are complied with in respect of any person carrying out the construction work; and

    (c) any structure designed for use as a workplace has been designed taking account of the provisions of the Workplace (Health, Safety and Welfare) Regulations 1992 which relate to the design of, and materials used in, the structure.

(2) The client shall take reasonable steps to ensure that the arrangements referred to in paragraph (1) are maintained and reviewed throughout the project.

CDM Regulation 9

The client must, therefore, ensure that the arrangements for health and safety management are clear. Where a project is notifiable, the CDM co-ordinator is available to advise and assist in this matter. Where a project is non-notifiable (and consequently has no CDM co-ordinator), it is hoped that the client can check that adequate provision has been made for health and safety management. If not, the client can consider approaching their organisation's appointed competent person (under Regulation 7 of the Management of Health and Safety at Work Regulations 1999).

Whether the client has a CDM co-ordinator or an appointed competent person, they still retain the liability for ensuring that effective arrangements are in place and maintained throughout the project. This regulation, therefore, should ensure that the client pays adequate regard to the health, safety and welfare of those carrying out the construction work and those affected by the activities undertaken.

Providing relevant health and safety information

It is the responsibility of the client to provide those designing, tendering, resourcing and planning the project with relevant information relating to the proposed work. This also needs to include the minimum amount of time afforded to the appointed contractors, prior to works commencing, to allow for planning and preparation for construction work.

Every client shall ensure that

(a) every person designing the structure; and

(b) every contractor who has been or may be appointed by the client is promptly provided with pre-construction information . . .

Extract from CDM Regulation 10(1)

Where the project is notifiable, the regulations require the client to supply all pre-construction information to the appointed CDM co-ordinator for dissemination to the relevant team members.

The extent of information that the client is expected to make available is qualified in the regulations as follows:

> The pre-construction information shall consist of all the information in the client's possession (or which is reasonably obtainable), including—
>
> (a) any information about or affecting the site or the construction work;
> (b) any information concerning the proposed use of the structure as a workplace;
> (c) the minimum amount of time before the construction phase which will be allowed to the contractors appointed by the client for planning and preparation for construction work; and
> (d) any information in any existing health and safety file . . .
>
> Extract from CDM Regulation 10(2)

This may sound like an obvious requirement but clients have a duty to proactively provide details on the proposed site. The client must provide information in his possession or information which is 'reasonably obtainable'. The following are all examples of valuable pre-construction information:

- the presence, location and condition of hazardous materials, such as asbestos or waste chemicals;
- activities on or near the site, which will continue during construction work, e.g. retail shops, deliveries and traffic movements, railway lines or busy roads, public access to a retail store;
- requirements relating to the health and safety of the client's employees or customers, e.g. permit-to-work systems in a petrochemical plant, fire precautions in a paper mill, one-way systems on site, means of escape, 'no-go' areas, smoking and parking restrictions;
- access and space problems, such as narrow streets, lack of parking, turning or information about means of access to parts of the structure, e.g. fragile storage space; materials and anchorage points for fall arrest systems; about those that are concealed, such as underground services; culverts, where this might affect the safe use of plant, e.g. cranes, or the safety of groundworks, e.g. the construction of trenches; unintentional collapse;
- available information about site services and their location, in particular, ground conditions and underground structures or water courses, such as

buildings, other structures or trees which might be unstable or at risk of uncontrolled collapse;

- previous structural modifications, including weakening or strengthening;
- fire damage, ground shrinkage, movement or poor maintenance which may have adversely affected the structure;
- any difficulties relating to plant and equipment in the premises, such as overhead service gantries whose height restricts access;
- health and safety information contained in earlier design, construction or 'as built' drawings, such as details of pre-stressed or post-tensioned structures.

This provision of information is the first hazard management process on a project. It begins the flow of information and hazard management action by the initial members of the team.

Ensuring the construction phase plan has been suitably developed

Given the client has arguably the greatest influence on the project, they are given a significant statutory duty under these regulations prior to the construction phase starting. The client must ensure that the construction work does not begin until the principal contractor has prepared a construction phase plan which is suitably developed and compliant with CDM Regulation 24. The construction phase plan is the fundamental driver for health and safety management during the construction phase as it sets out the approach to ensure that nobody undertaking construction work or who it affected by the project is hurt or suffers ill health.

Obviously, the client may not be sufficiently competent to make such an assessment of the construction phase plan and the CDM co-ordinator will provide suitable and sufficient advice to the client.

> Where the project is notifiable, the client shall ensure that the construction phase does not start unless—
>
> (a) the principal contractor has prepared a construction phase plan . . .
> Extract from CDM Regulation 16

Significant, too, is that whereas much of the CDM Regulations carry exemption from civil proceedings in the event of a breach of duty, this requirement does not. If a client is found to be in breach of Regulation 16(a) and allows construction work to start without a suitably developed construction phase plan, they are open to civil proceedings. Please refer to Regulation 45 in Appendix 1.

Ensuring adequate provision for welfare facilities

Over and above not allowing work to begin on site until a compliant construction phase plan is in place, the client cannot permit the construction phase to start until adequate welfare facilities are available.

Competent contractors will make provision for adequate facilities; however, there is evidence to suggest that other contractors do not see a requirement to provide people with minimum welfare standards.

Schedule 2 of these regulations specifies minimum requirements for sanitary conveniences, washing facilities, drinking water, changing rooms and lockers and facilities for rest.

> Where the project is notifiable, the client shall ensure that the construction phase does not start unless—
>
> (b) he is satisfied that the requirements of regulation 22(1) (c) (provision of welfare facilities) will be complied with during the construction phase.
>
> Extract from CDM Regulation 16

It is not necessary for the client to provide the welfare itself or, indeed, to make a decision as to what facilities are necessary for a project. However, the client must be assured that adequate provision has been made. Clients should actively ask contractors or the CDM co-ordinator, if appropriate, to confirm that welfare facilities are on site prior to construction work commencing and that the facilities are sufficient.

Here, too, if the client is guilty of a breach of this regulation there is no exemption from any possible civil proceedings being taken against them.

The client and the health and safety file

As discussed in Chapter 1, the health and safety file is a repository of information, held by the client, to assist those planning to undertake work on a structure such as general maintenance, cleaning windows, curtain walling, component replacement, warranty inspections, alteration and refurbishment, demolition or dismantling and so on.

As we know, the client has a statutory duty to provide information to others to facilitate health and safety management during design, planning and execution of a project. Where a project is notifiable (i.e. the construction phase is likely to involve more than 30 days or 500 person days), the client needs to provide the health and safety file to the CDM co-ordinator.

> The client shall ensure that the CDM co-ordinator is provided with all the health and safety information in the client's possession (or which is reasonably obtainable) relating to the project which is likely to be needed for inclusion in the health and safety file, including information specified in regulation 4(9)(c) of the Control of Asbestos Regulations 2006(a).
>
> CDM Regulation 17(1)

This regulation also calls for the client to provide information required under a further statutory instrument in relation to asbestos management in non-domestic premises. Where relevant to a project the client shall therefore ensure:

> (c) . . . that information about the location and condition of any asbestos or any such substance is—
>   (i) provided to every person liable to disturb it . . .
> Extract from Control of Asbestos Regulations 2006

It is estimated that approximately 4,000 people die each year from asbestos-related diseases. The provision of information to the CDM co-ordinator will allow those designing and planning any relevant work to consider, and potentially eliminate, any interface and, consequently, risk of exposure for contractors.

An existing health and safety file is, therefore, a valuable source of information for the project team and a starting point for the client to demonstrate a proactive approach to the provision of pre-construction information.

Following a construction project the client also has a duty to make available the health and safety file to those who may need it. They must also ensure the health and safety file is kept up to date with any new information.

Finally, in terms of the client duty in relation to the health and safety file, we need to understand what happens if a client relinquishes his interest in a structure. The regulations require the health and safety file to be handed over to any new client who takes ownership of the structure.

> It shall be sufficient compliance with paragraph (3)(a) by a client who disposes of his entire interest in the structure if he delivers the health and safety file to the person who acquires his interest in it and ensures that he is aware of the nature and purpose of the file.
> CDM Regulation 17(4)

It would be prudent for a formal handover procedure to be undertaken at an appropriate time so the client can demonstrate compliance with this requirement. The incoming, new client can also ensure the health and safety file is made available immediately to those who may need to consider its content.

3 The role of the CDM co-ordinator

Introduction

The original European Communities Directive 92/57/EEC on which the United Kingdom legislators based the CDM Regulations called for the client to appoint a 'coordinator for health and safety matters'. This appointee's key objective would be to co-ordinate health and safety matters during the various stages of designing and preparation for a project. Consequently the UK law makers invented the CDM co-ordinator to fulfil this role.

The fundamental role of the CDM co-ordinator is to assist and advise the client in ensuring that effective arrangements are in place to facilitate health and safety management throughout the design, planning and execution on site.

The introduction of the CDM co-ordinator function was seen, among the more cultured and forward-thinking in the construction industry, as a huge opportunity to improve pre-construction health and safety management. This was achieved through advising the client on appointments and information required and early involvement with the designers ensuring that hazards are being considered, eliminated and subsequent risks reduced. Sceptics, however, believed that the creation of the CDM co-ordinator introduced an unnecessary tier of bureaucracy and even a duplication of duties that were already undertaken by the lead designer, lead consultant, project manager or contract administrator.

Who then is best placed to assume the role of the CDM co-ordinator? The client needs to ensure that the CDM co-ordinator is competent and adequately resourced for any project likely to involve more than 30 days or 500 person days (i.e. a notifiable project). A selection of skills and knowledge required should include:

- knowledge of health and safety in construction, including all relevant legislation
- a thorough understanding of the respective design processes
- knowledge of the various construction processes and materials used in construction
- an understanding of how to evaluate designer and contractor competence to design and construct with respect to the statutory provisions
- a sound understanding of how construction health and safety management should be implemented
- good interpersonal and communication skills.

The CDM co-ordination duties are undertaken by lead designers, architects, engineers, health and safety professionals, project managers, contract administrators, quantity surveyors, CDM consultants, clients and even the principal contractor (on design-and-build schemes, for example).

The CDM co-ordinator can be an individual or an organisation. The CDM co-ordinator can also be an existing member (or members) of the project team or completely independent. Many believe that best practice would see the CDM co-ordinator as an independent appointment (or at least with sufficient independence from the team). Arguably, then, they would be more willing to professionally challenge the design team's health and safety contributions and give the client a more realistic status report on the effectiveness of the arrangements for health and safety management.

Also, on more complex, multi-faceted and possibly larger construction projects, there may well be a necessity for more than one individual to be able to undertake all the statutory duties of the CDM co-ordinator. If it is the case that more than one person is required to satisfy the skill set required it is important that this is clearly defined and there is sufficient co-ordination of their activities.

However, on smaller, uncomplicated notifiable schemes it would be very disappointing if the competence to carry out the duties of the CDM co-ordinator did not exist within the immediate team.

Competence of the CDM co-ordinator can, therefore, only be assessed for any intended project. Industry experience, chartered memberships and certain qualifications in health and safety law go some way towards establishing competence but are no guarantee.

Memberships of non-professional bodies, listings on certain CDM co-ordination registers, and use of their logos are also no guarantee of competence. Specific assessments should be made for each project.

Also, for a CDM co-ordinator to be fully effective, their appointment must be secured during the earliest design stages, or even pre-design if they are to be in a position to advise on the competence and adequacy of resources of the design team. The late appointment of the CDM co-ordinator has been a major failing in the industry and regulations to date. All too often a great deal of design work is undertaken without the ability of a competent entity to holistically assess the health and safety implications of a project's construction, use, future maintenance and even eventual demolition or dismantling.

Another requirement for the CDM co-ordinator is to ensure the design team co-operates and works as a team in its health and safety management function. The CDM co-ordinator will need to ensure that the design team is comfortable, for example, with the arrangements for health and safety management at the respective design stages, which ideally will be integrated into the entire design management process. The skills of communication to be able to present the case for an inclusive role will generally lead to a harmonious relationship with the design team. The CDM co-ordinator does not wish the project team to view them simply as a CDM policeman and must strive for practical involvement and co-operation.

Before we look in detail at the actual functions of the CDM co-ordinator, the point must be made that, in terms of these duties, they hold significant *potential* to contribute to a well-designed, planned and managed scheme from a health and safety management perspective. But you will note that, in real terms, the CDM co-ordinator has little statutory influence and generally is required to delicately articulate the benefits of their persuasion in the major decisions taken.

Significant lost opportunities can occur in terms of successful health and safety planning when CDM co-ordinators:

1. are appointed late
2. are not competent
3. are not adequately resourced
4. do not possess adequate resources
5. do not receive genuine client support
6. are not provided with relevant information from the client
7. are not provided with relevant information from designers
8. fail to secure and facilitate a working design risk management strategy
9. fail to adequately advise and assist the client with the holistic arrangements for health and safety management.

It is fair to say that the above list of CDM co-ordinator issues are all too common as the construction industry still tries to get to grips with this key health and safety management opportunity. Many claim that the role of the CDM co-ordinator has been misrepresented to the client, who often sees the position as an unnecessary overhead and as additional red tape.

However, although clarity as to the role of the CDM co-ordinator clearly exists in such documents as the Approved Code of Practice, CDM co-ordinators are still widely perceived as CDM facilitators and *not* as 'coordinators for health and safety matters' as defined in the original EU directive.

Many CDM co-ordinators provide the client with a fee proposal and associated service level agreement for consideration. In a competitive construction environment where CDM co-ordinators are selected solely on their price or the service is 'thrown in' as part of the project management consultancy service, a minimalist approach is sometimes delivered. A minimalist service can arguably ensure the client and CDM co-ordinator are seen to be addressing their statutory duties but this frequently adds no value in real terms. A minimalist service inevitably involves limited proactive advice and assistance to the client and little or no direct contact or influence with the designers. The client and their project team must appreciate the opportunity the competent CDM co-ordinator brings and ask themselves what they can do to assist the CDM co-ordinator in terms of eliminating harm and minimising risk.

Project notification

If it has been established that the project meets the criteria for notification, in that the construction phase is likely to exceed 30 working days or that the construction work will involve more than 500 person days, the project details need to be provided to the Health and Safety Executive.

This requirement falls to the CDM co-ordinator and is generally their first action upon appointment. No other duty holder shall attempt to make the notification as this is solely the CDM co-ordinator's statutory duty.

> The CDM co-ordinator shall as soon as is practicable after his appointment ensure that notice is given to the Executive containing such of the particulars specified in Schedule 1 as are available.
>
> CDM Regulation 21(1)

The standard Health and Safety Executive form for notification is called the F10 and is available on the HSE's website, where it can be completed electronically. There is no legal requirement to use the online notification and many organisations will use their own stationery. However, the information notified must contain the information listed in Schedule 1 of the regulations, as illustrated below:

CDM Schedule 1: Particulars to be notified to the Executive

1   Date of forwarding.
2   Exact address of the construction site.
3   The name of the local authority where the site is located.
4   A brief description of the project and the construction work which it includes.
5   Contact details of the client (name, address, telephone number and any e-mail address).
6   Contact details of the CDM co-ordinator (name, address, telephone number and any e-mail address).
7   Contact details of the principal contractor (name, address, telephone number and any e-mail address).
8   Date planned for the start of the construction phase.
9   The time allowed by the client to the principal contractor referred to in regulation 15(b) for planning and preparation for construction work.
10   Planned duration of the construction phase.
11   Estimated maximum number of people at work on the construction site.
12   Planned number of contractors on the construction site.
13   Name and address of any contractor already appointed.
14   Name and address of any designer already engaged.
15   A declaration signed by or on behalf of the client that he is aware of his duties under these Regulations.

Notification needs to be made as soon as is practicable following the appointment of the CDM co-ordinator. If not all of the details for the initial notification are known then any additional information must be sent to the Health and Safety Executive as soon as it is known. It is often the case that on a traditional procurement route the principal contractor will not be known until post-tendering.

Finally, and significantly, in relation to the notification to the enforcement authority (i.e. the Health and Safety Executive), the client must make a signed declaration, or it may be made on their behalf, that they are aware of their duties under these regulations.

Assisting and advising the client with their duties

Much of what the CDM co-ordinator must do on a project to contribute to the health and safety management arrangements are by their duty to advise and assist the client. As discussed in Chapter 2, the client has several major statutory duties themselves under these regulations, and the CDM co-ordi-nator is their key advisor in this regard when the project is notifiable. The nature of the relationship between the client and their CDM co-ordinator is critical if they are to succeed jointly in setting the tone for effective health and safety planning, design and construction. It may be necessary for the CDM co-ordinator, depending on the respective competence of their client, to consider these regulations as being more than simply criminal legislation; rather, as a genuine opportunity to integrate health and safety in to the project management process. However, the regulations themselves give us the following:

> The CDM co-ordinator shall—
>
> (a) give suitable and sufficient advice and assistance to the client on undertaking the measures he needs to take to comply with these Regulations during the project (including, in particular, assisting the client in complying with regulations 9 and 16).
>
> CDM Regulation 20(1)(a)

It must be understood that many clients, including many so-called profes-sional clients, will not fully understand their statutory health and safety obligations under these regulations and they will become heavily dependent on the advice and assistance provided by the CDM co-ordinator. However, the CDM co-ordinator needs to be somewhat sympathetic to other require-ments and pressures imposed on clients when undertaking construction work. This is where the successful CDM co-ordinator will develop a diplomatic approach to working with the client and convince them not to undervalue these regulations and the position they hold to affect health and safety deci-sions. An approach that will consider compliance with these regulations as a minimum requirement and where the client pushes the team towards best practice in terms of safe design, planning and management is highly recommended and rewarding.

The arrangements for health and safety management

First, we shall look at the CDM co-ordinator in terms of advising and assisting the client with the holistic project arrangements for health and safety management. The CDM co-ordinator must appreciate the liability they hold in terms of this duty as well as the opportunity to influence the approach. To clarify this, the Approved Code of Practice, when discussing the management arrangements for a notifiable project, tells the client:

> Having appointed a competent CDM co-ordinator, the client is entitled to rely on their advice when making these judgements.
>
> ACoP

Therefore, as soon as is practicable – when the CDM co-ordinator has a good understanding of the project's risk profile, available pre-construction information and the project team's competence and approach to design risk management and embracing of the principles of prevention – the CDM co-ordinator should be in a position to take action and advise accordingly.

It would be considered advisable and good practice to draft a set of health and safety management arrangements that are proportionate to the project needs in terms of compliance and even principles of best practice. This approach would be an opportunity to set the tone for health and safety management and introduce achievable key performance indicators. If high standards are set in these arrangements, which are considered achievable by the CDM co-ordinator, then we do not have to settle for mere compliance with these regulations as the end goal.

These draft arrangements would need to be presented to the client for endorsement and then distributed to the team for implementation.

Such arrangements would include, for example:

- a statement of intent from the client in relation to project health and safety goals;
- clarity as to the duties and responsibilities of the project team in relation to health and safety requirements and deliverables;
- how pre-construction information is to be communicated to the relevant duty holder for consideration in a timely manner – this would include any client-specific requirements;
- the arrangements for the team to adopt a co-ordinated approach to risk management and co-operate/communicate with each other and others affected by the project, including any adjoining sites – this includes making provision for communication information on significant residual risk

  – for the construction phase, and
  – for inclusion in the health and safety file for future reference;

- arrangements to facilitate change management if relevant, e.g. during a design-and-build contract where a new design team is introduced;
- procedures for ensuring the standards set in these arrangements are monitored and reviewed throughout.

Such management arrangements for health and safety provide a focal point for the CDM co-ordinator to proactively advise and assist the client with their duties. Monitoring contributions and reacting accordingly, whether by offering advice to team members, promoting suggestions for best practice, alerting the team to new industry initiatives, or even by having to advise the client of any shortcomings with the arrangements, can truly make the CDM co-ordinator involved.

This documented approach, therefore, has considerable benefits, not least of which is to provide a clear audit trail of the CDM co-ordinator's contributions.

The start of the construction phase

A second significant area where the CDM co-ordinator needs to assist and advise the client is immediately prior to the beginning of the construction phase. As discussed in Chapter 2, the client cannot legally allow the construction work to commence until two conditions are met:

1. the construction phase plan, prepared by the principal contractor, must be suitably developed for construction work to commence;
2. the client must be satisfied that appropriate welfare facilities are to be made available during the construction phase.

The construction phase plan sets the standards for health and safety management and execution of onsite activities. It is developed from pre-construction information provided and the principal contractor's own standards and arrangements for eliminating and reducing risk. It is hoped that the principal contractor will engage the CDM co-ordinator during the construction phase plan development to work together on the standards and arrangements that need to be included. The CDM co-ordinator, too, has an opportunity to proactively approach the principal contractor and assess the project's key health and safety implications. Either way, the CDM co-ordinator needs sufficient time to assess the plan and ensure it is compliant with the regulations and ideally follows the format promoted in the Approved Code of Practice (available in Chapter 5, where we further discuss the construction phase plan).

However, it has been known for CDM co-ordinators to receive ill-prepared and poorly considered construction phase plans with insufficient time to satisfy the requirements of this regulation with regard to the construction phase beginning on its intended planned date.

Therefore, the lack of a proactive and co-ordinated approach between the CDM co-ordinator and the principal contractor when ensuring the suitability of the construction phase plan can potentially lead to:

1. an ill-conceived approach to health and safety planning and management during the construction phase, which has not taken the pre-construction information into consideration;
2. the CDM co-ordinator having to advise the client that the construction phase plan is not suitably developed for works to commence in that it does not comply with the relevant regulation;
3. the client having to delay the start of the onsite activities until the principal contractor provides an appropriate construction phase plan.

In these circumstances the client would not and should not look favourably upon the principal contractor and the CDM co-ordinator. A proactive and co-ordinated approach, where the respective duty holders work co-operatively best suits the holistic project.

In reporting findings to the client, the CDM co-ordinator would benefit from using a pro forma to demonstrate that all the plan's contents have been assessed and also to set comments against any weak areas recommending further development.

The comments on the construction phase plan can be weighted to emphasise to the principal contractor the importance of the omission. For example, if the name of a consultant was not included in the plan, a simple note and no further action would be satisfactory. However, if there were no arrangements in the plan for temporary works design and co-ordination on a large highway concrete retaining wall, then the comment would advise the client not to allow work to start until the issue is ratified within the plan and re-assessed by the CDM co-ordinator.

In summary, there are four general objectives the construction phase health and safety plan must achieve for the CDM co-ordinator to deem it suitably developed for work to start. The plan must:

- address the significant residual hazards identified by the designer;
- address any issues identified by the client in respect of site rules, restrictions and interfaces;
- demonstrate the potential and resources for the principal contractor to manage health and safety, and co-ordinate health and safety issues between contractors throughout the construction phase;
- have arrangements to collect health and safety file data and deliver as specified to the CDM co-ordinator for assessment and delivery to the client.

Facilitating co-operation and co-ordination pre-construction

On all but the simplest of projects, design development and planning is a team effort, and as with all aspects of this phase health and safety requires a collaborative approach. Initially, to comply with this duty, the CDM co-ordinator can set up arrangements to monitor co-operation with the client and, depending on the project size and complexity, the approach can vary from reading design review meeting minutes to attending design team meetings and hazard identification workshops.

> The CDM co-ordinator shall—
>
> (b) ensure that suitable arrangements are made and implemented for the co-ordination of health and safety measures during planning and preparation for the construction phase, including facilitating—
> (i) co-operation and co-ordination between persons concerned in the project . . .
> (ii) the application of the general principles of prevention . . ..
>
> Extract from CDM Regulation 20(1)

Depending on the CDM co-ordinator's position (e.g. they could be lead designers, or a consultant or an independent CDM co-ordinator with limited resources) the approach obviously requires a judgement and would benefit from clarification in a service level agreement with the client.

Tools and methods to facilitate co-operation can vary, from informing the lead designer or consultant with examples of concerns to design programme Gantt charts highlighting hazards, resources and design responsibility, and risk registers leading with hazards and recording design action taken and future design action to be taken by whom and when.

CDM co-ordinators with limited design or experience need to be aware that competent, experienced designers naturally co-operate with other designers in solving all types of design problems and issues. It should not be assumed that because there is not a formal, visible strategy for co-operation that the team is not complying with this duty. Design experience and experience in contributing to design team meetings where issues are debated and resolved is invaluable for any CDM co-ordinator to discharge their duties efficiently and add value.

In assessing the pre-construction health and safety contributions and CDM compliance, the following is a list of the issues the CDM co-ordinator should be looking for in holistically evaluating a team's health and safety input:

•   Clear evidence of the project designers identifying significant hazards at different stages of the design, e.g. an architect considering site access and special design / footprint layout options at concept and feasibility stages, and M&E interface with the structure during the scheme and detail stages of design.

- Evidence that the designers have a strategy, whether formal or not, for considering hazards associated with the construction processes and assumed construction processes. The strategy should demonstrate to the CDM co-ordinator that they will consider hazards at all stages of the design and potentially review the design health and safety contributions at the recognised service stages.
- Evidence that design actions have been taken to avoid, reduce, control and transfer hazards.
- Evidence that designers are co-operating in respect of their design contributions to avoid, reduce, control and transfer hazards. This co-operation may involve simple arrangements to define the zones for the service runs within a false-ceiling void. The structural engineer and services engineer would need to work together to avoid conflicts and potentially any additional retrospective penetrations. They could, for example, discuss utilising risers and cast in situ perpetrations.
- Other problems could involve access during construction with badly planned service runs and potential access issues for maintaining plant.
- Evidence that information and actions, as an output of their risk assessment, are being managed by the respective recipient. Information for additional design contributions, collation in the health and safety plan by the CDM co-ordinator and for inclusion on the health and safety file for future maintenance considerations. Evidence that designers know how the residual hazard is to be managed, and by which CDM duty holder, is valuable and, in most cases, essential.
- Evidence that the client is supporting the team, allowing sufficient time for the design process and providing all pre-construction information in his possession or information that is reasonably obtainable.

Identification and provision of pre-construction information

It is obviously important for those designing, planning and constructing any project to have suitable and sufficient information available to them to consider when making critical decisions. The responsibility, on a notifiable project, to identify, collect and ensure that designers and contractors appointed by the client are furnished with such information is that of the CDM co-ordinator. If the CDM co-ordinator is to be instrumental in facilitating effective hazard identification and risk management this duty in relation to pre-construction information is fundamental. The regulations provide the following:

The CDM co-ordinator shall—

(a) take all reasonable steps to identify and collect the pre-construction information;

(b) promptly provide in a convenient form to—
   (i) every person designing the structure, and
   (ii) every contractor who has been or may be appointed by the client (including the principal contractor),

such of the pre-construction information in his possession as is relevant to each.

CDM Regulation 20(2)(a) and (b)

The proactive CDM co-ordinator will assess the requirements for information from a very early stage and liaise with the design team to see what they have perhaps already been provided with, prior to the appointment of the CDM co-ordinator. Such information as site investigations, contaminated land surveys, topographical surveys and asbestos surveys, for example, may already be in the presence of those who need it initially.

It would also be extremely helpful for any CDM co-ordinator to have an aide-memoire or relevant checklist to assist them in identifying potential requirements for any project. This is provided in the Approved Code of Practice.

1   Description of project

(a) project description and programme details including:
   (i) key dates (including planned start and finish of the construction phase), and
   (ii) the minimum time to be allowed between appointment of the principal contractor and instruction to commence work on site;

(b) details of client, designers, CDM co-ordinator and other consultants;

(c) whether or not the structure will be used as a workplace (in which case, the finished design will need to take account of the relevant requirements of the Workplace (Health, Safety and Welfare) Regulations 1992);

(d) extent and location of existing records and plans.

2   Client's considerations and management requirements

(a) arrangements for:
   (i) planning for and managing the construction work, including any health and safety goals for the project,
   (ii) communication and liaison between client and others,
   (iii) security of the site,
   (iv) welfare provision;

   (b) requirements relating to the health and safety of the client's employees or customers or those involved in the project such as:

       (i) site hoarding requirements,

      (ii) site transport arrangements or vehicle movement restrictions,

     (iii) client permit-to-work systems,

      (iv) fire precautions,

       (v) emergency procedures and means of escape,

      (vi) 'no-go' areas or other authorisation requirements for those involved in the project,

     (vii) any areas the client has designated as confined spaces,

    (viii) smoking and parking restrictions.

3 Environmental restrictions and existing on-site risks

   (a) Safety hazards, including:

       (i) boundaries and access, including temporary access – for example narrow streets, lack of parking, turning or storage space,

      (ii) any restrictions on deliveries or waste collection or storage,

     (iii) adjacent land uses – for example schools, railway lines or busy roads,

      (iv) existing storage of hazardous materials,

       (v) location of existing services particularly those that are concealed – water, electricity, gas, etc,

      (vi) ground conditions, underground structures or water courses where this might affect the safe use of plant, for example cranes, or the safety of groundworks,

     (vii) information about existing structures – stability, structural form, fragile or hazardous materials, anchorage points for fall arrest systems (particularly where demolition is involved),

    (viii) previous structural modifications, including weakening or strengthening of the structure (particularly where demolition is involved),

      (ix) fire damage, ground shrinkage, movement or poor maintenance which may have adversely affected the structure,

       (x) any difficulties relating to plant and equipment in the premises, such as overhead gantries whose height restricts access,

      (xi) health and safety information contained in earlier design, construction or 'as-built' drawings, such as details of pre-stressed or post-tensioned structures;

   (b) health hazards, including:

       (i) asbestos, including results of surveys (particularly where demolition is involved),

　　　(ii) existing storage of hazardous materials,
　　　(iii) contaminated land, including results of surveys,
　　　(iv) existing structures containing hazardous materials,
　　　(v)   health risks arising from client's activities.

4   Significant design and construction hazards

　　(a) significant design assumptions and suggested work methods, sequences or other control measures;
　　(b) arrangements for co-ordination of ongoing design work and handling design changes;
　　(c) information on significant risks identified during design;
　　(d) materials requiring particular precautions.

5   The health and safety file

Description of its format and any conditions relating to its content.

appendix 2 CDM ACoP

Any CDM co-ordinator who fully understands the legal significance of the Approved Code of Practice will generally follow this recommended layout. The level of detail provided in the plan should also be proportionate and relevant to the risk profile of the project.

CDM co-ordinators historically have added value to projects by liaising with the client in respect of their site activities where applicable, undertaking investigations with the architect and through site visits to obtain more information.

Those who plan and design without considering relevant information would need to be challenged and asked what provision has been made for so-called 'known unknowns'. Such designs and preparations can introduce risk and potentially require late modifications resulting in delay and often increase costs for the client.

In terms of promptly making such pre-construction information available to contractors appointed by the client, including the principal contractor, much will depend on the project procurement strategy. If a principal contractor, for example, is asked to tender on a traditional, fully designed scheme then the CDM co-ordinator must prepare such information that will allow them to fully understand and consider the health and safety objectives and resource accordingly. However, on such ventures as, say, collaborative design and build, where the principal contractor and other contractors become more involved in the early design and planning stages, they can become an excellent cohort with whom to discuss pre-construction information requirements.

Noteworthy, too, is that pre-construction information is not an entity that stops when a principal contractor is engaged. A strategy must be adopted by the CDM co-ordinator to consider how the flow of information will continue during the construction phase, particularly if the design phase is continuing.

The golden rules of providing pre-construction information for the principal contractor are:

- Don't include information which one would expect a competent contractor to be able to manage effectively.
- Don't include general generic statements about health and safety standards.
- Include design and site information that will facilitate the contractor in undertaking suitable and sufficient risk assessment and developing method statements to promote safe systems of work on site.
- Set standards for what is expected by the client and CDM co-ordinator in respect of health and safety management. A principal contractor and contractor will benefit from clarity as to what is acceptable in relation to the development of a construction phase plan.

When we summarise regarding pre-construction information we are mindful of the key statement made in the Approved Code of Practice:

> [Y]our focus should always be on action necessary to reduce and manage risks. Any paperwork produced should help with communication and risk management. Paperwork which adds little to the management of risk is a waste of effort, and can be a dangerous distraction from the real business of risk reduction and management.

Ensuring designers comply with their duties

This is arguably where the CDM co-ordinator can play another significant role in terms of their contribution to reducing a project's risk profile. This is also where the client will find out whether the assessment of the design team's competence and resources was effective and whether the client's interpretation of any advice given was heeded.

The ability to work closely with designers from an early project stage to ensure that hazards are identified and eliminated or reduced can be a vital contribution to onsite health and safety. Risks associated with future maintenance, use as a workplace and even eventual demolition or dismantling of a structure can also be designed out or significantly reduced following appropriate involvement from the CDM co-ordinator. The regulations require:

> [T]he CDM co-ordinator shall—
>
> > take all reasonable steps to ensure that designers comply with their duties . . .
>
> Extract from CDM Regulation 20(2)

Early on the CDM co-ordinator will need to consider an appropriate strategy to carry out this duty effectively. This is generally dictated by the size of the project in terms of the number and variety of designers involved, the procurement route and the CDM co-ordinator's own perception of the level of risk involved.

The main routes to assess the designer's health and safety contributions are:

- By attending design review meetings and assessing the designer's contributions and health and safety considerations. In these design environments where the design options are discussed with the client and other consultants, the CDM co-ordinator can, but is not legally required to, enter the discussions on design solutions that avoid or reduce the hazard and add value.

- Requesting significant residual risks from the design team unless already issued to the CDM co-ordinator in compliance with their duty to co-operate. Evaluation of these contributions should provide sufficient evidence of designer's health and safety effectiveness or failings. These contributions on residual risk should be assessed along with the drawings and/or specifications.

- Calling a CDM design review meeting to formally discuss the designer's contributions and strategies. This provides the ultimate opportunity to explore all aspects and interfaces of the design and the respective designer's health and safety considerations. This environment provides the opportunity for the CDM co-ordinator, lead designer or lead consultant responsible to manage health and safety through a risk register, for example.

- Reviewing design meeting minutes and contributions.

- Again, for the CDM co-ordinator to be in a position to ensure the designer is providing adequate information in or with their designs, an assessment of the project and the presumed information should be made first. Designers do not need to provide information on every hazard or assumption but on the unusual and difficult-to-manage issues that are not likely to be obvious to a competent designer or contractor.

The contributions by the design team to a health and safety risk register are valuable supporting information that should be included as pre-construction information. Typical information a competent designer should be providing with their designs include detailed drawings for difficult-to-assemble or difficult-to-replace elements of the building or structure, information on residual maintenance hazards, e.g. confined spaces, heavy components, difficult-to-access light fittings and so on. Many of these hazards should be supported by a proposed sequence of erection demonstrating how the hazard can be managed safely.

In assessing designer compliance and contributions the CDM co-ordinator is also assessing their competence in the field of design health and safety, and based on this initial assessment the CDM co-ordinator can evaluate their strategy to further assess the designer's contributions. For example, if a designer has not identified deep excavations in a restricted area as a significant risk, will they identify the access issues in relation to the plant located on the roof?

As with all duties 'to ensure', as a CDM co-ordinator, the report to the client, project manager or client representative should highlight areas of concern that have not been addressed fully by the design. These residual risks or issues concerning the CDM co-ordinator should be of a nature where it was reasonably practicable for the designer to have taken design action to avoid or reduce the risk to a more manageable level.

The extent of this duty is qualified by 'take all reasonable steps to ensure'. This does not require the CDM co-ordinator to evaluate all aspects of the designer's health and safety contributions but should provide a basis for a strategy that is based on the project's risk profile. It would be considered on a smaller, lower-risk project to adopt a minimalist strategy whereas on a large, complex design and high-risk project a more detailed and investigative approach which explores the design areas and construction activities in more detail would be advisable.

Working with the principal contractor

The CDM co-ordinator, over and above their general duty to co-operate and co-ordinate their activities with other duty holders, needs to develop a good relationship with those representing the principal contractor as soon as is practicable. The regulations provide the following:

The CDM co-ordinator shall—

(c) liaise with the principal contractor regarding—
   (i) the contents of the health and safety file,
   (ii) the information which the principal contractor needs to prepare the construction phase plan, and
   (iii) any design development which may affect planning and management of the construction work.

Extract from CDM Regulation 20(1)

The early involvement and discussions with the principal contractor, therefore, can only facilitate robust arrangements for health and safety management.

The pre-construction information should have included the requirement for the health and safety file and the diligent CDM co-ordinator will further bring these to the attention of the principal contractor. They should discuss an approach that will provide all necessary information before or at practical completion. As part of the project arrangements the CDM co-ordinator can ask or advise on the principal contractor's strategy for identifying, collating and providing such information deemed necessary for the health and safety file.

The CDM co-ordinator can also take the opportunity to discuss, in a proactive and helpful manner, the quality of the available pre-construction information and whether this is sufficient to facilitate a compliant construction phase plan. The earlier the appointment of the principal contractor is made by the client, the greater the opportunity to minimise risk and plan for safety onsite.

Again, depending on the timing of the appointment of the principal contractor and the contractual arrangements for the project's design, there may be an opportunity for the principal contractor to contribute towards the design risk management process. If the contract is of a design-and-build nature, the principal contractor will need to ensure arrangements for the designers, either novated or otherwise engaged, are in place to continue to identify hazards and embrace the general principles of prevention. Often it has been suggested that a minimal service agreement between the principal contractor and the novated design team does not lend itself to the requirements of the regulations. Poorly resourced architects, engineers and other designers in a design-and-build environment do not always have the opportunity to effectively undertake their design risk management duties. The CDM co-ordinator would be required to monitor the arrangements and is liable for ensuring that designers comply with these duties.

The health and safety file

Health and safety people have argued for a long time about the risks during construction versus the risks during future maintenance. Statistically, you are six times more likely to be killed on a construction site than in most other jobs, but, as a product of the building's life, the maintenance operations and management of associated hazards go on for the structure's existence. Therefore, the CDM document that provides the information to facilitate the future health and safety management is a valuable resource. All maintenance and future projects would benefit from a suitable developed and readily accessible health and safety file. The regulations regarding the file initially state that:

> [T]he CDM co-ordinator shall—
>
> (e) prepare, where none exists, and otherwise review and update a record ("the health and safety file") containing information relating to the project which is likely to be needed during any subsequent construction work to ensure the health and safety of any person . . . and
> (f) at the end of the construction phase, pass the health and safety file to the client.
>
> Extract from CDM Regulation 20(2)

The CDM regulations, therefore, require the CDM co-ordinator to prepare the health and safety file. It is more than useful if the process of defining the health and safety file structure and format is discussed initially with the client and then brought into the project-wide arrangements for health and safety management.

In setting up the health and safety file, the CDM co-ordinator could consider the following issues for facilitating development:

• Setting up a checklist for the designers and contractors of typical information, e.g. types of components that will be difficult to replace, e.g. air handling units, large window/glass sections, etc.; access arrangements, e.g. mobile elevation work platforms, man-safe systems, etc.; as installed M&E drawings, 'as built' drawings, hazard data sheets for hazardous substances like finishes or materials used, contact detail of specialist contractors, etc.
• Where possible discuss the operational and maintenance health and safety issues with the client's facilities manager or safety representative, review risk assessments and accident reports.
• Discuss the format of the file with the client and offer advice on version control and accessibility with information technology options.

The CDM co-ordinator is best placed to monitor the health and safety file's development through the audit function of monitoring the outputs of design risk management and other information provided in or with designs. The CDM co-ordinator also has the opportunity to define the arrangements for the file's development in the pre-construction. Certain complex projects require development and access to the file throughout the project. Other projects may require parts of the file to be handed over to tenants or occupiers when parts of a building are handed over for fit-out by other or respective client contractors.

4 Designers and CDM

Introduction

This section has been designed to provide designers with support in developing the knowledge and day-to-day skills to comply with their CDM duties as designers. The chapter covers the theoretical solutions to common design-related health and safety problems, the ability for designers to assess their own competence and designer CPD development and, where possible, to see the opportunities to add value to their service and the project as a whole through a commitment to CDM compliance.

The designer's CDM duties apply to all construction projects irrespective of the size or CDM status, i.e. notifiable or non-notifiable. Designers' duties apply to competition work, pre-planning work, town planning and so on, where there is sometimes no definable project.

As we are talking about criminal law, any professional designer or practice manager operating in Britain today wishing to comply with their CDM duties would be advised to ask themselves the following questions as part of a review:

- What is CDM competence and am I competent to comply with CDM 2007?
- With respect to occupational health and safety in construction, future maintenance and final demolition, how do I design safely?
- How do I clearly communicate relevant health and safety information to contractors, other designers, CDM co-ordinators and the client?

The following chapter will assist the designer in answering these questions and developing an action plan to address any concerns.

The statutory duties imposed on designers by the CDM Regulations are designed to set a health and safety agenda at the earliest stages of design during a project and to take advantage of the opportunities that exist at pre-planning and early design that are lost in the detailed design stages. Examples include spatial design to avoid or reduce risks associated with restricted access for construction or maintenance, contamination, poor ground conditions, integration of mechanical and electrical systems and associated plant and so on. In the real world one could argue that the issues of planning and funding are so high on the agenda that CDM is difficult to apply, but the relationship between the initial design layout and interfaces becomes a real cost issue if not addressed in the early design stages. The application of the designers' CDM duties is qualified in the CDM Approved Code of Practice with the following statement:

> Designers have to weigh many factors as they prepare their designs. Health and safety considerations have to be weighed alongside other considerations, including cost, fitness for purpose, aesthetics, buildability, maintainability and environmental impact. CDM2007 allows designers to take due account of other relevant design considerations. The Regulations

do not prescribe design outcomes, but they do require designers to weigh the various factors and reach reasoned, professional decisions.

Extract from CDM ACoP

This statement and the Health and Safety Executive appreciate that designers have many standards and codes to follow, and health and safety considerations must be applied in a balanced and reasonable way on projects. Having said that, the regulations and Approved Code of Practice require, through the design process, the avoidance of foreseeable risks as far as is reasonably practicable, taking into account other relevant design considerations.

It is true to say that the design fraternity and the CDM Regulations have not had the closest of relationships since they came together in 1995. It was widely thought that many design practices did not perhaps fully appreciate the contribution they could make to construction health and safety. Whether designers were mis-sold the principles of CDM or whether they misunderstood what was required of them, the fact remained that numerous practices did not go far enough in embracing this legislation. One could argue that without the legislation having any legal gateways like planning and building regulations approval, it did not rate highly on the priority list. It is hoped by many CDM advocates that the duties placed on the client to ensure there are CDM designer arrangements in place on a project will drive the issue up the agenda and promote more application of design risk management.

This chapter will also discuss the strategy and arrangements a designer will need to have in place to address the health and safety challenges on the project and demonstrate compliance. There is a move away from design risk and an encouragement in the CDM Approved Code of Practice to apply a simpler design risk management strategy that accepts a direct application of risk avoidance and reduction without the holistic audit trail. Also covered is how the designers will need to interact with the CDM co-ordinator in respect of co-operation, design co-ordination and implementing the client's project-specific CDM arrangements for design risk management and the development of the health and safety file.

High-level project safety standards for design CDM compliance that suit a project's particular risk profile are potentially set before the start of the design phase by the definition of the CDM arrangements which can be an output of the CDM co-ordinator's advice to the client. Arrangements can vary from detailed standards that require CDM design review workshops, a common risk register, defined design risk management responsibilities within the design team for high-risk projects, to simple arrangements of notes on drawings and design statement in stage reports for low-risk projects. Fundamentally the CDM arrangements and practice operating procedures of any competent design practice should take advantage of the early opportunities that exist to proactively address any health and safety issues that are to be managed by designers, through identifying significant hazards, recording these as a design CDM agenda and taking appropriate direct design action or design management action, including co-ordination, to avoid or reduce the risks or obtain additional site or client information. Examples of design action categories can include programming, e.g. phasing works, requesting more pre-construction information, e.g. asbestos Type 3 survey (now called Demolition and Dismantling Survey) when only a Type 1 exists; design co-ordination, e.g. planning mechanical and electrical services interface and penetrations to avoid hazards associated with drilling and chasing concrete; and, obviously, direct design actions that can include specification, spatial design, layout, etc., to reduce onsite risks of manual handling, restricted access, etc.

Significantly, too, the designer's and contractor's duties apply to all construction projects where the HSE are the enforcing authority, which is the majority of construction projects. This suggests that even on the smallest of projects a designer must and can contribute to avoiding and reducing risks on site. In the opinion of the authors, the designer's belief and understanding that there is a direct relationship between a design and onsite health and safety is fundamental to effective compliance.

It could be argued that competent, experienced designers subconsciously comply with their CDM duties as an integrated part of their service. They consider building issues and spatial design for contractors to access site, for mechanical and electrical plant to be installed and removed safely, and the phasing of the works to minimise the impact on the client's business. However, the regulations promote a proactive and CDM-integrated design strategy that requires designers to critically assess their designs throughout the design and not retrospectively. This assessment must initially identify significant construction, maintenance and final demolition risks associated with the design. Then, where it is reasonable to do so, the designer, through designing and the design service, must avoid or reduce the risk to a manageable level. Then, where this is not practicable, the designer must specify a sequence of work, specify a control measure and transfer the risk to the contractor, other designer and CDM co-ordinator with supporting information so it can be managed by others. The CDM Approved Code of Practice provides invaluable guidance for designers on the extent of this duty, how far they are required to go and how information can be communicated to other duty holders for action. The principles of the guidance apply a common-sense filter and only require the designer to communicate health and safety information on unusual and difficult-to-manage risks, and not on risks one would expect a competent designer or contractor to manage effectively. More detail on the application and design strategies associated with communicating health and safety information will be discussed later in this chapter.

The issues of designer CDM competence will also be discussed in this chapter and the importance of the relationship between the experience of the designer and the design risk management process will be emphasised. The CDM regulations have identified competence as a fundamental requirement and those clients engaging designers are having to focus on the standards set for competence in the CDM Approved Code of Practice. This includes

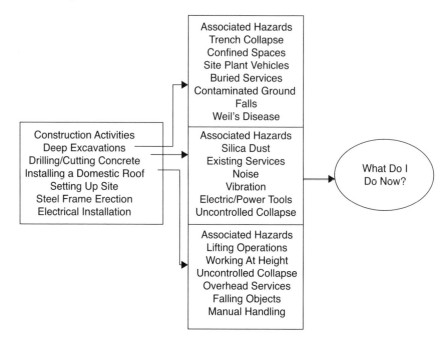

Figure 4.1 The relationship between construction activities and associated hazards

individual and organisational assessments of task knowledge, experience, continuous professional development, training and the overall approach to design risk management.

In simple terms, the designers on any project must have the design and health and safety skills and knowledge to proactively identify significant health and safety problems (hazards) and through their design service take action to ensure the structure can be constructed, and maintained, safely. Below is an illustration highlighting the relationship between construction activities and associated hazards.

Finally, in appreciating the challenging questions at the start of this chapter, a design practice or lone designer must have advice and training or instruction from a competent source, based on the risk profile of the projects worked on regarding their CDM system to address:

- CDM competence (both in-house and when engaging external designers);
- arrangements for checking clients are aware of their CDM duties;
- applied design risk management to avoid and reduce risk and communicate significant residual risks that are unusual and difficult to manage, associated with the construction, maintenance, use (workplace only) and eventual demolition of the structure;
- co-ordinate their design work with others to reduce health and safety risks;

- co-operate with the CDM co-ordinator regarding design risk management and health and safety file information.

Who are CDM designers?

With a clear understanding that designers have legal duties and in complying with them have real opportunities to contribute to the health and safety on projects and throughout the life cycle of a structure, one important question should be, 'Who are designers?' The influences on and contributions to a design are not solely under the control of the traditional architects and engineers. To clarify this issue for organisations and clients setting standards and service arrangements on projects, the regulations have a broad definition of a 'designer':

> Designers are those who have a trade or a business which involves them in:
> - preparing designs for construction work including variations – this includes preparing drawings, design details, specifications, bills of quantities and the specification of articles and substances, as well as all the related analysis, calculations, and preparatory work; or
> - arranging for their employees or other people under their control to prepare designs relating to a structure or part of a structure.
>
> Extract from CDM ACoP

This definition can be more accurately broken down to include a wide variety of designers with a set of CDM duties and potential to manage and contribute to health and safety. Examples of who these include are:

- architects, civil and structural engineers, building surveyors, landscape architects, and design practices (of whatever discipline) contributing to, or having overall responsibility for, any part of the design, e.g. drainage engineers designing the drainage for a new development;
- anyone who specifies or alters a design, or who specifies the use of a particular method of work or material, e.g. a quantity surveyor who insists on specific material or a client who stipulates a particular layout for a new production building;
- building service designers, engineering practices or others designing fixed plant which people can fall more than 2 metres from (this includes ventilation and electrical systems), e.g. a specialist provider of permanent fire extinguishing installations;
- those purchasing materials where the choice has been left open, e.g. people purchasing building blocks and so deciding the weights that bricklayers must handle;

- contractors carrying out design work as part of their contribution to a project, e.g. an engineering contractor providing design, procurement and construction management services;
- temporary works engineers, including those designing formwork false work, scaffolding, and sheet piling;
- interior designers, including shop-fitters who also develop the design;
- anyone specifying or designing how demolition, dismantling work, structural alteration, or formation of openings, is to be carried out;
- and heritage organisations who specify how work is to be done in detail, e.g. providing detailed requirements to stabilise existing structures.

Extract from CDM ACoP

As a rule any official, for example a building control officer, or planning officer who is appointed and authorised under a specific Act or regulation, is not a CDM designer irrespective of their influence over the design and its risk profile. How the designer addresses professional concerns on projects regarding these issues is covered later in this section, but the designer is responsible for managing the health and safety aspects of that change brought about by the official.

A lead designer, project manager who may not have any specific CDM duties, the client and the CDM co-ordinator on any project would benefit from identifying the extent of potential design services so the flow of health and safety information can be clearly predicted and monitored. These more obscure designers can include temporary works designers, landscape designers, fit-out graphical designers and contractor design portions.

Designers' duties explained

There are five designer-specific duties for all projects, three additional duties for notifiable projects and four general duties that are also covered in Chapter 1. The specific designer duties applicable to all projects are to:

- make sure that they are competent and adequately resourced to address the health and safety issues likely to be involved in the design;
- check that clients are aware of their duties;
- when carrying out design work, avoid foreseeable risks to those involved in the construction and future use of the structure, and in doing so, they should eliminate hazards and reduce risk associated with those hazards which remain;
- provide adequate information about any significant risks associated with the design;
- co-ordinate their work with that of others in order to improve the way in which risks are managed and controlled.

Extract from CDM ACoP

The additional duties applied to a notifiable project include:

- ensure that the client has appointed a CDM co-ordinator;
- ensure that they do not start design work other than initial design work unless a CDM co-ordinator has been appointed;
- co-operate with the CDM co-ordinator, principal contractor and with any other designers or contractors as necessary for each of them to comply with their duties. This includes providing any information needed for the pre-construction information or health and safety file.

Extract from CDM ACoP

The general duties applied to the designers and all duty holders are:

- to ensure those with duties under the CDM regulations must satisfy themselves that they are competent and those engaged are competent to comply with their CDM duties;
- to ensure those with duties under the CDM regulations take account of the principles of prevention when considering what controls to select to control risks;
- to ensure those with duties co-operate and co-ordinate with others to ensure they can comply with their duties.

We will now examine in detail how the designer should comply with these duties.

Ensuring competence

CDM Regulation 4 and appendix 4 of the CDM Approved Code of Practice set standards for achieving competence to comply with the CDM Regulations. In simple terms the designer and design practice must have, in most cases documented, procedures for compliance with the designer's CDM duties. They must have evidence of CDM training or instruction in the application of design risk management and be aware of their CDM duties.

But fundamentally the important criteria for competence are experience and professional qualifications associated with the particular area of design and project types.

The main evidence a designer or practice would need in demonstrating competence should consist of:

- a company CDM manual or set of policy arrangements;
- evidence of CDM training or instruction on the CDM duties – this can be via CPD commitments or by in-house training or CDM briefings;
- CVs of main designers;

- arrangements for obtaining health and safety advice, e.g. subscription service or appointed health and safety professional depending on size of practice and nature of construction work.

A design organisation may wish to set up in-house induction and training courses to promote CDM design risk management and best practice from previous projects. Some practices have set up annual CDM training courses with pre-reading, tests and pass marks to drive competence standards up and demonstrate a high commitment to CDM to their potential and existing clients.

Clients and their advisors on CDM-notifiable projects are advised to make a judgement on competence of designers and the assessment should focus on the particular project and be proportionate to the risks and complexity of the work. Clients and their CDM co-ordinators do not need to issue lengthy questionnaires for simplistic low-risk projects and, conversely, an interview with the design team would be valuable for a more complex high-risk project.

The CDM regulations cater for designers who can't currently demonstrate CDM competence due to lack of experience or language issues and they can still continue to work under the CDM supervision of a competent designer.

Informing clients of their duties

This duty generally is imposed on the initial designer and requires them not to commence designing on a project unless the client is aware of their duties. This is not required when designers have worked with clients before and are aware the client knows his duties.

Not one of the regulations, CDM Approved Code of Practice or industry guidance state what action should be taken if the client is not aware of their CDM duties, but a reasonable approach would be to offer them some information, for example the HSE leaflet 'Having Construction Work Done?' or meeting with them and explaining the CDM Regulations using the CDM Approved Code of Practice as a guide. The Construction Skills CDM industry guidance for clients also provides valuable information to discharge the duty in a reasonable manner. For notifiable projects one could argue that it is reasonable to assume the client is aware of their duties if a CDM co-ordinator, who is their advisor, has been appointed. The designer should assess the level of existing client CDM knowledge so a sensible approach is adopted to advising the client and commencing work legally. One problem can exist with large or complex client bodies in identifying who the client actually is. With PFIs (private finance initiatives), PPP (Public Private Partnerships) initiatives, joint ventures and local authorities, for example, it may not be obvious and inquiries will be required. The CDM Regulations have anticipated this potential problem and CDM Regulation 8 states where there is more than one client the election of a client or clients in writing is required, and this client is the CDM duty holder.

To demonstrate compliance it is advisable that a record of the action taken is kept by the designer. This interaction with the client should be seen as an integrated part of the design service and an opportunity to clarify the extent of the design service in relation to CDM compliance. Issues like efficiently obtaining, recording and communicating health and safety information and the issues of as-built drawings for the health and safety file can be discussed early in the project's life.

It should be noted that this regulation makes no reference to contract or appointment but purely to designing on a project, and designers and practices would benefit from making the execution of this duty a pre-design action in any quality plan, practice procedures or service level agreement. Also, it should be noted that there is no duty to advise the client of their duties but there is a duty not to commence designing unless the designer checks that the client is aware of their CDM duties. However, the Construction Skills CDM industry guidance for designers actively promotes the idea of making clients aware of their duties which seems a valuable contribution on any project, especially a non-notifiable one where there is no formal health and safety advisor.

Integrating health and safety into the design process

The management of health and safety through the design service is a skill that designers must understand and apply to comply with their CDM duties and contribute in managing risk on the project. In designing safely it is important to understand some basic rules and terminology associated with design risk management. First, the duty to avoid and reduce foreseeable risks is qualified by 'reasonably practicable', which means there must be a balance between cost and health and safety. An example of this could be installing parapets on a roof that maintenance contractors would only access every two years to carry out warranty inspections. A contractor-supplied portable 'man-safe' system would be a suitable recommendation from the designer to demonstrate CDM compliance. A designer would never be expected to identify all significant hazards, only those that are reasonably foreseeable given their area of design expertise and information provided by the client and CDM co-ordinator on a project. Designers are not required by the CDM Regulations to produce risk assessment and record design actions that have resulted in the avoidance or reduction of risk on site; however, if a design action or assumption in relation to safety needs to be communicated clearly to another designer or contractor, then it should be recorded, e.g. the selection of a particular structure or material or a phasing sequence to solve a health and safety problem. Finally, in the provision of health and safety information to other designers and contractors, the extent of detail is qualified in the CDM Approved Code of Practice to discourage bureaucracy and encourage designers to only report on hazards that are unusual and difficult to manage, in their opinion. They do not have to report on information relating to hazards that one would expect a competent designer or contractor to be capable of managing effectively. It is felt that understanding these points dispels some of the myths that have evolved throughout the life of the CDM Regulations and provides designers with some valuable guidance regarding design risk management.

Design risk management could be defined as the integrated design approach to managing health and safety. To be confident in applying a design risk management strategy some other terminology needs qualifying. The words hazard, significant hazards and risk are all used in design risk management activities. A hazard can be defined as anything with the potential to cause harm. A significant hazard could be defined as or refer to the hazards that cause fatal and major accidents, e.g. falls from height, collapsing structure or hazards that could cause multiple casualties, e.g. collapsing scaffolding or fire. A risk is a qualifying term for a hazard that brings in factors of likelihood that the accident could occur and the severity of the accident. This terminology is important because design risk management initially requires a process of hazard identification before a design consideration is made of the risk and best design action to avoid, reduce or transfer the risk to another party for action. This brings us on to the detail of applied design risk management and the appropriate strategy for compliance and making a real health and safety contribution on site. A strategy based on the risk profile of the project and the extent of the design service provides the designer with sensible parameters to form a CDM agenda and to comply with their CDM duties effectively and efficiently.

One of the keys to effective design risk management strategy is identifying the opportunities early on in the project for health and safety contributions. Spatial design, density and orientation are fundamental design and architectural considerations and their relationship with health and safety offer opportunities to:

- provide unrestricted access to all areas of the structure;
- provide access and space for the contractor to deliver materials with plant and avoid or reduce manual handling operations;
- avoid or reduce the interface with existing services and utilities infrastructure or plan for their removal;
- provide the opportunity for contractors to have a one-way traffic management plan to avoid or reduce risk associated with reversing;
- provide space for site welfare, materials lay-down areas, crane positions, etc.;
- consider general arrangements for access for maintenance.

All the above health and safety issues are difficult to manage at the detailed stage of the design so the designer's strategy for a site layout is something contractors would like designers to plan with full consideration of the site and logistical building operations. Similarly, an engineer designing a water treatment plant or upgrade to a pump set would need to consider similar issues in respect of layout, positioning, interfaces and future maintenance activities.

With respect to early design opportunities, one could argue a potential problem in the construction industry exists regarding conceptual designs for competitions and funding, which are not always produced by competent designers, and therefore limited considerations for buildability and health and safety have been made. The problem also potentially exists, in under-pressure architectural studios, in the pre-planning and production of planning drawings where little commercial opportunity is given to the practice to consider CDM as thoroughly as the designer or practice would like.

Another issue in relation to design risk management strategy is the influence of the client and for notifiable projects their advisor, the CDM co-ordinator, in defining the design CDM arrangements. There could be design risk management standards that are different from the designer's or practice's own and require training or briefing before design starts. Some clients require notes on drawings, which on more complex and dynamic designs can be difficult to track and manage change. Some clients prefer common live risk registers, managed by their CDM co-ordinator and CDM meetings or CDM co-ordinator attendance at design meetings to manage the register. Finally, some client and CDM co-ordinator strategies require designers to send their design risk assessments to the CDM co-ordinator for appraisal and inclusion in tender and pre-construction information document updates. One could strongly argue positively for the common risk register approach, as it places the CDM co-ordinator in a position where they can assess designer CDM compliance, advise the designer on compliance in real time and co-ordinate health and safety information between designers and contractors via the register. This provides an opportunity for all parties to demonstrate compliance, for co-ordination and co-operation and avoids multiple systems of communicating health and safety information. In summary it is important for the team to understand what the arrangements are for high-level health and safety management through the design element of the project. The arrangements need to clarify the recording and communicating arrangements, the duties and responsibilities and the review and action management arrangements. Figure 4.2 is an example of a typical risk register.

Clients can also have specific design standards to address health and safety issues associated with their particular business, site or activities. Some clients have policies on access for maintenance where, for example, man-safe systems and/or mobile elevation work platforms are not permitted; early consideration to low-maintenance or perhaps permanent gantries may be necessary in such situations. Other standards include floor finishes and slip-resistance requirements, no plant at ground level for security reasons and component replacement strategies requiring no hard/permanent wiring of units that will require replacement within the building's or system's life. It is worth checking if clients have management and or design health

X Project Design Risk Register						
Hazard Ref No	Hazard Ownership	Design Area/ Construction/ Maintenance Activity	Hazard/Issue	Design Action To date	Further Design Action	Comments & Supporting Information
1.1	A Company	Ground / Foundations	New structure clashing with existing piles	Carry out accurate survey of existing pile locations to determine relationship with new structure.	Survey existing piles Fix setting out of new building in world co-ordinates. Co-ordinate existing piles with new structure.	?????? to arrange structural design CDM review meeting before end of May.

Figure 4.2 A typical risk register

and safety standards so they can be built into the overall CDM approach to the project.

This is a good time to discuss how far it is necessary to go, which is covered in the CDM Approved Code of Practice. The code reminds designers that they need to comply with regulation 3 of the Management of Health and Safety at Work Regulations 1999, which places a duty to undertake a suitable and sufficient risk assessment. However, it is accepted that if designers comply with the requirements of the code, this will generally suffice in terms of demonstrating compliance. This promotes a more direct design application of avoiding and reducing risk and transferring significant residual risk, and construction and maintenance methods for promoting health and safety by others. The code discourages unnecessary paperwork and encourages the application of the principles of prevention; therefore designers don't necessarily or legally have to produce design risk assessments.

The health and safety output of designing safely – in other words, what information is supplied to contractors and other designers – is covered later in this chapter, but generally only requires information on unusual and difficult-to-manage hazards to be communicated, not all hazards.

The application of this more simplistic and direct approach is promoted by the Construction Skills Industry CDM Guidance for Designers, using the acronym ERIC – Eliminate, Reduce, Inform and Control – which is expanded on below. This can be seen as a précised version of the principles of prevention covered in Chapter 1 and defines the hierarchy of action to take in managing a hazard.

Eliminate: To eliminate a hazard altogether one must generally design or programme to avoid the associated activity, environment or interface. This can be done through spatial design, planning, specification, etc. The most fundamental design actions can eliminate hazards. The best examples and generally the most simplest, e.g. planning significant structural work in a school during the summer holidays to avoid interface with the children, specifying a non-toxic paint or adhesive, spatially positioning a building to allow the contractor to have independent access with no reversing required, and positioning non-opening windows so they can be cleaned by a reach-clean system to avoid access via a flat roof. To eliminate a significant hazard is best practice but when the cost of eliminating the hazard is prohibitive and places the project at risk, then the designer should consider reducing the risk to a manageable level for the contractor or designer to continue.

Reduce: Risk reduction involves evaluating the design options to reduce the severity and/or likelihood associated with the hazard and the number of people involved. Designing to reduce the time maintenance or construction workers spend at height through specification of pre-installed or low-maintenance elements will reduce the likelihood of falling. Reducing the amount of drilling the structure to accommodate the mechanical and electrical systems through specifying engineered joists and pre-forming penetrations in concrete structures will reduce the risks of the associated hazards, e.g. working at height, noise, vibration, structural collapse associated with potential weakening of key structural elements and hazardous substances, e.g. concrete dust. Where a significant risk remains and it is unusual or difficult to manage, the next duty holder in the design or construction chain must be notified.

Inform: This promotes the provision of information to assist the future management of the risk during future design, construction, maintenance and demolition. The information can be purely regarding a hazard or hazards associated with an activity or area or can be supporting information involving a sequence or phasing of work or a design assumption that is critical to safety. The general project CDM arrangement should cover the methodology for communicating information. The main options include risk registers and notes on drawings. The information can also cover health and safety strategies for persons using and maintaining the building in the form of maintenance access strategies for cleaning, general access, component replacement and dismantling.

Control: Consultants or high-level designers are not generally directly involved in specifying onsite control measures however many designers do become involved in this practice. Temporary works designers and co-ordinators set control measures for integrated edge protection and safe systems of work in relation to permits to undertake safety critical actions.

A practical understanding and application of ERIC contributes significantly to demonstrating competence and compliance with the design's duties to avoid or reduce foreseeable risks.

In the mindset of applying a design risk management approach, the following illustrations have been developed to (a) illustrate the activities and interfaces, and (b) the hazards associated with the following construction issues:

1. Surrounding environment
2. Site set-up and management
3. Building/construction
4. Maintenance.

Historically designers have been encouraged to record their, sometimes obvious, mitigation and through poor application of CDM have recorded obvious risks for contractors to consider on site. Recording and communicating the hazard of working at height in relation to a roofing contractor

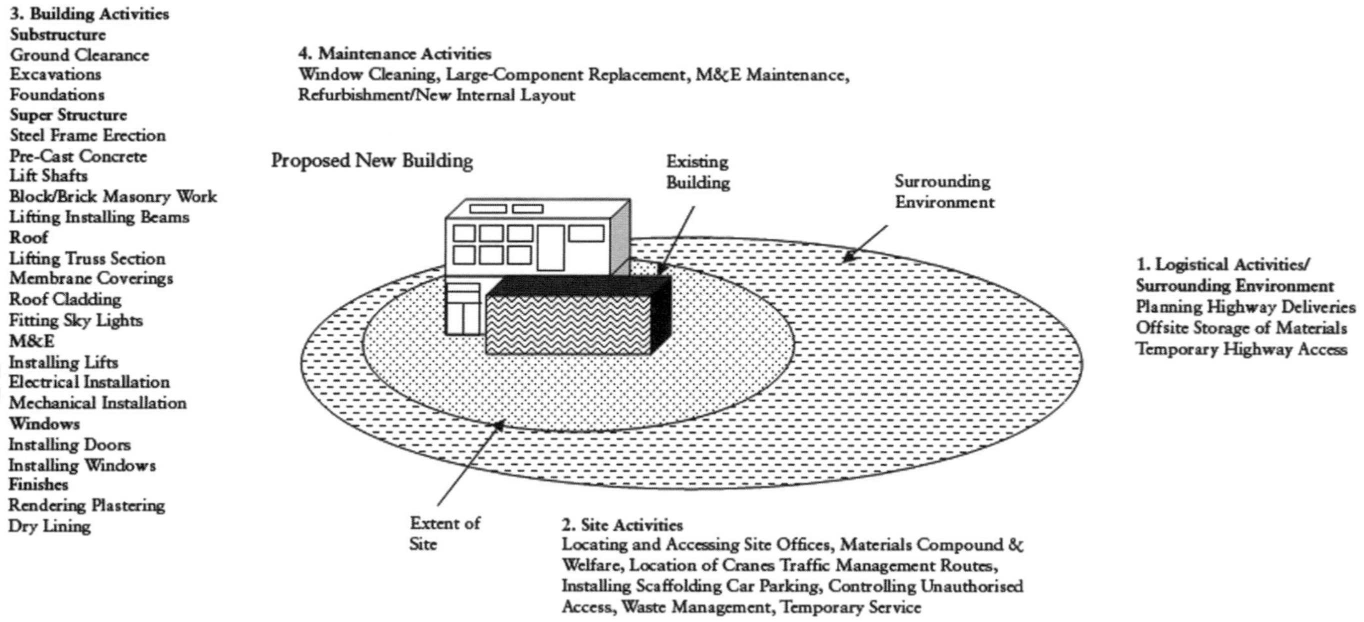

Figure 4.3 The activities and interfaces around a new building

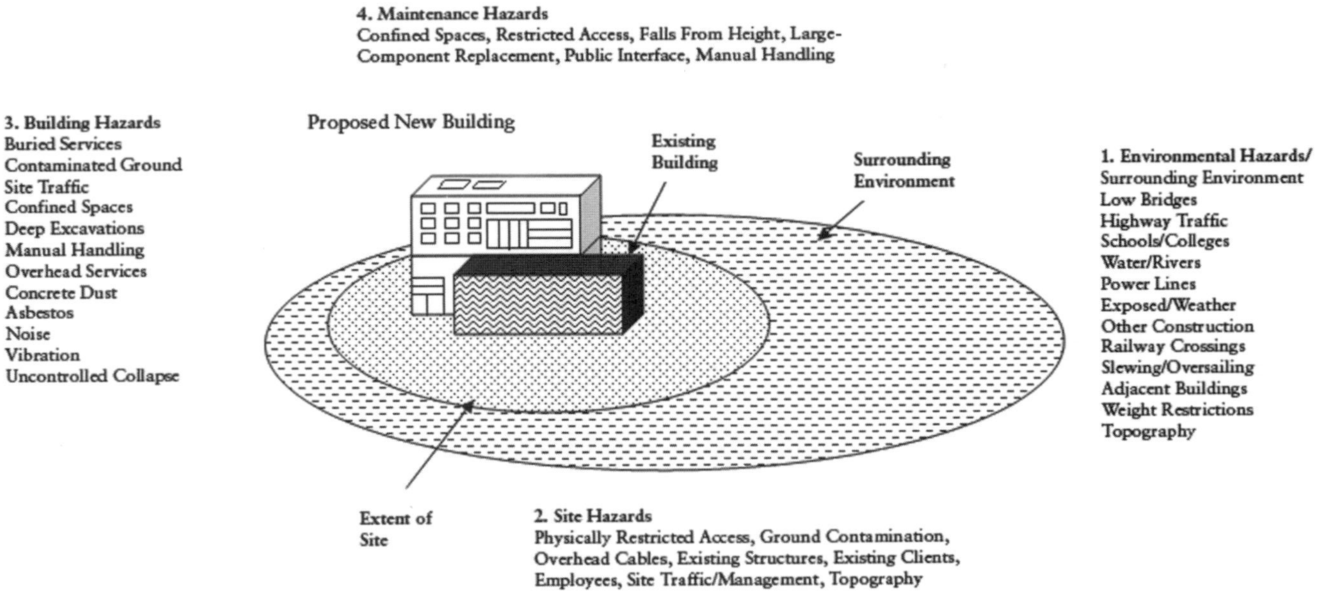

4. Maintenance Hazards
Confined Spaces, Restricted Access, Falls From Height, Large-
Component Replacement, Public Interface, Manual Handling

**1. Environmental Hazards/
Surrounding Environment**
Low Bridges
Highway Traffic
Schools/Colleges
Water/Rivers
Power Lines
Exposed/Weather
Other Construction
Railway Crossings
Slewing/Oversailing
Adjacent Buildings
Weight Restrictions
Topography

Proposed New Building

Existing Building

Surrounding Environment

Extent of Site

2. Site Hazards
Physically Restricted Access, Ground Contamination,
Overhead Cables, Existing Structures, Existing Clients,
Employees, Site Traffic/Management, Topography

3. Building Hazards
Buried Services
Contaminated Ground
Site Traffic
Confined Spaces
Deep Excavations
Manual Handling
Overhead Services
Concrete Dust
Asbestos
Noise
Vibration
Uncontrolled Collapse

Figure 4.4 Hazards associated with the activities

and stating that issue to be covered in the method statement is not helpful or legally required. These designer health and safety contributions detract from the design risk management exercise and as stated in the CDM Approved Code of Practice 'obscure the significant issues'.

The individual designer's fundamental strategy for design risk management, to demonstrate CDM compliance, should simply start with a review of an initial design programme or brief and the identification of hazards associated with the construction, maintenance and future demolition. Key to hazard identification is competence in the field of design and construction. Designers don't have to be experts in the construction and maintenance activities but they can't design structures that can't be built safely so they need a general understanding of the relationship between design and the associated activities. The pro forma shown in Figure 4.5 is a typical hazard identification checklist to promote the exercise in a systematic way.

The main construction and maintenance hazards for consideration are listed in Table 4.1 with guidance on some of the main associated construction and maintenance activities and environments on the building site.

In relation to this exercise, and setting the agenda for health and safety through the design, it is good practice to include the design team and CDM co-ordinator at the first design team meeting. The team should be briefed by the CDM co-ordinator or lead designer to review their design for hazards before attending and highlight the significant hazards at the meeting. In some cases it is advisable to invite the client or client's facilities maintenance team to contribute to the exercise. They often have experience of problems that have been identified during the maintenance and use of the building associated with their working activities that designers wouldn't necessarily be aware of. On smaller, more simple projects this can be done over the phone; however, the principles are the same.

Through this initial exercise, which does not have to be separate from the design meeting but in the authors' opinion should be integrated, the team should have the following outcomes:

- a list of significant hazards on the project that the design team believes can be avoided or reduced through collective or individual designer action;
- a list of significant hazards that they don't believe can be designed out, which the contractor or another designer will need to be made aware of;
- defined designers responsible for managing the design risk management process.

This initial list can set the agenda for real-time design risk management, for example:

- when the architect is setting out house positions they can consider the locations in respect of known services or topography to avoid or reduce risks from deep excavations;

Project...3 Storey School Extension/ St Davids...............Design Stage.......Scheme................Date......15th April 2010..............
Designer/Organisation......A Designer & Co.................

Design Area & Activity Insert reference No in appropriate box.	Hazardous Substances	Confined Spaces	Fall From Height	Falling Objects	Site Plant Vehicles	Collapsing Structure	Manual Handling	Moving Objects	Electricity Services	Gas Services	Fire Explosion	Noise & Vibration	Cuts & Abrasions	Asbestos & MM Minerals	Fire Means of Escape	Highway Traffic	Adverse Weather	Access for Cleaning	Access for Maintenance	Designer/ Company Responsible
Site Set-Up																				
Site Workface Access																				
Deliveries																				
Welfare Location																				
Pedestrian Routes																				
Temp Services																				
Car Parking																				
Materials Storage																				
Hording																				
Construction &																				
Excavating																				
Piling																				
Strip Foundations																				
Slab																				
Superstructure																				
Windows & Atria																				
Maintenance Work																				
Window Cleaning																				
Component Replacement																				
Light Fittings																				

Hazards (NB: only select hazards with significant risks)

Figure 4.5 Hazard identification checklist

Table 4.1 Construction and maintenance hazards

Hazards	Some associated construction or maintenance activities and environments (general and specific)
Falls from height (including falling objects)	Deep excavations, erecting/constructing structures, block work, metal and timber frames, surface coating and finishing, cladding, roof work, windows, mechanical and electrical works, demolition and refurbishment.
Hazardous materials	Residual contaminated or stored materials in a building or ground. An output of construction activities, e.g. silica/concrete dust from cutting pre-cast concrete products or drilling for mechanical and electrical services. Also toxic fumes from spray-painting elements.
Asbestos	Demolition/dismantling and mechanical and electrical works.
Lead	Roof works, plumbing and paint removal.
Confined spaces	Basements, attics/roof voids, fuel and water tanks, ducting, excavations.
Uncontrolled collapse	Excavations, wall and superstructures construction, timber frame combustion, temporary works, e.g. propping and concrete formwork.
Fire	Hot works, e.g. flame cutting during demolition and dismantling and plumbing, mechanical and electrical commissioning.
Site transport/plant	Deliveries, reversing vehicles, site access, groundworks, piling, lifting operations, mobile elevation work platforms, e.g. during fit-out.
Manual handling	Block and brick works, plaster boarding, floor boarding, timber and steel frame erection, roof covering, mechanical and electrical works.
Noise and vibration	Using power tools, operating mobile plant, working in industrial facilities, e.g. factories, power stations, etc.
Crush/entrapment	Lifting operations, temporary works, e.g. propping and concrete formwork.
Poor/restricted access/egress	General workface access and egress, confined spaces working, roof work in voids and truss erection, basements, mechanical and electrical works in false ceilings, risers and lift shafts.

Table 4.1 Construction and maintenance hazards (*continued*)

Hazards	Some associated construction or maintenance activities and environments (general and specific)
Interface with public and other persons at work	Inner-city/town projects, working in live workplaces, site access, deliveries, lifting operation slewing/ oversailing, highways/ street works, shops.
Uneven ground/conditions and challenging topography	Ground works, traffic management, working near water courses.
Adverse weather	Traffic management, working near or over water, external works, roofing, cladding, frame erection, lifting operations, deep excavations.
Hazardous construction operation	Diving, demolition, explosives, working over or near water, temporary works, stressing structures, cofferdams and caissons, strand and conventional jacking, rock bolting, dynamic compaction ground treatment, decontamination, sea defence structures, station plant modifications and upgrades.

• when a mechanical and electrical engineer is specifying and designing the system he can co-ordinate the design spatially to avoid or reduce restricted access hazards for plant installation and maintenance and reduce hazards associated with retrospectively drilling and chasing through spatial design and specification.

Strategically a process of applying design risk management consists of managing health and safety at a hazard's level and at a higher level managing the design process to manage health and safety as lead designers do with all design service subjects. Please remember that a competent CDM co-ordinator can, as part of their combined auditing and co-ordinator role, play a valuable part in administering the design risk management process via a risk register, which could add value in having someone competent advising more directly in design team meetings rather than desktop auditing and reporting findings retrospectively.

The simplification and management of this process can be supported through the use of pro formas in the form of checklists and registers to track, prompt an action and to communicate health and safety information. Some simple mindsets to guide the designer can include a problem and solution, which is illustrated below.

Problem = Hazard

Hazard = 'Something with the potential to cause harm or losses'

• Existing construction hazards (e.g. asbestos, restricted access)

- Designed in construction hazards (e.g. confined space, heavy blocks or beams in basement where mechanical lifting can't be utilised)
- Maintenance hazards (e.g. rooftop access for skylight cleaning)
- Workplace hazards (e.g. slippery floor when wet, traffic and pedestrians interfacing at a delivery point)
- Demolition and dismantling hazards (e.g. complicated cantilevered structure which requires a precise sequence to dismantle without collapsing).

Solution = Design Action

Direct design action:

- drawings
- specifications
- bills of quantities.

Design management action:

- programming
- surveys
- design co-ordination meetings
- requests for information (RFI), technical queries (TQ), architect's instructions (AI) management.

In pursuance of a simple and more direct approach to compliance, a checklist of company design health and safety standards can be used, as illustrated below, to assess the design at the various design stages.

To assist the design fraternity, the inspectorate, the Health and Safety Executive published a set of design health and safety traffic-light-type standards in categories, called RAG lists.

Red lists

Lists of known high-risk/hazardous building materials, construction activities and procedures to be eliminated from the project without compromise by designers. This list can also include CDM arrangements or CDM gateways for a project where no action can be taken unless a necessary statutory action has been executed.

Examples

- Pre-construction information not to be issued until detailed structural surveys, asbestos surveys, etc., completed or arrangements set for delivery through contract.
- Scabbling of concrete ('stop ends', etc.).

Table 4.2 Design health and safety checklist

# Health and safety issue and considerations Please tick as Appropriate ✔	RIBA stage				Comments and summary of residual risks
	A/B	C	D	E	E+	

1 Initial design layout/density and orientation
Position building/structure to consider temp access to allow access on to site and around site to avoid or reduce interface with contamination, buried structures, highway vehicles and reversing vehicles.
Also design to facilitate site set-up to include welfare, offices, and traffic routes, lay down areas, crane positions, scaffolding interface, etc. Control risks by specifying enabling works to remove services and structures, remediate contamination, provide temporary access, liaise with highways, authority, etc.

2 Groundworks substructure
Design and co-ordinate with engineers applying spatial opportunities and engineering design principles to avoid or reduce deep excavations, interface with buried structures and to provide access for plant and temporary works.

3 Superstructure
Design to avoid or minimise difficult-to-manage temporary works, co-ordinate design with engineers to consider structural stability/erection method and interface with existing buildings. Consider lifting operations and offsite fabrication solutions for restricted sites.

4 Roof system
Design to avoid confined spaces, construction problems in installing fall protection/netting, etc. Consider system and materials that reduced working at height, stability during erection and facilitates access for maintenance and warranty conditions.

Continued

Table 4.2 Design health and safety checklist (*continued*)

#	Health and safety issue and considerations Please tick as Appropriate ✓	RIBA stage					Comments and summary of residual risks
		A/B	C	D	E	E+	
5	**Mechanical and electrical systems** Early design co-ordination with M&E engineers to identify special requirements, access for maintenance, additional imposed loads on structure and main service entries, openings and runs to avoid and reduce restricted/difficult access for installation and maintenance, pre-formed openings to avoid/reduce working at height, noise, dust, vibration and affecting structural integrity during grinding and cutting concrete and steel. Plant location at low level.						
6	**Windows, curtain walling and atria** Consider unitised offsite fabricated and finished systems to reduce working at height. At early design stages plan strategic access strategy and consider reach clean, cleanable from inside, access for cherry picker (MEWP), building maintenance units and rope access as last resort.						
7	**Secondary structures and finishes** Consider in the finish access and logistics for construction and maintenance, also scaffolding and crane positions. Product life in restricted areas and component replacement must be considered. Brick, fabricated finished cladding, colour render, etc., all reduce maintenance activities, working at height and risks of falling objects. Metal section internal walls instead of block work, floating flooring instead of screed and false ceilings can reduce risks with manual handling and future access for M&E modifications.						
8	**Refurbishment** Obtaining sufficient site information for consideration at an early stage is valuable to avoid asbestos, structural, party wall, and interface with third parties. Site set-up and construction sequencing including enabling/early works/demolition should be considered at an early design stage. Generally this involved working the client and the CDM co-ordinator for advice on the initial pre-construction information.						

#	Health and safety issue and considerations — Please tick as Appropriate ✓	RIBA stage					Comments and summary of residual risks
		A/B	C	D	E	E+	
9	**Access for maintenance** Early design consideration to include access for maintenance and warranty conditions for: • windows, curtain walling • all mechanical and electrical systems • roof and rainwater systems • voids • water tanks • external cladding Access options include: • permanent access, gantries, steps, etc. • integrated parapet solution, plant well • MEWP: Mobile elevation work platform • Reach clean • Man-safest system Note: Solution based on frequency and nature of work, e.g. rooftop lights, mansafe and planton leading edge or hand rail protection.						
10	**Workplace (HS & W) Regulations 1992** Main considerations for compliance include: • Maintenance/cleaning – access for cleaning, capable of being cleaned/material and maintenance and liaison with client regarding use • Space – 11 m³ per person • Workstations – fit for purpose • Floors and stairs – clear thoroughfare • Traffic routes • Windows/glass walls – manifestation to prevent accidents • Toilets and washing – fit for purpose • Lockers and changing rooms • Meals and restrooms						

- Demolition by hand-held breakers of the top sections of concrete piles (pile-cropping techniques are available).
- The specification of fragile roof lights and roofing assemblies.
- Processes giving rise to large quantities of dust (dry cutting, blasting, etc.).
- Onsite spraying of harmful particulates.
- The specification of structural steelwork which is not purposely designed to accommodate safety nets.
- Designing roof-mounted services requiring access (for maintenance, etc.), without provision for safe access (e.g. barriers).

Source: www.hse.gov.uk

Amber lists

Products (as on the red list but lower risk), processes and procedures to be eliminated or reduced as far as possible and only specified/allowed if unavoidable. Amber list items are by inclusion unusual and/or difficult to manage for other designers, the contractor or facilities maintenance contractor and therefore require information to be provided. The list does not include the classification of hazards that one would expect a competent contractor or designer to be aware of, e.g. the risk of falling off a standard roof for a roofing contractor.

Examples

- Internal manholes in circulation areas.
- External manholes in heavy used vehicle access zones.
- The specification of 'lip' details (i.e. trip hazards) at the tops of pre-cast concrete staircases.
- The specification of shallow steps (i.e. risers) in external paved areas.
- The specification of heavy building blocks, i.e. those weighing >20 kg.
- Large and heavy glass panels.
- The chasing out of concrete / brick / block work walls or floors for the installation of services.
- The specification of heavy lintels (the use of slim metal or concrete lintels being preferred).
- The specification of solvent-based paints and thinners, or isocyanates, particularly for use in confined areas.
- Specification of curtain wall or panel systems without provision for the tying of scaffolds.
- Specification of block work walls >3.5 m high and retarded mortar mixes.

Source: www.hse.gov.uk

Green lists

These lists promote a positive design-in culture and include products, processes and procedures that are to be positively encouraged on the project or as part of the in-house design standards.

Some of the advantages of this proactive and organised approach include the efficient management and decision-making process during design that can cause designers concern when investigating solutions to a hazard via a risk assessment process. Other advantages include a uniformity of approach and as long as the lists and the arrangements for their management are flexible and evolve throughout projects to provide a continuously improving set of design standards, there will be reduced risk for builders and maintenance operatives on the associated projects.

Examples

- Adequate access for construction vehicles to minimise reversing requirements (one-way systems and turning radii).
- Provision of adequate access and headroom for maintenance in plant rooms, and adequate provision for replacing heavy components.
- Thoughtful location of mechanical/electrical equipment, light fittings, security devices, etc., to facilitate access and exit from crowded areas.
- The specification of concrete products with pre-cast fixings to avoid drilling.
- The specification of half board sizes for plasterboard sheets to make handling easier.
- Early installation of permanent means of access, and prefabricated staircases with hand rails.
- The provision of edge protection at permanent works where there is a foreseeable risk of falls after handover.
- Practical and safe methods of window cleaning (e.g. from the inside).
- Appointment of a Temporary Work Co-ordinator (BS 5975).
- Offsite timber treatment if PPA- and CCA-based preservatives are used (boron or copper salts can be used for cut ends on site).

Source: www.hse.gov.uk

In respect of supporting the design risk management exercise we have discussed hazard identification pro formas, design risk registers, red, amber and green lists and the top 10 checklists. Other valuable risk management exercises for more complex structures or environments include HAZID and HAZOP studies. HAZID studies are similar to risk assessment and are designed to invite the relevant team players to identify what could go wrong, i.e. the hazards, measure them against a defined list or benchmark of hazards and plan what can be done to avoid or control the resultant risks. The HAZOP study was historically derived from the chemical industry and promotes a

systematic examination of a process and evaluates what problems could happen, why and what can be done to avoid the problem. For complex structures and temporary works, these studies provide an opportunity to demonstrate compliance and add value to the project through design risk management.

The key designer design risk management issues could be summarised as:

- identifying the hazards associated with the construction, maintenance, 'in use' and demolition and identifying who can address them through design;
- transferring hazards that are significant and there is no design opportunity to manage the associated risk;
- designing individually and collaboratively to eliminate or reduce the risks in line with the principles of prevention;
- designing to comply with the Workplace Health Safety and Welfare Regulations 1992;
- engaging the CDM co-ordinator as a part of the design team and providing them with evidence of applied design risk management, providing pre-construction information for other designers and contractors and information for the health and safety file.

Table 4.3 illustrates some appropriate examples of information required as part of the design risk management process:

The CDM Approved Code of Practice qualifies the extent of health and safety information a designer would need to provide with their designs in a practical way to avoid over-production and anyone missing critical data. The ACoP states that designers should provide project-specific information and the information should concentrate on significant risks, which should not be obvious to those who use the design. Designers have to provide information on significant risks that are:

(a) not likely to be obvious to a competent contractor or other designers;
(b) unusual; or
(c) likely to be difficult to manage effectively.

Extract from CDM ACoP

An example of not applying the above guidance would be to provide a roofing contractor with information on the risk of falling off a roof. A competent contractor should be capable of managing these risks. However, knowledge of a structural defect or location of a fragile covering would be valuable to the contractor for health and safety planning and development of a method statement.

The designer's method of communicating information to support significant health and safety risks is also covered in the code and states:

Information should be brief, clear, precise, and in a form suitable for the users. This can be achieved using:

Table 4.3 Typical construction hazards

Example	Type of information
A site with poor or no access from the road.	Where possible, a temporary access route illustrated on the drawing.
Bespoke structural design to address an irregular shape.	Provide information to support installation, e.g. pre-assembly instructions, installation methodology based on known structural environmental conditions for temporary works, weights of components to facilitate lifting plan development by contractor.
Installation of large beam into a confined/restricted space.	Provide weight of beam and assumed access route or method for contractor so lifting plan, risk assessment and method statement can be developed.
Interface with the public at a busy shopping centre.	Define the extent of space allowed to work, lay down materials and equipment. Where possible negotiate restrictions to activities within certain times, e.g. driving access equipment during client's operational hours, and ensure these are stated clearly.
Installation of partition walls where asbestos is present.	Provide asbestos survey or commission/advise client to obtain information. Either recommend enabling works to remove asbestos or suggest alternative fixing method that avoids drilling/disturbing asbestos.
Installation of large curtain walling units over highway.	Supplier/designer information on installation/lifting arrangements to reduce time by lifting section pre-assembled onsite. Also designer could supply traffic and road closure information to facilitate development of risk assessment, and method statements regarding working over highway.
Access for maintenance in a confined space/void.	Highlight hazard to client for inclusion as a residual risk in health and safely file.
Component replacement – air handling unit on a building roof.	Provide as installed drawings and lifting arrangements for inclusion in health and safety file. Where significant restrictions exist, provide outline method statement.
Specified a hazardous substance as a finish.	Provide hazard data sheet on material and, where applicable, safe application instructions.
Large eccentric truss.	Provide centre of gravity guide for contractors/ competent lifting appointed person planning a lift.
Demolition of buttress walls on an old part of occupied building.	Provide existing surveys and drawings for temporary works designer and co-ordinator to consider when designing a solution.

(a) **notes on drawings** – this is preferred, since the notes will then be immediately available to those carrying out the work. They can refer to other documents if more detail is needed, and be annotated to keep them up to date;

(b) **written information provided with the design** – this should be project specific, and should only contain information which will be useful to those constructing or maintaining the structure;

(c) **suggested construction sequences** showing how the design could be erected safely, where this is not obvious, for example suggested sequences for putting up pre-cast panel concrete structures. Contractors may then adopt this method or develop their own approach.

The industry has developed the use of an SHE (Safety, Health and Environment) box for placing notes on drawings. The box is a method of referencing and highlighting the issues on a drawing, as illustrated in Figure 4.6.

SHE Information		Key-RR = See CDM Risk Register	
Haz Ref	Hazard & Description	RR	Other Associated DWGs

Type 2-For smaller lower risk profile* projects

SHE Information
Hazard & Description

Figure 4.6 An SHE box

Designing for maintenance access

The requirement to design structures that can be safely maintained and to demonstrate compliance with the Workplace (Health, Safety and Welfare) Regulations 1992 through design requires a suitable design strategy. From the early design philosophy to completion the requirement to identify the access and maintenance requirements is essential to avoid retrospective, and sometimes costly, design changes. The categories associated with the access activity issues that should be considered in the early planning stages and throughout the design are:

- component replacement (consumables and building fabric)
- cleaning requirements
- warranty requirements
- statutory maintenance and inspections.

As this is a design risk management strategy issue, the identification of the associated hazards and design actions to eliminate, reduce or provide information on the significant residual risks is required to demonstrate compliance and support the client in managing their structure.

The access design solutions should be based on risk and the level of risk should take into account the frequency or work, number of persons involved, the nature of the work, e.g. whether equipment and tools are required, the duration of the task, etc.

As a guide when designing to address access for maintenance the following three questions provide a valuable rule of thumb to apply a reasonable design solution. In this instance we are using roof access as the example.

1. Why do maintenance operatives need to access, enter the environment? (Warranty, component replacement, statutory inspection, cleaning, etc.)
2. If the access requirement can't be avoided, how can the maintenance operatives safely access the environment?
   (Fixed ladder, cherry picker, rope access, reach clean pole, man-safe system, extended stair core and level access, portable tower scaffolding, etc.)
3. How is the safety of the maintenance operatives supported when they are working? (Installed man-safe, contractor supplied portable man-safe with dead-weight system, installed eye bolt, fixed edge protection, non-fragile glass, secondary means of escapee, etc.)

The one-solution-fits-all philosophy can promote a lack of early consideration at the concept stage and encourages the specification of more reactive solutions. This is best illustrated in the construction industry with the specification of man-safe systems when there is little or no need to walk on the roof. The inspections and gutters can be accessed from a mobile elevation work platform every two years and the man-safe system can increase the risks and frequency to access the roof due to the required inspections of the safety system.

All health and safety strategies should be developed with the design team, CDM co-ordinator and client where possible and the supporting information provided to the CDM co-ordinator for inclusion in the health and safety file.

Designing workplaces

The CDM Regulations require the designer to take account of other legislation, which includes the Workplace (Health, Safety and Welfare) Regulations 1992

(WHSW). These regulations also apply to employers who are in control of work-places so the designer's approach to providing the potential for them to provide a compliant premises is a key design deliverable. The main issues covered in the regulations and how designers can deal with them is covered below.

WHSW Regulation 5 – Maintenance

Designers need to consider the requirements for maintenance, including cleaning, and the opportunities to provide through specification, collaborative design and spatial design the environment, equipment, safe access and information to support future maintenance and the management of residual risks, e.g. how to safely access an environment or change a component. This information on a low-risk project could be an entry on a risk register or note on a drawing for the CDM co-ordinator to reference or install in the project health and safety file. On a more complex project, the development of an operational and maintenance manual will be required to collate and communicate the relevant information.

WHSW Regulation 6 – Ventilation

A workplace must be adequately ventilated with fresh air that has no risk of being contaminated. The ventilation must be designed by a competent engineer or specifier to suit the environment and must have an alarm system where the risk of failure could cause harm to the workforce.

WHSW Regulation 7 – Temperature

The temperature in workrooms should provide reasonable comfort without the need for special clothing.

WHSW Regulation 8 – Lighting

Lighting should be sufficient to enable people to work safely, use plant and equipment and move from place to place safely. Stairs and fixed ladders should be well lit in such a way that shadows are not cast over the main part of the treads. Where necessary, local lighting should be provided at individual workstations, and at places of particular risk, such as pedestrian crossing points on vehicular traffic routes. Outdoor traffic routes used by pedestrians should be adequately lit after dark.

WHSW Regulation 9 – Cleanliness and waste

Designers need to consider both how the structure, components and finishes need to be cleaned and how waste materials are managed, which includes safe storage and disposal.

WHSW Regulation 10 – Room size

Workrooms should have enough free space to allow people to get to and from workstations and to move within the room with ease. The number of people who may work in any particular room at any one time will depend not only on the size of the room, but on the space taken up by furniture, fittings, equipment, and on the layout of the room. Workrooms, except those where people only work for short periods, should be of sufficient height (from floor to ceiling) over most of the room to enable safe access to workstations. In older buildings with obstructions such as low beams, the obstruction should be clearly marked. The associated Approved Code of Practice guidance specifies 11 m³ per person, assuming the room is 3 m high.

WHSW Regulation 11 – Workstations and seating

Workstations should be arranged so that each task can be carried out safely and comfortably. The worker should be at a suitable height in relation to the work surface. Work materials and frequently used equipment or controls should be within easy reach, without undue bending or stretching.

Workstations including seating, and access to workstations, should be suitable for any special needs of the individual worker, including workers with disabilities.

WHSW Regulation 12 – Floors and traffic routes

Floors and traffic routes should be designed to promote segregation and be of sound construction and should have adequate strength and stability taking account of the loads placed on them and the traffic passing over them. Floors should not be overloaded.

The surfaces of floors and traffic routes should be free from any hole, slope, or uneven or slippery surface, which is likely to:

(a) cause a person to slip, trip or fall;
(b) cause a person to drop or lose control of anything being lifted or carried; or cause instability or loss of control of vehicles and/or their loads.

WHSW Regulation 13 – Falls or falling objects

Designers need to design so far as is reasonably practicable to avoid or reduce risk of falls to prevent:

(a) any person falling a distance likely to cause personal injury;
(b) any person being struck by a falling object likely to cause personal injury.

So far as is reasonably practicable, the measures required above shall be measures other than the provision of personal protective equipment, information, instruction, training or supervision.

WHSW Regulation 14 – Glass, windows

Designers must design to ensure every window or other transparent or translucent surface in a wall or partition and every transparent or translucent surface in a door or gate shall, where necessary for reasons of health or safety—

    (a) be of safety material or be protected against breakage of the transparent or translucent material; and

    (b) be appropriately marked or incorporate features so as, in either case, to make it apparent.

WHSW Regulation 15 – Opening windows

Designers must design to ensure no window, skylight or ventilator, which is capable of being opened, shall be likely to be opened, closed or adjusted in a manner which exposes any person performing such operation to a risk to his health or safety. No window, skylight or ventilator shall be in a position when open which is likely to expose any person in the workplace to a risk to his health or safety.

WHSW Regulation 16 – Cleaning windows

Designers must design to ensure all windows and skylights in a workplace shall be of a design or be so constructed that they may be cleaned safely. Account may be taken of equipment used in conjunction with the window or skylight or of devices fitted to the building to facilitate cleaning.

WHSW Regulation 17 – Organisation of traffic routes

Designers must design to ensure every workplace can be organised in such a way that pedestrians and vehicles can circulate in a safe manner. Traffic routes in a workplace shall be suitable for the persons or vehicles using them, sufficient in number, in suitable positions and of sufficient size. Any traffic route, shared by both pedestrians and vehicles should be wide enough to enable any vehicle likely to use the route to pass pedestrians safely.

WHSW Regulation 18 – Doors and gates

Designers, including specifiers, must ensure that doors and gates, which swing in both directions, should have a transparent panel, except if they are low enough to see over. Conventionally hinged doors on main traffic routes should also be fitted with such panels. Panels should be positioned to enable a person in a wheelchair to be seen from the other side.

Sliding doors should have a stop or other effective means to prevent the door coming off the end of the track. They should also have a retaining rail to prevent the door falling should the suspension system fail or the rollers leave the track.

Upward opening doors should be fitted with an effective device such as a counterbalance or ratchet mechanism to prevent them falling back in a manner likely to cause injury.

Power-operated doors and gates should have safety features to prevent people being injured as a result of being stuck or trapped.

WHSW Regulation 19 – Escalators and moving walkways

Designers, including specifiers, ensure that escalators and moving walkways—

(a) function safely;
(b) be equipped with any necessary safety devices;
(c) be fitted with one or more emergency stop controls which are easily identifiable and readily accessible.

WHSW Regulation 20 – Sanitary conveniences

The designer must ensure suitable and sufficient sanitary conveniences shall be provided at readily accessible places. The details and number of facilities required is covered in the WHSW Approved Code of Practice.

WHSW Regulation 21 – Washing facilities

Designers are required to facilitate compliance with the client's duty to provide suitable and sufficient washing facilities, including showers if required by the nature of the work or for health reasons, which shall be provided at readily accessible places.

WHSW Regulation 22 – Drinking water

Designers must consider the facilities to ensure the client can supply an adequate supply of wholesome drinking water shall be provided for all persons at work in the workplace.

WHSW Regulation 23 – Accommodation for clothes

Designer to consider the clients requirements for suitable and sufficient accommodation shall be provided—

(a) for the clothing of any person at work which is not worn during working hours; and
(b) for special clothing, which is worn by any person at work but which is not taken home.

WHSW Regulation 24 – Facilities for changing clothes

Designers to consider the client's requirements for changing room or rooms, which should be provided for workers who change into special work clothing and where they remove more than outer clothing. Changing rooms should also be provided where necessary to prevent workers' own clothing being contaminated by a harmful substance.

WHSW Regulation 25 – Facilities to rest and eat meals

Designers to consider the client's requirements for suitable and sufficient rest facilities shall be provided at readily accessible places.

Rest facilities provided should include suitable facilities to eat meals where food eaten in the workplace would otherwise be likely to become contaminated.

Rest rooms and rest areas shall include suitable arrangements to protect non-smokers from discomfort caused by tobacco smoke.

Suitable facilities shall be provided for any person at work who is a pregnant woman or nursing mother to rest.

Suitable and sufficient facilities shall be provided for persons at work to eat meals where meals are regularly eaten in the workplace.

Additional duties when projects are notifiable

The additional CDM duties imposed on the designer consist of ensuring the client has appointed a CDM co-ordinator before detailed design starts and does not start design other than initial design work until one is appointed.

As a notifiable project has a CDM co-ordinator, the regulations require the designer (that covers all designers) to co-operate with them in the provision of evidence that the designer is designing in accordance with their duties and providing health and safety information for co-ordination and the health and safety file information

Summary and conclusions

In conclusion the contributions of the designer from a health and safety perspective can contribute significantly to lowering the risk profile of a project. The relationship between the design and health and safety can be controlled sufficiently to add real value to a project and a client's investment.

The keys to compliance and adding value are based on the design team's CDM competence, clear arrangements for design risk management on the project that are proportional to the risk profile, and the co-operation and co-ordination between all duty holders to facilitate compliance.

In summary, the designer's structures and design elements must be capable of being constructed, maintained and eventually demolished with respect to health and safety. The designer's health and safety contributions are qualified by being reasonably practicable, which provides a balance between health and safety and cost. However, there is no timescale on the designer's liability. So it is recommended that all designers have answers to the questions posed at the start of this chapter to ensure they add value, demonstrate compliance and, as professionals, provide the best service to their clients.

- What is CDM competence and am I competent to comply with CDM 2007?
- With respect to occupational health and safety in construction, future maintenance and final demolition, how do I design safely?
- How do I clearly communicate relevant health and safety information to contractors, other designers, CDM co-ordinators and the client?

5   The principal contractor

Introduction

On every notifiable project, the principal contractor is ultimately responsible for the management and co-ordination of health and safety throughout the construction phase of a project. They are at the sharp end of the project and challenged with managing the residual design and environmental hazards. They are very much removed from the comfort of the design studio and the client's offices. The theory of a well-planned and well-designed project would suggest that many significant risks will have been eliminated or reduced pre-construction, and the principal contractor would be required to manage the residual hazards on site.

If the client, designers and the CDM co-ordinator have been diligent and carried out their own CDM responsibilities effectively, the rewards should be evident at this stage. If they have not, then unusual and difficult-to-manage health and safety issues on site or for future maintenance could be identified by a competent contractor, but the opportunity for a design change could be lost. The difference between a principal contractor having time to proactively manage a planned interface with the client's staff, e.g. the moving of offices, planned client's maintenance work on site, etc., or finding out on the day, can significantly affect work and reduces the opportunity to undertake a suitable and sufficient risk assessment to avoid or reduce risks as required.

A competent principal contractor will legally and contractually control their site. This control from a health and safety perspective and all the associated standards and arrangements for safety management should be defined specifically in the construction phase plan.

It is valuable to appreciate that the term '*principal* contractor' is purely applicable to the statutory responsibilities of this duty holder as per the CDM Regulations. The principal contractor, therefore, is a legal entity in its own right and is not to be confused with such terms as 'main contractor' or 'contractor'.

It could be argued that the CDM regulations has had less impact on organisations carrying out the role of principal contractor as many contractors, particularly the larger companies, were already familiar with the principles of risk assessment, hazard management and health and safety legislation. The regulations did, however, bring a framework to construction health and safety management that has been largely welcomed by contractors and allowed the more cultured of them to discuss health and safety with clients and designers and formally request information using the framework of responsibilities imposed on the other duty holders.

It is generally, although not always, the case that the main contractor carries out the duties of the principal contractor. They are obviously well placed to holistically co-ordinate and manage health and safety during construction. However, there are examples of the client themselves either acting as the principal contractor or even arranging for a project management team to fulfil the role. Other examples of how the role is discharged by the client involve changing the principal contractor throughout the project so that the main or largest contractor takes responsibility, based on the fact that they are most competent in managing the risks associated with their work. Best practice would dictate that for continuity and clarity one principal contractor throughout the project would have more opportunity to set, implement, monitor and review health and safety standards throughout the project.

Competent contractors that are adequately resourced manage safety proactively with risk assessment exercised. They plan their work by producing method statements with planned health and safety actions of identifying services, sampling soil conditions, liaising with existing occupiers and third parties, etc. Under-resourced and less competent principal contractors do not take this approach and the effects of this impact on the client, designers and CDM co-ordinator from a CDM compliance perspective.

Principal contractors fail to discharge their duties effectively for many reasons, not all of which are obviously under their control. Possible causes that should be considered when setting up a contract include:

1. Principal contractors are appointed so late that they cannot plan for safety.
2. They are not competent to manage health and safety and do not have suitably competent health and safety advisors, management or supervisors with sufficient knowledge, experience and training to develop project-specific arrangements.
3. They do not possess adequate resources to set, implement, monitor and audit the appropriate health and safety standards for the project.
4. They are not provided with relevant pre-construction information.
5. They are not provided with relevant information from designers on unusual or difficult-to-manage hazards or are provided with irrelevant information on hazards that a competent contractor could manage effectively that could obscure significant issues.
6. They fail to secure a healthy working relationship with designers.
7. They fail to secure a working relationship with and control subcontractors.
8. There is a lack of control on site, with clients controlling their own operations without the principal contractor's input or knowledge.

In summary, the principal contractor is a legal CDM position with the sole purpose of securing the health, safety and welfare of anyone who works on or resorts to the site including third parties who may be affected by the operations on or adjacent to the site.

The principal contractor's duties explained

Appointment of contractors and designers

As we have heard above, if the principal contractor is to appoint contractors or designers they must ensure that they are both competent and adequately resourced to address the health and safety issues likely to be involved in the project. This duty requires a judgement to be made based on an assessment of information obtained from the contractor that can be collected in an interview, via a questionnaire or both.

> No person on whom these Regulations place a duty shall—
>
> (a) appoint or engage a . . ., designer . . . or contractor unless he has taken reasonable steps to ensure that the person to be appointed or engaged is competent;
> (b) accept such an appointment or engagement unless he is competent;
> (c) arrange for or instruct a worker to carry out or manage design or construction work unless the worker is—
>   (i) competent, or
>   (ii) under the supervision of a competent person.
>
> CDM Regulation 4(1)

The principal contractor should avoid an overly bureaucratic approach to assessing competence and resources as this is unnecessary. However, at the same time they must be confident that they have sufficient evidence of any designer's or contractor's ability to comply with their legal health and safety responsibilities. Also the amount of information requested or checks made should be proportionate to the risks likely to have to be managed. One of the key factors here, like so many of the CDM Regulations, is the competence of the person making the decisions. Assessing competence and resources is by its very nature subjective, so the strategy must have essential performance indicators to measure or benchmark organisations being assessed.

Appendix 4 of the CDM Approved Code of Practice has been developed to assist those who need to make such judgements of competence.

The construction phase plan

The vehicle used to manage, communicate and co-ordinate the health and safety aspects of the construction phase is the construction phase plan. It should be seen as the master health and safety policy for the project during the construction phase. The document should have the objectives of the plan, the organisation for its implementation and the project-specific arrangements for managing health and safety on site. Also the principles of successful health and safety management apply (as promoted by HSG65, *Successful Health and Safety Management*) where any policy must have the review and audit arrangements to make it work. Therefore, the construction phase plan must have the arrangements for revision. The arrangements should include reactive, i.e. accident and near-miss investigations, and proactive, i.e. onsite monitoring and audits of management systems, safe systems of work and reacting to changes in design and so on.

The principal contractor must develop the plan throughout the construction phase of the project. The plan should build on the pre-construction information provided, describe just how health and safety will be managed and co-ordinated during construction and clearly demonstrate how any project-specific health, safety or welfare issues will be addressed.

The level of detail in the construction phase plan will need to be proportionate to the project's specific risk profile. The Approved Code of Practice suggests a list of the minimum information that should be in place from the start of the construction work, which can be used as a guide when developing plans, management systems and when discussing the development of a plan with a client or CDM co-ordinator. The minimum information is listed as:

(a) general information about the project, including a brief description and details of the programme;
(b) specific procedures and arrangements for the early work;
(c) general procedures and arrangements which apply to the whole construction phase, including those for the management and monitoring of health and safety;
(d) arrangements for communication; and
(e) the health and safety file.

These initial requirements are further extended in appendix 3 of the ACoP 'where they are relevant to the work proposed'. The headings in Table 5.1 act as a checklist to assist the principal contractor when planning for health and safety. These headings are supported by guidance on an application that is not in the ACoP.

The construction phase plan is designed to be a live document and should continue to evolve throughout the construction phase; it must reflect any changes in the management or health and safety arrangements for the project. To this end an amendments section in the initial part of the document provides an opportunity to manage and inform users of the changes.

There has been evidence, since the introduction of the regulations of non-project-specific, almost generic, plans being developed with insufficient thought given to the significant hazards associated with the scheme. In defence of the principal contractor, if they are starved of project-specific information from the team the development of the construction plan may feel rather more like paper management than a realistic hazard management exercise.

Table 5.1 The principal contractor's health and safety checklist

1. Description of work

a. Project description and programme details

Guidance on application

Simply include a brief description or overview of the project description, covering the basic construction principles and based on the nature of the project. Programme details can vary from a detailed Gantt chart to start and finish dates for a simple project.

Objectives

To provide contractors and others who may interface with the project with an understanding of what the project is and its extent and sufficient information to consider the impact of the project on their activities, e.g. client, maintenance team on site, etc., or contribution to the project, e.g. start of demolition, opening of new road, removal of asbestos, etc.

b. Details of client, CDM co-ordinator, designers, principal contractors and other contractors

Guidance on application

Full contact details of all parties including contractors can be helpful so all readers can contact any party as necessary. Arrangements with contractors should include providing this information and any planned changes to the key personnel for safety which can also be checked at induction by the principal contractor.

Objectives

To provide up-to-date information and contact information on key health and safety personnel to promote and facilitate health and safety co-operation and co-ordination.

c. Extent and location of existing records and plans

Guidance on application

This information could include an existing health and safety file for an existing structure, reports of surveys undertaken, and information on how to access this information if it is not contained within the plan. Most of this information should be referenced in the pre-construction information which should be derived from the client making reasonable enquiries about the existing site or structure. Important information to have, or to reference, in the plan is existing services surveys, structural or conditional surveys, asbestos surveys and existing drawings or method statements of historical construction works.

This information is invaluable when the principal contractor starts undertaking risk assessments for the project and setting up arrangements for induction training, briefing on the safety plan and providing information to relevant contractors so they can plan for safety.

A competent principal contractor should also question any potential omissions and feed back to the client or CDM co-ordinator any concerns they may have regarding health and safety.

Continued

Objectives

To provide a focus for the principal contractor in setting site safety standards and information to support the selection of contractors and approval of method statements before work starts. Also information on significant unforeseen hazards, e.g. buried services, structural defects, etc., that contractors will need to consider in undertaking risk assessments of their activities and in developing method statements.

2. Communication and management of the work

a. Management structure and responsibilities

Guidance on application

The implementation of the construction phase plan requires the illustration of the project's organisation, with key health and safety skills clearly defined. A list of appointments and/or an organogram or family tree best illustrates the hierarchy. The extent of detail on key personnel and their duties obviously depends on their role and the size and nature of the project. On a small project, simply recording the construction managers, site supervisors and/or senior tradesmen's names and responsibilities will be adequate. On large, complex projects where there are interfaces with the client's activities, many design packages in a design-and-build project, then the structure may need to be as illustrated below:

- construction manager/project manager
- health and safety advisor
- design manager/co-ordinator
- purchaser
- site supervisors
- site foremen
- appointed person (lifting operations)
- permit controller
- temporary works co-ordinator
- security manager
- fire safety co-ordinator
- first aiders.

Duties and responsibilities can start with the initial and continuous development and overseeing the implementation of the construction phase plan and can be as simple as maintaining the first aid provisions on site. The duties should address the arrangements for implementing the plan itself, emergencies and any contingencies.

Objectives

To clearly define the organisation to implement the construction phase plan and manage health and safety on site.

b. Project health and safety goals and arrangements for monitoring health and safety performance.

Guidance on application

In respect of project health and safety goals, it is valuable to define the objectives of the project in respect of health and safety. Examples of these could be:

- to ensure an accident- and injury-free project;
- to have a zero tolerance on non-compliance with the site health and safety rules;
- to have weekly/monthly health and safety initiatives to promote a positive health and safety culture;
- to operate a 'Stop Me/Don't walk by' policy to promote contractor participation in maintaining high health and safety standards;
- to have safety incentive schemes, e.g. hazard busters, where site personnel are encouraged to report hazards for a prize or even money;
- to contribute to national health and safety schemes, e.g. working well together;
- to set specific key performance indicators for high-level elements of the construction phase plan, e.g. method statement receipt and approval, permit management, access platform inspections, etc.

All safety targets must be realistic, achievable and driven by the senior management. For the monitoring of health and safety on site, arrangements need to cover:

- the person responsible for auditing and monitoring;
- the nature and frequency of audit;
- the management of output action from the audit.

And the fundamental targets for auditing and monitoring compliance should cover:

- the relevant health and safety regulations applicable to the project;
- the applied arrangements for selection and management of contractors;
- the selection and management of designers' health and safety contributions;
- the site rules contained within the construction phase plan;
- accident, dangerous occurrence and near-miss reports;
- hazards reported under the hazard-stopping incentive scheme;
- high-risk environments, e.g. working platforms, cofferdams, confined spaces, highways engineering, deep excavations, roof work, working over or near water, contaminated sites, etc.;
- high-risk activities, e.g. lifting operations and cranes, piling, live electrical work, asbestos removal, traffic management on site, using cartridge-operated power tools;
- training, results of awareness tests, induction tests, etc.;
- feedback from toolbox talks and talking to contractors at work during audits;
- method statements and risk assessments;
- permits to work;
- lifting plans;
- site co-ordination registers.

Monitoring of health and safety standards is generally undertaken by safety advisors and managers but involvement of all the team is good practice and promotes health and safety throughout the project team. The use of standard pro formas to prompt the auditor and record the findings is effective for site monitoring, and more management system-focused pro formas are used for auditing the implementation of the construction phase plan. Accidents and near-miss investigations are also invaluable tools to assess the effectiveness of the plan.

Continued

Certain inspections of working platforms, cofferdams, excavations, etc., should be undertaken again with a checklist or pro forma but recorded on a formal register to assist in the management of the exercise. Systems like 'scaff tag' (a safety sign label that is attached to scaffolding to record the inspection and status of the scaffolding) are used to communicate the results of inspections and facilitate the management and outputs of the exercise. If scaffolding fails a weekly inspection, the sign will read 'Do Not Use' with a red prohibition sign.

The extent to which the principal contractor needs to go in setting auditing and monitoring standards as with all safety management arrangements, depends on the risk profile of the project. At the lower end of the scale a simple safety inspection using a standard pro forma is adequate and for more complex projects a strategy based on the list above will be required.

The most important issues in being successful with auditing is to have competent trained auditors, a strategy for identifying what to audit based on risk and a method of integrating the outputs into the management of the business or project.

Objectives

The fundamental objectives of this section of the plan are to describe to all on site who is auditing what and when. Also how health and safety problems and remedial actions are implemented on site. The section should reinforce the principal contractor's commitment to implementing the standards set in the safety plan.

---

c. Arrangements for:

---

i. Regular liaison between parties on site

Guidance on application

Arrangements for liaison with all parties on site to facilitate the management of health and safety on site should include structured meetings, agendas and the parties. Examples of the types of arrangement this section could cover include:

- project meetings with the client
- consultants/design co-ordination team meetings
- daily site co-ordination meeting with contractors
- safety forums with contractors
- safety report issues to all
- monthly newsletter
- health and safety executive via statutory notification
- emergency planning meetings with emergency services
- method statement development and briefings
- reactive safety meetings
- safety notice board.

The size, nature and complexity of the project should provide a guide to the development of this section. Principal contractors should amend this section as certain contract packages will require more liaison than others. A formal presentation on this section at a pre-start meeting is advisable even for the smallest project.

Objectives

To provide a structured set of arrangements for health and safety to be an integrated element of the project. Also to promote a positive, proactive health and safety culture by providing opportunities for effective liaison between parties.

Table 5.1 The principal contractor's health and safety checklist (*continued*)

ii. Consultation with the workforce

Guidance on application

Consultation with the workforce on a project on site can provide an invaluable source of health-and-safety-related information from issues regarding occupational health to hazardous site conditions or contractors who could be putting themselves or other workers at risk. Many site workers know about problems on site associated with the environment and work activities and legally and practically must be provided with the opportunity to discuss these issues with the principal contractor. Options for complying with this duty can range from having regular onsite toolbox talks on general health and safety on site, to having structured meetings with the contractors or their representatives. In creating a positive health and safety culture on the project, the effective implementation of any reasonable recommendations demonstrates to the workforce that they are part of the health and safety team. Consultation with the workforce could be considered for the following:

- developing and amending emergency plans and traffic routes
- undertaking risk assessments and developing/amending method statements
- planning a training session or programme
- during site health and safety inspections
- in developing and amending site rules
- before ordering materials that are hazardous to use or difficult to lift
- during an accident or near-miss investigation (persons not as witnesses but with site experience to discuss arrangements to prevent reoccurrence).

Objectives

To harness the invaluable experience, site knowledge and co-operation of the workforce as part of the arrangements to manage health and safety on the project. To further promote a positive health and safety culture on a project.

iii. The exchange of design information between the client, designers, CDM co-ordinator and contractors on site

Guidance on application

This section requires the formal arrangements to clearly define the communication, consultation and approval of design information, which is key to any project's success. Design managers, architects, engineers and contractors obviously need design information to price, plan and build but also to manage their respective duties under the CDM Regulations. This section in the construction phase plan could also benefit from defining who a designer is and what a design contribution is, which are not always clear. Typical information in relation to health and safety could include a detailed design of a component that is difficult to install, weights of an awkward or heavy component to assist the contractor in developing a lifting plan, information from designers to contractors on hazards one would not expect a competent contractor to be aware of, a contractor request for information (RFI) from a specific designer, etc. Arrangement could include:

- design information register to manage RFIs and the outputs, i.e. inclusion in method statement, action for purchaser, inclusion in lifting plan, consideration/ design amendment by other designer, etc.;

Continued

- an RFI pro forma;
- the inclusion of a 'health and safety information' column on a design team meeting minutes template;
- a policy on what information is to be provided and what information is not required to avoid unnecessary bureaucracy;
- a policy defining the CDM co-ordinator's method of auditing the health and safety element of design.

Objectives

To set up arrangements to manage the health and safety element of the design. To take proactive advantage of the team's potential to design and plan for health and safety and to ensure key parties receive safety-critical information to facilitate onsite health and safety and the development of the health and safety file.

iv. Handling design changes during the project

Guidance on application

As above, design changes need formal arrangements for approval before being actioned on site. The change will need to be subject to the same scrutiny as all design work and this section in the plan must avoid changes bypassing the formal system. The CDM co-ordinator must also be provided with the opportunity to assess the health and safety contributions of the designer. A design change can have a significant impact on health and safety so arrangements for this section would benefit from project gateways to formalise the consultation and sign-off procedure.

Objectives

To control and prevent design changes not being subject to the necessary health and safety contributions from the team and supported by the designer's supporting information on residual risk.

v. The selection and control of contractors

Guidance on application

This section must define who is responsible for the task. This could be an individual or a position within a principal contractor's team, like assistant team leaders. The section also must explain the procedure for the following examples:

- subcontractors
- designers
- suppliers who design
- self-employed
- plant and equipment suppliers.

Arrangements must cover or reference the type of questionnaire or interview agenda and the method of appraisal.

In respect of controlling contractors, the principal contractor on any project must have robust procedures with gateways. The following is a list of control issues that should be considered, depending on the nature of the project, before the contractor starts work or starts a new phase of the work:

- signing on and off site, swipe cards, etc., to prevent unauthorised access to site or areas of site;

- receipt and approval of selection information in pursuance of the duty to engage competent and adequately resourced contractors and designers;
- induction training covering the site arrangements for safety and activity hazards;
- provision of relevant health and safety information to the organisation, e.g. copy of, or relevant section of, or access to, construction phase health and safety plan, or relevant method statement that may interface or conflict with their activities, etc.;
- receipt and approval of method statements and risk assessments for their activities;
- issuing of any permits to work;
- attending site co-ordination meeting;
- work added to live programme;
- approval for work to commence granted by principal contractor.

Site co-ordination registers provide principal contractors with the potential to manage these procedures, act as an aide-memoire and demonstrate that a control procedure is in place for the project. On simple, relatively low-risk projects with one or two contractors a simple method statement approval process is sufficient.

Objectives

To ensure only suitably competent and adequately resourced contractors and designers are engaged on the project. To set standards for health and safety from the onset of the project.

vi. The exchange of health and safety information between contractors

Guidance on application

Information between contractors must be co-ordinated as on most sites the activities' interface or access to an area is shared. In planning and managing safety, generally undertaken through the development of method statements and risk assessment exercises, the contractor must consider the impact on other contractors and what safety and management arrangements are needed. This valuable information can be co-ordinated by the principal contractors on large and complex projects or passed directly to contractors and audited by the principal contractor as part of the arrangements. The exchange of information must be made mandatory and this should form part of the arrangements for auditing health and safety on site. Good practice and these arrangements on site can result in a subcontractor inviting other contractors to attend method statement briefings to obtain information for them to pass on to their team and consider when planning for health and safety.

Objectives

To ensure contractors share valuable health and safety information and proactively promote co-operation between contractors so their work activities do not affect the health and safety of others on site.

vii. Security, site induction and on site training

Guidance on application

Employers, like principal contractors, are required to provide information, instruction and training, and also a safe place of work. This section of the plan requires arrangements that could be addressed in the following manner.

Continued

Security: In assessing what arrangements for security are needed as an output of a risk assessment the following should be considered:

- pedestrian access security and health and safety
- vehicular access security and health and safety
- fencing/hording
- lighting
- CCTV
- out-of-hours security arrangements
- alarm systems
- onsite security to control access to certain areas
- compound location and access or authorisation
- access for emergency services.

Site induction: Site induction is the necessary training one would need to safely access the site, work on site and respond to an emergency; however, many principal contractors extend this training to cover environmental and quality issues. Such training obviously needs to be suitable and sufficient and on a small, relatively low-risk site will cover the site rules, location of welfare facilities and highlight some of the typical site hazards. On larger sites the training may also include an introduction to the fire plan, traffic plan, method statement approval procedures, work programme and planning procedures, design management procedures – almost a presentation on the construction phase plan. To ensure the trainee has understood the training and can work safely, a test can be incorporated with a pass mark. Many principal contractors require contractors and self-employed persons to resit the induction as a part of a health and safety offence on site to reinforce the knowledge.

Onsite training: Onsite training should be an output of a risk assessment and/or training needs analysis. Typical training courses given on site can vary from health and safety awareness to competent training and assessment for plant operatives. The types of training and refresher training a principal contractor should consider are:

- health and safety awareness training and passport scheme training
- training on safety management system
- plant operator training
- site managers health and safety training
- inspectors training for scaffolding, excavations, etc.
- slingers and banksmen training
- first aid training
- confined spaces training
- appointed person for lifting operations
- scaffolding and tower scaffolding erection.

Objectives

- Security to a standard to ensure the health and safety of third parties and site personnel and also to control personnel and traffic access.
- Site induction to be provided for any new person on site and any person who is found not to comply with the site rules to ensure they have sufficient knowledge to work safely on site without risk to themselves and others affected by their activities.

Table 5.1 The principal contractor's health and safety checklist (*continued*)

- Onsite training to ensure compliance with statutory provisions and that workers are safe and competent to perform their task on site without risk to themselves and others affected by their activities.

---

viii. Welfare facilities and first aid

Guidance on application

In setting standards for the provision of welfare facilities, a risk assessment of the work activities and assessment of numbers of facilities required will be necessary. The main standards and issues in planning for welfare facilities on site are listed in Schedule 2 of the regulations and include:

- provision of toilets, the number to be based on the number of people on site (the facilities must have associated wash basins with water, soap and a means of drying hands, and can be connected to the mains sewer or have a self-contained tank for waste and one for water);
- provision of washing facilities in the form of basins large enough to allow users to wash their hands, faces and forearms (all basins should have a clean supply of hot and cold running water and a means of drying);
- provision of rest facilities for taking breaks (these should be heated, and provided with a table, a means of boiling water and heating food);
- provision of drinking water;
- provision for storage, drying clothing and personal protective equipment.

For short duration work the Health and Safety Executive also provides guidance on acceptable standards for principal contractors and contractors.

First aid must be addressed by the provision of competent first aiders in the ratio of at least one appointed person if fewer than five on site, and at least one first aider for 5–50 on site. For more than 50 on site, one additional first aider per additional 50 employed is required.

Arrangements must also cover the provision of sufficient equipment to cope with the numbers on site and cover signage of facilities and appointed persons so they can be contacted.

Objectives

To provide and maintain adequate welfare facilities on site to address the needs of the project. To provide adequate first aid resources to address the site.

---

ix. The reporting and investigation of accidents and incidents including near misses

---

Guidance on application

These arrangements will require all accidents and near misses to be reported to the principal contractor for investigation immediately by the quickest practicable means, but the employers are generally responsible for statutory reporting under the Reporting of Diseases and Dangerous Occurrence Regulations 1995 (RIDDOR). The arrangement will also need to cover who, within the principal contractor's team, is responsible for undertaking an immediate investigation to assess the situation to prevent reoccurrence and assess site health and safety compliance. It is in the interests of the principal contractor to make these arrangements and especially the requirement to report near misses clear at the start of the project.

Continued

Arrangements concerning subcontractors on site generally require the follow information to be supplied to the principal contractor:

- a copy of the report in the accident book;
- the subcontractors' accident investigation containing any remedial action and supporting witness statements (which should be made compulsory);
- a copy of the RIDDOR report if applicable;
- any revised risk assessments or method statements.

Objectives

To comply with the statutory requirements to report accidents and obtain all information on accidents and near misses as part of measuring the construction phase plans performance. To react appropriately to these issues to ensure the site and working practices are safe.

---

x. The production and approval of risk assessments and method statements

---

Guidance on application

The production and approval methodology for risk assessments and method statements is critical to health and safety planning and these arrangements must set standards to achieve the following:

- project-specific risk assessments and method statements that are suitable and sufficient to control the risks to all those affected;
- all the necessary organisational, resource and logistical elements to implement, monitor and review the safe systems of work;
- an approval process, managed by the principal contractor, that allows sufficient time to assess the submission, comments and revision if necessary, consideration of interfaces and impact on site and presentation to the workforce;
- an appreciation of the procedural gateway that ensures no work starts without the principal contractor's formal approval.

Objectives

To control contractors and set standards for the proactive planning and management of health and safety as an integrated part of the contractors' service. To take advantage of the information to assess the impact of the activities on the sites risk profile.

---

d. Site rules

Guidance on application

The site rules on any project should be made up of a set of principal contractors' company health and safety rules and site-specific rules that are derived from the pre-construction information. The key for the principal contractor is ensuring the rules are kept up to date, brought to the attention of all on site and enforced effectively. Relaxation in site rules can cause problems, e.g. not wearing hard hats in hot weather, so any relaxation must be authorised by the principal contractor's site representative.

Objectives

To set and enforce clearly defined health and safety standards to avoid accidents, ill health and losses.

---

e. Fire and emergency procedures

Guidance on application

Fire and emergency plans for rescue from confined spaces or from scaffolding, for example, will require the following considerations:

- the emergency controller
- key personnel and emergency telephone numbers
- alarm systems
- illustrated plans
- training and testing of plan
- equipment
- specific arrangements.

Objectives

To design and test suitable emergency plans to secure life in the event of an emergency situation.

3. Arrangements for controlling significant site risks

a. Safety risks

---

i. Services, including temporary electrical installation

Guidance on application

This section is designed to cover the safety standards for existing services and the safety issues associated with supplies for task lighting and onsite equipment and supplies to welfare facilities and onsite offices. The main issues to be addressed in this section are:

Temporary services

- liaison with utilities and others, e.g. Environmental Agency, local authorities, etc.;
- installation standards, e.g. BS7671 IEE Wiring Regulation for electrical supplies;
- competent persons to undertake work;
- marking, identification and mechanical protection from site vehicles;
- testing to appropriate standards.

Objectives

To ensure the site establishment and work activities consider the interface with existing services and competent persons install and test to the required standards.

---

ii. Preventing falls

Guidance on application

Falling from height, even low height falls, account for the majority of fatalities. This section must clearly set out the minimum standards for the following:

Continued

- undertaking work at ground level to avoid or reduce working at height;
- safe use of ladders, scaffolding including towers, all types of mobile elevation work platforms (MEWPs), harnesses and fall arrest systems and trestles;
- access control and control of contractors;
- open excavations;
- roof work;
- openings in floors;
- risers;
- inspections and reports on equipment, e.g. scaffolding, mewps, and fall arrest equipment, etc.;
- leading edge protection;
- soft landing systems;
- working over or near water;
- materials management;
- falling objects and public safety;
- emergency rescue;
- safety signage;
- training, awareness, safety monitoring, supervision and competence;
- risk assessments and method statements approval.

Objectives

To ensure this significant risk is managed effectively and all work is planned to avoid or set acceptable control measures to the appropriate standards.

iii. Work with or near fragile materials

Guidance on application

Safety standards for fragile materials, particularly roofing material, should be addressed in this section. The following issues need consideration:

- risk assessment to identify the hazards and plan installation, replacement access, etc.
- asbestos
- existing services
- access methodology
- fall protection
- emergency rescue
- safety signage.

Objectives

To ensure this significant risk is managed effectively and all work is planned to avoid or set acceptable control measures to the appropriate standards.

iv. Control of lifting operations

Guidance on application

Safety standards for all lifting operations should be addressed in this section. The following issues need consideration:

- risk assessment to identify the hazards and plan all lifting operations, etc.
- development of lifting plan to manage risks and implement safety standards

- appointed person(s) to manage the lifting operations
- checks, inspection, thorough tests of plant, etc.
- formation of a crane team to manage lifts
- existing services
- third-party safety
- ground conditions
- materials stability
- structural integrity of loading platforms or structure receiving materials
- man-riding equipment, communication, access control, signalling and rescue
- weather conditions and wind speeds.

Objectives

To ensure all lifting operations are planned, executed in a safe manner and residual risks managed by competent appointed persons as required by the Lifting Operations and Lifting Equipment Regulations 1998.

v. Dealing with services (water, electricity and gas)

Guidance on application

This section is designed to cover the safety standards for existing services, the main issues to be addressed in this section are:

- existing services
- liaison with utilities and others
- location, identification and marking of buried services
- safe digging procedures
- marking and barriers for overhead services to avoid contact
- supervision and control with permits
- physical/mechanical support
- emergency plan.

Objectives

To ensure the site establishment and work activities consider the interface with existing services and liaise with the appropriate authorities.

vi. The maintenance of plant and equipment

Guidance on application

This section required clear arrangements for the maintenance of plant and equipment on site. Most equipment on building sites required maintenance and all work equipment falls under the scope of the Provision and Use of Work Equipment Regulations 1998 (PUWER) which addresses maintenance requirements for equipment to be safe. The main issues and areas the principal contractor should focus on in this section to set standards are:

- requesting copies of maintenance reports or schedules for hired or contractors' equipment before work activities start – these arrangements could be part of the procurement process and also defined as a site rule;
- setting up a maintenance schedule for site plant;
- site facilities and a suitable safe area for undertaking maintenance on site;

Continued

- allocating responsibility to a principal contractor's representative;
- linking these arrangements with the inspection for specific salutatory inspections and tests, e.g. PAT testing for portable electrical appliances, lifting equipment through test and examination, etc.;
- PUWER compliance inspection as part of the health and safety auditing regime;
- competence and arrangements of maintenance personnel.

Objectives

To ensure all work equipment meets the requirements of the Provision and Use of Work Equipment Regulations 1998 and that all equipment and plant is maintained to a standard to ensure safe operation by a competent person.

vii. Poor ground conditions

Guidance on application

Arrangements for ground conditions need to take account of slopes, water, stability and existing buried structures. All these issues should be subject to or derive from a risk assessment and the arrangements set in the construction phase health and safety plan need to address the following:

- flooding, tidal and wet ground where vehicles and site operatives could become trapped;
- site access and access and temporary roads and paths for plant and pedestrians on site;
- unstable ground where falling rocks or mud slides are a risk;
- steep slopes and the risk of plant overturning is a risk;
- excavation support;
- voids, buried tanks and wells;
- temporary retaining walls, sheet piling;
- geotechnical surveys.

Objectives

To set standards to address the health and safety problems associated with hazardous ground conditions.

viii. Traffic routes and segregation of vehicles and pedestrians

Guidance on application

Arrangement for managing traffic and pedestrians on site need to apply the principles of prevention and wherever possible segregate site workers from mobile plant by high visibility fencing as a minimum standard. The site rules also play an important part in managing these risks with speed limits and competent authorised persons only using and driving plant on site. The main areas of the plan this section needs to focus on is:

- illustrated traffic management plan to communicate the pedestrian and traffic routes, site access and egress points, lay down areas, parking facilities, etc.
- deliveries
- one-way traffic systems to avoid reversing
- speed limits and hazard warning signs

- crossing points
- access control
- blind spots
- training banksmen
- limits on vehicle size, height and weight
- overhead services and structures.

Objectives

To establish a set of safety standards to promote the safe communication of pedestrians and site traffic avoiding an interface between the two where practicable. Also to define crossing points and safety rules to manage the risks where there is an interface.

ix. Storage of hazardous materials

Guidance on application

The standards for the storage of hazardous materials should be derived from risk assessments and the associated hazard data sheets. Also environmental consideration could be addressed here in respect of spillage control. The main issues the principal contractor should consider when planning for storage of hazardous substances are:

- risk assessment
- restricted/authorised access and security
- segregated defined storage areas
- safety equipment and personal protective equipment
- fire safety arrangements
- safety signs
- emergency plans
- training and information for users, first aiders and handlers
- additional first aid arrangements.

Objectives

To provide facilities and the safety arrangements to manage the storage of hazardous substances on site.

x. Dealing with existing unstable structures

Guidance on application

In respect of setting standards for existing unstable structures the principal contractors will need to cover in this section the arrangements for temporary works, the competence of the temporary works designer and co-ordinator and site safety issues associated with temporary works. The main consideration the principal contractor must address in managing risks associated with unstable existing structures are:

- obtaining a structural survey to plan either permanent or temporary structural works;
- engaging the services of a competent structural engineer/designer;
- engaging the services of a competent temporary works engineer;
- public safety, access control and security arrangements to site;
- associated services;
- falling objects and structural collapse as significant hazards;

Continued

- the structures status, i.e. whether the building is occupied;
- emergency planning;
- protection and control of contractors via a permit procedure;
- risk assessment and method statements.

Objectives

To ensure the appropriate actions are taken to make the working and public environments safe and to ensure the works on the structure are planned by competent persons in respect of the design and construction.

xi. Accommodating adjacent land use

Guidance on application

When sites have no space for the site accommodation, welfare facilities and/or materials storage the principal contractor will often use adjacent land or facilities. These facilities will require health and safety arrangements that, owing to their location and contractual conditions, may require additional health and safety arrangements to manage the risks. The main issues the principal contractor should consider are:

- access and egress interfaces with highways, client/occupier activities, etc. and security;
- transporting material from a lay-down area off site;
- temporary and existing services;
- pedestrian traffic segregation and interface with highways traffic;
- emergency communication and response.

Objectives

To ensure that suitable health and safety standards are set and maintained on adjacent land used on the project.

xii. Other significant safety risks

This section is designed to cover additional safety risks, for example:

- delivery and removal of materials from site
- working over or near water
- working on highways
- working in confined spaces
- roof works
- erecting structures
- groundworks
- demolition.

b. Health risks

i. Removal of asbestos

Guidance on application

Asbestos arrangements will need to cover identified asbestos as part of a survey from a client or in the pre-construction information and reactively when identified by site personnel. The arrangement will need to address the competence of operatives, control of contractors, the working standards, notification to the HSE, waste management and third-party health and safety. Reference in this section could be made to a specific set of asbestos health and safety rules and awareness training. The principal contractor or contractor could also, as an output of a risk assessment, consider the programming of the works to avoid interface with the other contractors or the client, e.g. removing asbestos in a school during school holidays. Difficult-to-manage issues with asbestos standards on site concern when an HSE-licensed removal contractor is needed to remove the material. HSE guidance should be used to ensure licensed contractors are used for all removal except work on asbestos cement sheet, or asbestos cement products like duct and pipe work; however, the work must be done in compliance with the Control of Asbestos Regulations 2006.

Objectives

To ensure minimum health and safety standards in relation to asbestos on site and avoid any exposure to site workers, members of the public and future building users.

---
ii. Dealing with contaminated land

Guidance on application

The standards for working safely on contaminated land site must control contamination and contain it to the site and transfer site and must address hygiene and occupational health issues. The risks can vary from relatively low-risk inert waste materials to highly dangerous chemicals. The site rules, induction, training and access control will be key areas to manage the risk. To control contamination, vehicle wheel wash stations, hygiene facilities for site workers, suitable personal protective equipment and enforced safety rules regarding eating and working practices will need to be addressed in this section. Awareness and induction training will need to cover the hazards and controls and auditing frequencies will need to monitor the standards.

Objectives

To ensure those workers on site, the general public and anyone accessing the site is aware of the risks, control measures and emergency procedures.

---
iii. Manual handling

Guidance on application

The risks associated with manual handling on site will require a strict set of conditions in this section enforced by the principal contractor and contractors. The conditions can be company specific and produced as a result of a manual handling operations risk assessment. The main issues the principal contractor will need to cover in this section are:

- the minimum acceptable weights to lift on site for one-man and two-man lifts to provide operatives with a rule-of-thumb guide;
- training on manual handling hazards and lifting techniques;
- provision of lifting equipment and guidance on its application either through training or via safety posters;
- manual handling risk assessment;
- occupational health arrangements to monitor personnel and advice.

Continued

Objectives

To ensure no site operative suffers from an injury as result of inappropriate manual handling.

iv. Use of hazardous substances

Guidance on application

This section will need to cover the risk assessment requirements and minimum standards for products that contain hazardous substances and by-products of construction operations that contain hazardous substances. The standards for personal protective equipment (PPE), disposal, storage and emergency procedures including first aid will also need to be derived from risk assessments by the respective contractors. Hazardous substances registers may need to be developed to ensure a suitable emergency or first aid response is effective. Also the principal contractor will need this information to undertake appropriate audits to evaluate the contractor's risk assessment, selection and use of control measures and effects on other site workers possibly affected by any substances.

Objectives

To ensure that all potentially hazardous substances are subject to a risk assessment and, where products or activities cannot be reasonably prevented, suitable control measures are developed and employed on site to control exposure to acceptable levels.

v. Reducing noise and vibration

Guidance on application

The principal contractor will require in this section arrangements for contractors to undertake risk assessments of activities involving noisy equipment and equipment that has the potential to cause occupational health problems associated with exposure to vibration. The assessments will be based on previous knowledge, information supplied with equipment and monitoring results on site. The competence of the assessor will be defined in this section with the requirement to periodically monitor the activities. Principal contractors and contractors will also need to share this health and safety information. Noise operations can cause problems in not being able to hear alarms or safety instructions. Again planning and co-ordination of contractors can provide opportunities for certain activities that cause potential problems to other workers or affect the client's operations to be undertaken out of normal working hours. It is advisable for principal contractors to have their own noise and vibration monitoring arrangements to monitor levels and occupation health arrangements to monitor the contractor's health and safety performance.

Objectives

To ensure that noise and vibration hazards are identified and assessed and, where they cannot be reasonably avoided, adequate control measures developed and implemented on site to protect operatives and others affected by their activities.

vi. Other significant health risks

Other significant health hazards that one could provide arrangement for in detail in this section are:

Table 5.1 The principal contractor's health and safety checklist (*continued*)

- lead paint
- lasers
- radiation
- leptospirosis
- whole body vibration
- anthrax
- zoonoses
- excessive heat
- arsenic in paint.

4. The health and safety file

a. Layout and format

Guidance on application

The layout or structure of the health and safety file should be defined in the pre-construction information. If this is not the case, arrangements should be detailed here on liaison with the relevant parties, generally the client's representative, to plan the file's structure and also the format, e.g. electronic, hard copy, both, web-based, numbers of copies, etc.

Objectives

To ensure a user-friendly health and safety file is developed for use during the project and for providing information in managing health and safety on future projects and maintenance work.

b. Arrangements for the collection and gathering of information

Guidance on application

This section must identify the key personnel and arrangements for obtaining, approving and collating the file information. This information then needs to be provided to the CDM co-ordinator to assemble the health and safety file.

Objectives

To ensure all contractors and suppliers supply appropriate health and safety information for the development of the health and safety file as a part of their contract and services.

Once the principal contractor believes that the plan has sufficient information for work to begin on site, the document must be sent to the client for assessment who may be responsible for advising the client on the plan's suitability. Only when confirmations from the client that the construction phase plan is acceptable, and confirmation that adequate provision for welfare has been established, can the construction phase start.

Ensuring co-operation between contractors

The control of contractors is one of the primary functions of the principal contractor and ensuring they co-operate on site and when planning for health and safety is essential. The requirement to co-operate with other contractors should, where practicable, start before work on site starts. As part of the risk assessment process, and in developing method statements, contractors must consider the impact on other persons on site and issues like access, deliveries, lifting operations, production of dusts and demolition. all impact on other contractors' health and safety.

So the principal contractor must set up the appropriate arrangements to ensure co-operation. These arrangements should form part of the construction phase health and safety plan, which in turn can form part of the contractor's form of contract. The arrangement generally involves attending site co-ordination meetings, sharing risk assessments and method statements and liaising on site as part of the day-to-day managing of health and safety.

> The principal contractor for a project shall—
>
> (a) plan, manage and monitor the construction phase in a way which ensures that, so far as is reasonably practicable, it is carried out without risks to health or safety, including facilitating—
> (i) co-operation and co-ordination between persons concerned in the project . . .
>
> Extract from CDM Regulation 22(1)

If the principal contractor is to accurately co-ordinate and manage the health and safety aspects of the project then the interrelationship between the respective contractors' activities must be fully and proactively assessed from this holistic position as part of the project planning to avoid conflicts and access problems on site. One would hope that information on potential pinch points or restricted access, if associated with a difficult-to-manage construction activity, would be provided to the principal contractor via the pre-construction information.

In summary, principal contractors must set up and enforce arrangements to promote co-operation between contractors and sharing of relevant health and safety information. To achieve this, a co-ordination role must be played by the site, construction or project manager.

Controlling site access

The principal contractor needs to ensure that only authorised people access the construction site and are aware of the site rules, hazards and emergency procedures as a minimum. Conversely, the principal contractor must ensure that no unauthorised persons gain access to the site or certain areas of the site.

The principal contractor for a project shall—

(l)   take reasonable steps to prevent access by unauthorised persons to the construction site.

Extract from CDM Regulation 22(1)

To emphasise the significance of this duty, if a principal contractor is found to breach this regulation the path is open for civil action against them as there is no exclusions from civil liability (see CDM Regulation 45).

The principal contractor will, therefore, be required to introduce authorisation procedures for all workers and site visitors. The extent of control over site access will be based on an assessment of risk considering such issues as the site location, the surrounding environment and the type of construction activity being undertaken.

Suitable control measures are then necessary to ensure that unauthorised cohorts do not gain access to the site. It is suggested that all sites should be physically defined, where practical, by suitable barriers. Additional consideration should be given if there is evidence of children playing on or near the site.

Safety signs, signing-in and -out books, stickers on hard hats indicating that induction training and authorisation to site has been given, access control swipe cards and security guards are common arrangements on projects.

Displaying the project notification

It is the responsibility of the principal contractor to clearly display on site, in a prominent position, the project information notified to the Health and Safety Executive. More often than not the principal contractor will make a copy of the original notification sent to the HSE (F10) and attach it where it can be easily read by those working on the site or indeed affected by the work.

Enforcement of the site rules

The principal contractor, as the duty holder ultimately responsible for health and safety on site, has a duty to ensure all site rules are adhered to.

The principal contractor for a project shall—

(d)   where necessary for health and safety, draw up rules which are appropriate to the construction site and the activities on it (referred to in these Regulations as "site rules");

Extract from CDM Regulation 22(1)

The 'rules', which may come from the client as well as the principal contractor, must be communicated to all relevant cohorts, ideally through the construction phase plan itself, site inductions, appropriate signage and toolbox talks. Procedures for non-compliance with any rules also need to be made clear. Site inspections and monitoring will generally assess the levels of compliance with the site rules.

Below is an example of a building project's rules extracted from the construction phase plan.

Workforce
- Make sure you have attended a site induction prior to commencing work.
- Safety helmets, high-visibility vests and safety footwear are mandatory on site.
- Make sure your supervisor has briefed you prior to starting work.
- Wear the personal protective equipment specified at all times.
- Do not operate plant or equipment without authorisation or correct PPE.
- If you have to use glues, oils, fuels, etc., ensure you have been briefed.
- No alcohol, drugs, radios or walkmans allowed on site.
- Only eat, drink or smoke in areas designated by management.
- Look out for your fellow workers and they will look out for you.

Work areas
- Do not cross barriers or enter no-go zones.
- Keep your work area tidy, put rubbish in piles or bins away from access routes.
- Keep all accesses clear of debris, materials and cables.
- Holes through floors MUST be covered, marked and adequately fixed.
- Some areas on site will require permits to access. These areas are clearly defined.

Permits
- Some activities need special permits; if you haven't received a briefing, ask.
- With hot work permits, know which extinguisher to use for different types of fire.

Plant and equipment
- Scaffolding is only to be erected, dismantled or altered by competent scaffolders.
- Mobile towers can only be erected or modified by approved erectors.
- Only appropriate certificated operators to drive or operate plant (including disc cutters).

- Electrical tools have date-tags to keep the machine safe; don't remove them.
- Do not pour old oil or other pollutants down the drain.

Unplanned events
- Report all accidents to the principal contractor so we can learn from our mistakes and prevent recurrence.
- Know the best means of escape from your work area, and your assembly point.
- Fight fires quickly with the correct extinguisher if competent, after raising alarm.
- We will not tolerate damage to company property, safety equipment or personal property, but we cannot be responsible for your own possessions or cars.
- Unsafe working will not be tolerated and positive action will be taken.

General
- Take notice of signs and instructions. Do not bring children or pets to site.
- Inform your supervisor if you think something is unsafe.
- Keep noise and dust levels down to the minimum and wear your PPE.

Incentive schemes that promote compliance with the site rules can help in a positive way but effective enforcement generally requires disciplinary action and, in the worst cases contractors or companies may be required to resit induction training, be removed from site or asked to stop work until they can demonstrate that remedial action has been taken to avoid re-offending.

Provision of relevant information to contractors (pre-construction)

It is important for all contractors working on a project to be provided with relevant information to help them plan for health and safety. The principal contractor needs to provide such information.

> The principal contractor for a project shall—
>
> (h) ensure that every contractor is given, before he begins construction work and in sufficient time to enable him to prepare properly for that work, access to such part of the construction phase plan as is relevant to the work to be performed by him.
>
> Extract from CDM Regulation 22(1)

Contractors are expected to provide risk assessments and associated method statements and are unable to effectively carry out this duty without project-specific information. The principal contractor must ensure that he only provides information that is relevant to the contractor's specific work area or shared area, activity or environment. The provision of irrelevant information for a contractor may obscure significant risks. The principal contractor's arrangement in the construction phase plan must identify who is responsible for providing this information.

Co-operation and consultation with workers

As well as being obviously good practice it is also a legal duty for the principal contractor to engage the workforce in terms of discussing health, safety and welfare issues. Many accident and near-miss investigations have identified that site workers were aware of a hazardous situation or working practice.

> The principal contractor for a project shall—
> (a) make and maintain arrangements which will enable him and the workers engaged in the construction work to co-operate effectively in promoting and developing measures to ensure the health, safety and welfare of the workers and in checking the effectiveness of such measures;
> (b) consult those workers or their representatives in good time on matters connected with the project which may affect their health, safety or welfare, so far as they or their representatives are not so consulted on those matters by any employer of theirs.
>
> CDM Regulation 24(a) and (b)

This two-way dialogue is an important contribution towards successful health and safety management on site. The combined experiences of persons working on site are a valuable asset and it is in everybody's interest to have this exchange of ideas.

The principal contractor should instigate site safety meetings with all relevant parties, discuss hazardous operations, safe systems of work and actively encourage dialogue.

Health and safety training and information

The legal duty and objective of the principal contractor in respect of training and information should be based on risk. Training in the form of induction training and awareness training is to ensure contractors are aware of the risks to their health and safety, the rules and arrangements to manage and control the risks. Induction training should generally cover the site rules, significant hazards, emergency procedures and security and site access arrangements.

The information to be issued to contractors is highlighted in the Approved Code of Practice which states:

> Good communication is essential to co-operation and risk control. Information about risks and precautions can be communicated by, for example:

(a) drawings that highlight hazards or unusual work sequences identified by designers, with clear advice on where to find more information;
(b) the relevant parts of the construction plan;
(c) meetings to plan and co-ordinate the work;
(d) effective arrangements to discuss the plan with those involved (section titled Information and training);
(e) making the plan available to workers and their representatives;
(f) induction training and toolbox talks to ensure workers understand the risks and precautions;
(g) providing a leaflet explaining the site rules that can be given to everyone at the induction training.

Formal procedures to record the receipt of information and briefings and even testing of induction training safety information can help focus the contractor's attention on the subject, especially if they appreciate that it is linked with authorisation to access site.

The health and safety file

The principal contractor is charged with the responsibility to collect the health and safety file information from the respective contractors, designers and suppliers they engage. The arrangement for the collection, which can be clearly defined in the contractors' contracts, must be entered in the construction phase plan and should identify the person responsible for collation. Arrangements can be made to ensure this requirement is a part of the project progress meetings or contractor co-ordination meetings to formalise the requests for overdue and unsuitable information.

The proactive principal contractor will also introduce a tracker system to identify, request and monitor health and safety contributions from their contractors, designers and so on.

The principal contractor for a project shall—

(j) identify to each contractor the information relating to the contractor's activity which is likely to be required by the CDM co-ordinator for inclusion in the health and safety file . . . and ensure that such information is promptly provided to the CDM co-ordinator.
Extract from CDM Regulation 22(1)

The structure of the file is generally defined in the pre-construction information to suit the clients and end users. It should also state the number of copies required and whether (or not) the information is required electronically.

6   The contractor

Introduction

As discussed in Chapter 1, the construction industry is both the largest industry in the UK and one of the most dangerous. On average two people have died every week on construction sites and hundreds have suffered major injuries and ill health over the past few decades. The majority of these people are clearly contractors.

> "[C]ontractor" means any person (including a client, principal contractor or other person referred to in these Regulations) who, in the course or furtherance of a business, carries out or manages construction work.
>
> Extract from CDM Regulation 2(1)

If CDM is to succeed in protecting people at work in the construction industry then contractors are among the very people it is aimed at protecting through solid design, planning, management and foresight. Contractors themselves must obviously contribute to the health and safety management process and have several significant duties under CDM itself.

Before we examine the CDM contributions expected from contractors it is worth reminding ourselves of the statutory duty imposed on them as employers in section 2 of the Health and Safety at Work etc. Act 1974, which states:

> It shall be the duty of every employer to ensure, so far as is reasonably practicable, the health, safety and welfare at work of all his employees.
>
> HSWA section 2(1)

Section 3 of the Act also emphasises the duty of an employer to conduct his work in such a manner, as far as is reasonably practicable, to ensure that his activities do not cause harm to people not in his employment. This is generally aimed at protecting the general public and other non-employees. Significantly these section 3 duties also apply to self-employed contractors who are widely found throughout the construction industry.

> Every self-employed person must conduct his undertaking in such a way as to ensure that persons not in his employment are not exposed to health and safety risks.
>
> HSWA, section 3(2)

Section 2 and section 3 of the Act are supported by Regulation 3 of the Management of Health and Safety at Work Regulations, which offers:

> Every employer shall make a suitable and sufficient assessment of:
>
> (a) the risks to the health and safety of his employees to which they are exposed whilst they are at work, and

(b) the risks to the health and safety of persons not in his employment arising out of or in connection with the conduct by him or his undertaking.

MHSW Regulation 3

Health and safety legislation applicable to contractors, including that detailed in Chapter 7, provides a framework for the health and safety management tools they use. Below are examples:

The contractor's duties explained

Contractors are CDM duty holders with a set of regulations to promote a safe working environment and, on notifiable projects, their interaction with the principal contractor. The extent to which a contractor must go to execute these duties generally is dependent on the risk associated with the activities they undertake and in the project's construction phase plan when the scheme is notifiable.

Now that we have an appreciation of the other health and safety duties imposed on contractors (employers and self-employed) by other legislation we will look in detail at the CDM requirements placed on them. The contractor's duties and general CDM duties are summarised below.

Plan, manage and monitor activities

The contractor has a duty under these regulations to ensure that all works they or their workers undertake are adequately planned, managed, supervised

Table 6.1 Examples of legislation and associated health and safety tools

Legislation	Health and safety tools
Construction (Design and Management) Regulations 2007 (see Chapter 7 for details)	Inspection register Checklists
Work at Height Regulations 2005	Working at height risk assessment template
Confined Space Regulations 1997	Permit to work/enter
Lifting Operations and Lifting Equipment Regulations 1998	Lifting plan template Lifting equipment checklist
Management of Health and Safety at Work Regulations 1999	Risk assessment pro forma Method statement template Traffic management plan Induction training programmes Toolbox talk programme

and monitored. The resources used to comply with this would need to be considered against the risk profile of the works to be undertaken as well as the competence and experience of those undertaking the activities.

> Every contractor shall plan, manage and monitor construction work carried out by him or under his control in a way which ensures that, so far as is reasonably practicable, it is carried out without risks to health and safety.
>
> CDM Regulation 13(2)

The contractor also needs to provide any contractors they engage with the minimum amount of time allowed for them to plan and prepare for their work. This again facilitates proper planning and consideration for the health and safety implications that will require management onsite.

Co-ordination with co-operating activities of others working on a project or affected by the work will also assist in the safe planning and preparation for construction work. Daily site meetings, sharing risk assessment and a main contractor operating a site co-ordination register are all examples of good planning.

The contractor, too, where the project is not notifiable and consequently no principal contractor is involved, must ensure that no construction work begins until there is adequate site security and all reasonable steps have been taken to prevent unauthorised access.

Appointing competent and adequately resourced contractors or designers

Many contractors will obviously appoint other contractors and designers themselves. When this is the case it is a requirement to ensure that they are both competent and adequately resourced to undertake the work. The contractor making the appointments will consequently need to comply with relevant duties imposed by the following regulation:

> No person on whom these Regulations place a duty shall—
>
> (a) appoint or engage a CDM co-ordinator, designer, principal contractor or contractor unless he has taken reasonable steps to ensure that the person to be appointed or engaged is competent;
> (b) accept such an appointment or engagement unless he is competent;
> (c) arrange for or instruct a worker to carry out or manage design or construction work unless the worker is—
>   (i) competent, or
>   (ii) under the supervision of a competent person.
>
> CDM Regulation 4(1)

The arrangements for compliance will need to demonstrate a process of assessing designers and contractors by obtaining information through embracing the requirements of the Approved Code of Practice. The information will need to be subject to an appraisal by a competent assessor, i.e. someone with the experience and skill to make a judgement on their competence and resources. The balanced approach to this exercise is to avoid any irrelevant questions and to focus the questions on to what is appropriate based on the risk profile of the project. For example, a painting company internally painting some flats does not require the same assessment as a steel frame company erecting a tower in the middle of a city. Likewise the information received should be proportionate. Standards questionnaires can promote bureaucracy and a statement at the top of the questionnaire requesting the respondent to only provide relevant information to the relevant questions or recommending to the respondent that they are not required to answer all questions can help. Having a select list of those whose competence has been established previously is also efficient and potentially only specific resources will need assessment for a particular project.

Training requirements and information for the workforce

An output of a suitable and sufficient risk assessment, undertaken by a competent person, will identify any requirements for training or other information needed by site workers. Initially, this might focus on site-specific issues such as fire safety, emergency and first aid arrangements, requirements for asbestos-containing materials awareness training, pedestrian routes around site, arrangements for welfare and other site rules. A project-specific site induction process would generally provide much of this information

This risk assessment approach would also identify any activity-based information or training requirements such as for manual handling operations, confined spaces training, training on the development of lifting plans (competent person), safe use of harness training, machinery plant operative training and so on.

Ensuring there are adequate welfare facilities for their workers

The requirements for adequate welfare provision are very explicit in the regulations and every contractor needs to ensure, as far as is reasonably practicable, this is available from those who work under their control. The following criteria are necessary for compliance:

•   Provision of toilets, the number to be based on the number of people on site. The facilities must have associated wash basins with water, soap and a means of drying hands. The facilities can be connected to the mains sewer or have a self-contained tank for waste and one for water.

- Provision of washing facilities in the form of basins large enough to allow users to wash their hands, faces and forearms. All basins should have a clean supply of hot and cold running water and a means of drying.
- Provision of rest facilities for taking breaks that are heated and provided with a table and a means of boiling water and heating food.
- Provision of drinking water.
- Provision for storage, drying clothing and personal protective equipment.

Additional duties when the project is notifiable

Co-operating with the principal contractor

The relationship between contractors and the principal contractor is essential to successful hazard management on site. Co-operation in relation to planning and programming work on site to reduce risk is a fundamental part of this duty. As part of the contractor's health and safety management process, generally achieved through risk assessment, the contractor can liaise with the principal contractor to assist them to manage health and safety on site. A simple example could be attending a site co-ordination meeting to plan the programme of what contractors can access what part of the site or to plan the assembly of a crane.

The principal contractor must have this co-operation if he is to comply with his own CDM responsibilities to ensure co-ordination of site activities and co-operation between contractors; to ensure that every contractor on the project complies with the rules laid down in the construction phase plan and the provision of information to the CDM co-ordinator.

Receiving information prior to starting work

The provision of information to the contractor is the end of the road in terms of filtering residual hazards through the project for the construction phase. The regulations place the onus on the employer or, indeed, self-employed (contractor) to ensure they do not carry out any work until:

> Where a project is notifiable, no contractor shall carry out construction work in relation to the project unless—
>
> (a) he has been provided with the names of the CDM co-ordinator and principal contractor;
> (b) he has been given access to such part of the construction phase plan as is relevant to the work to be performed by him, containing sufficient detail in relation to such work; and
> (c) notice of the project has been given to the Executive . . .
>
> Extract from CDM Regulation 19(1)

Remember that the name of both the CDM co-ordinator and principal contractor will be available in the construction phase plan and also displayed on the notice required under Regulation 21. It is for the contractor, though, to provide the information to employees and the self-employed.

The respective elements from the construction phase plan must also be articulated to the employees and self-employed by the contractor. The contractor will receive, from the principal contractor, comprehensive information on the specific health and safety risks, generally in the form of the construction plan. This must be assessed and communicated effectively. Depending on the specific risks, this can be achieved, for example, by toolbox talks, method statement briefings and induction and awareness training.

The principle of the contractor adopting an informative and inclusive policy in terms of their employees or self-employed when managing health and safety is a sensible regime. The relevant experiences of the contracting team will no doubt contribute towards managing the risks.

Providing information to the principal contractor

The contractor is required to provide the principal contractor, as soon as possible, with any information which may affect the health and safety of site workers or, indeed, others who may be affected by their activities such as the general public. The regulations offer the following to the contractor:

> Every contractor shall—
>
> (a) promptly provide the principal contractor with any information (including any relevant part of any risk assessment in his possession or control) which—
>   (i) might affect the health or safety of any person carrying out the construction work or of any person who may be affected by it,
>   (ii) might justify a review of the construction phase plan, or
>   (iii) has been identified for inclusion in the health and safety file in pursuance of regulation 22(l)(j).
>
> CDM Regulation 19 (2) (a)

As discussed earlier, risk assessments will need to be carried out by contractors to satisfy their duty under regulation 3 of the Management of Health and Safety at Work Regulations 1999. These may well form part of their strategy for complying with this responsibility of providing information to the principal contractor.

This duty also requires the contractor to provide information in respect of the health and safety file. Such information could include as built or installed drawings, operational and maintenance manuals, method statements for more complicated procedures, contact details of specialist suppliers and information on residual risks for any future maintenance, cleaning and refurbishment work.

Complying with directions from the principal contractor

To enable the principal contractor to manage health and safety and the regulations and to control contractors they are given duties that are supported by the duty for contractors to co-operate and comply with the directions of the principal contractor. To this end, it is a breach of the regulations for a contractor not to comply with the directions of the principal contractor to secure health and safety.

> (c) Comply with—
>   (i) any directions of the principal contractor given to him under regulation 22 (1) (e), and
>   (ii) any site rules.
>
> CDM Regulation 19(2)(c)

Assuming the directions are reasonable and necessary for the principal contractor to comply with his duties under the regulations, the contractor will need to comply. However, the general duty to co-operate should, if executed effectively, avoid the need for the principal contractor to enforce this duty. These directions can be directly related to health and safety action or can be higher-level programming and planning issues to facilitate health and safety on site.

Complying with relevant rules from the construction phase plan

These rules and standards obviously need to be presented to the contractors so they are aware of the responsibilities that must be addressed when developing risk assessments, method statements, lifting plans and so on. Again, if robust arrangements are in place for effective co-operation and co-ordination and the general principles of prevention are adhered to by all, complying with the construction phase plan would be an integral part of any contractor's approach to health and safety management.

Contractors will, however, need to take steps to ensure that they comply with this regulation. This is often undertaken and complied with by contractors inspecting and monitoring their own work to ensure that their employees, or, indeed, self-employed workers they are supervising, are complying with the regulations.

Contractors will also obviously need access to the construction phase plan amendments, updates and revisions to be able to comply with this requirement. Again, this is related to the close, informed working relationship that any contractor should seek with the principal contractor.

Reporting accidents and incidents to the principal contractor

If the contractor has to notify the Health and Safety Executive of an accident or incident as required by the Reporting of Injuries, Diseases and Dangerous

Occurrences Regulations (RIDDOR), CDM also provides them with an additional duty to promptly inform the principal contractor. As the principal contractor is responsible for health and safety throughout the construction phase then this information is required to monitor compliance levels with relevant health and safety legislation. Also, the proactive principal contractor will review existing health and safety management arrangements to ensure they are effective. These issues should be covered in induction and form part of the site rules.

7 Duties relating to onsite health and safety

Introduction

Following all the risk management opportunities and supporting project information provided to contractors and site workers, the fact is that there will always be risks to be managed on construction sites. The CDM Regulations 2007 define a set of high-level onsite health and safety standards to control risks and provide a safe working environment. These standards, defined in Part 4 of the regulations, fundamentally replace the Workplace (Health, Safety and Welfare) Regulations 1996, with the omission of the standards covering falls, now addressed in the Work at Height Regulations 1995 (see Appendix 2).

Part 4 of the regulations require all contractors and persons who control the way in which construction work is carried out by a person at work to comply with the requirements of Regulations 26 to 44. The details and how contractors must address these regulations is covered below.

Key to the management of health and safety onsite is the integration of health and safety into the construction phase planning process. At a high level the identification of the construction team, their competence and experience and the arrangements at the planning stages for how health and safety is to be managed is legally and practically essential. To start planning health and safety on site and not earlier is poor practice and only increases the holistic health and safety and business risk.

This process at a more detailed level can be driven through the development of the construction phase plan (if the project is notifiable) and method statement. The standard headings of these documents promote a systems approach to consider what is required to manage health and safety on site. Also due consideration must be given to the suitability and sufficiency of management arrangements in respect of the risk profile. This is also legally defined as 'reasonably practicable' which can be interpreted as a cost versus safety balance. The problem with overly bureaucratic health and safety management systems that have many irrelevant elements is obvious, but the approach must focus on the significant risk, contractual and statutory requirements.

Safe places of work

The provision and maintenance of a safe place of work is fundamental to health and safety on site as statistically one is more likely to have an accident travelling to the workface than doing any specific work.

The regulations (CDM Regulation 26) specifically require the contractor to provide and maintain safe access and egress, ensure the provisions are without risk to health and safety, access is adequately controlled to prevent unauthorised use and be of an adequate size to suit the working activity and equipment use in that area.

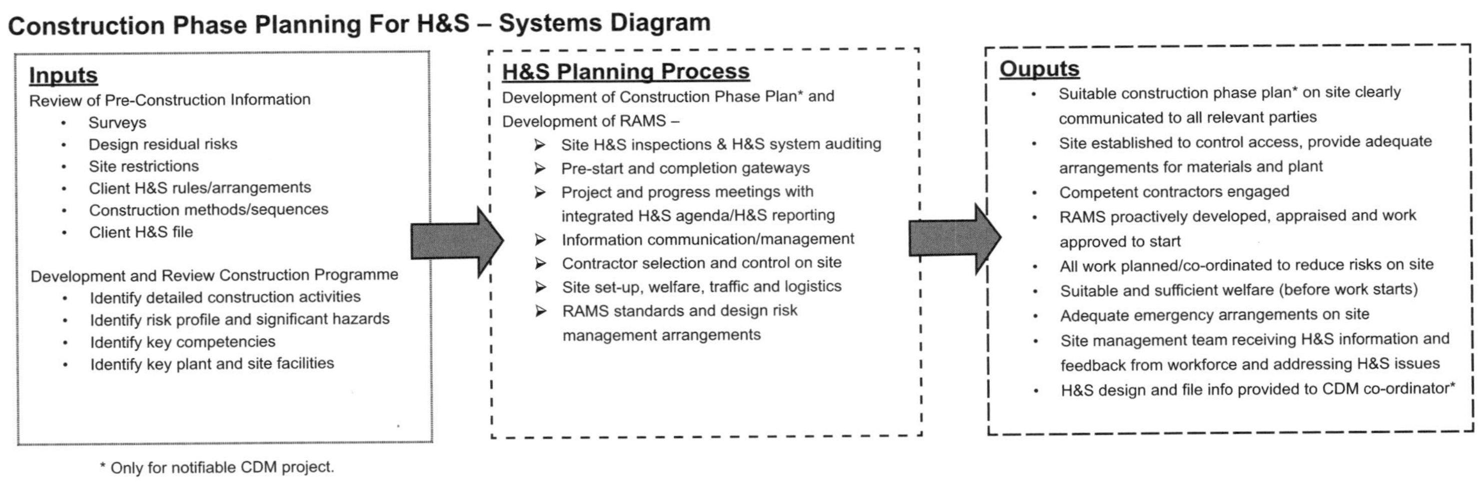

Construction Phase Planning For H&S – Systems Diagram

Inputs

Review of Pre-Construction Information
- Surveys
- Design residual risks
- Site restrictions
- Client H&S rules/arrangements
- Construction methods/sequences
- Client H&S file

Development and Review Construction Programme
- Identify detailed construction activities
- Identify risk profile and significant hazards
- Identify key competencies
- Identify key plant and site facilities

H&S Planning Process

Development of Construction Phase Plan* and
Development of RAMS –
- Site H&S inspections & H&S system auditing
- Pre-start and completion gateways
- Project and progress meetings with integrated H&S agenda/H&S reporting
- Information communication/management
- Contractor selection and control on site
- Site set-up, welfare, traffic and logistics
- RAMS standards and design risk management arrangements

Ouputs

- Suitable construction phase plan* on site clearly communicated to all relevant parties
- Site established to control access, provide adequate arrangements for materials and plant
- Competent contractors engaged
- RAMS proactively developed, appraised and work approved to start
- All work planned/co-ordinated to reduce risks on site
- Suitable and sufficient welfare (before work starts)
- Adequate emergency arrangements on site
- Site management team receiving H&S information and feedback from workforce and addressing H&S issues
- H&S design and file info provided to CDM co-ordinator*

* Only for notifiable CDM project.

Figure 7.1 Construction phase planning for health and safety

The application of this regulation at the planning stage of a project or task on a project should be managed by a risk assessment. The factors to be considered in developing the risk assessment could include:

- the duration of the project or task;
- the interfaces with hazards, e.g. site plant, falls from height, lifting operations, working over or near water, highways and other transport infrastructure, public and other working parties, etc.;
- the number of persons working on site requiring welfare facilities;
- the conditions on site, e.g. ground conditions, weather conditions, etc.;
- the significant construction activities requiring access and space to logistically be undertaken safely, e.g. groundworks, excavations and piling, storage of spoil, decontamination, demolition, asbestos removal, lifting operations, etc., all requiring isolation from the persons not directly involved;
- the execution on an emergency plan to allow emergency services access and facilitate a safe means of escape.

Other considerations when planning safe access, egress and spatial require-ments covered in these regulations should include Regulations 36 (Traffic routes), 37 (Vehicles), 39 (Emergency procedures), 40 (Emergency routes and exits) and so on.

As a guide to demonstrate compliance with this regulation and to support a suitable risk assessment, contractors would benefit from adopting a 'Site set-up checklist' as a safe system of work.

In conclusion, the provision of safe and controlled access and egress must be an initial consideration when putting people to work and is fundamental to health and safety on site. Also, the specific arrangements to control the risks must be clearly defined and communicated to the workforce. For a complex high-risk project; an illustrated plan is valuable for a low-risk scenario the arrangements for car parking, pedestrian routes and plant locations can be explained at the pre-start method statement briefing.

Good order and site security

This regulation requires contractors to maintain a safe workplace in respect of the maintenance and cleanliness of the workplace and controlling access onto the site or working area to prevent unauthorised access. It also specifies that any sharp materials projecting in such a way as to cause a risk must be prevented.

Health and safety issues associated with good order and site security have been historical problems in the construction industry, prompting the inspectorate to promote slips and trips campaigns and develop specific CDM regulations requiring principal contractors to manage access on to the site.

One of the industry terms for good order and cleanliness is 'housekeeping'. The main hazards associated with poor housekeeping that should be considered as part of a risk assessment include:

- slips and trips; associated with materials and waste materials stored in walkways and liquid spills not being cleaned up or managed with barriers following an accidental spill or during commissioning of M&E plant;
- falling objects; associated with uncontrolled storage of materials on scaffolding and adjacent to floor openings including excavations;
- fire, food poisoning, blocking means of escape and access to emergency equipment like fire alarms and extinguishers, first aid equipment and emergency telephones. Also, hazards associated with waste materials including nails through wood and projections of metal and sharp objects pose significant hazards.

Stability of structures

The stability of structures can be considered a high-risk issue in construction associated with temporary works, demolition and the erection of new structures. During construction the design of a building may be very stable when fully erected and all bracing and supports have been completed, but during the erection phase the columns and walls, for example, will be unstable before bracing or wind-bracing structures have been completed. A simple brick and block wall can be unstable during construction until the mortar has cured effectively to perform its bonding task, so the construction methodology and information supplied by the designer must be used to construct safely. Rules of thumb or best practice exist for brick and block wall construction that guide the builder not to construct a wall higher than 10 times its width until the mortar has cured to reduce risks of stability and quality.

Instability can also result from bad weather conditions and failure to consider and manage ground conditions effectively. Also poor site traffic management and crane management can damage structures during construction causing instability.

During demolition works the main hazard is uncontrolled collapse, and the demolition planner must be competent to identify the demolition method that reduces the risk of uncontrolled collapse, when a structural engineer is required for advice, what temporary works may be needed during demolition to control collapse risk and what supporting information in the form of surveys are required to facilitate the safe planning process.

The keys to controlling these risks are competence, co-operation and co-ordination. A competent designer and construction site manager should identify the hazards early on in the process and identify who is to manage the risks. For a timber roof or frame construction process the method statement must identify the permanent bracing requirements, i.e. the installation of key bracing internal walls and the temporary bracing requirements to ensure stability before the next level is constructed. Co-operation and co-ordination in practice should involve the designers placing notes on drawings, completing risk registers or producing erection methodologies to facilitate stability during construction.

On site, safe systems of work should identify maximum loadings on floors, roofs and walls when tying in scaffolding, etc. Loading out semi-constructed building with pallets of cement or plaster boards can cause structural collapse or at least damage to the structure.

Where there is more complex temporary works like facade bracing, complex and structural form work and so on, a temporary works designer and onsite co-ordinator will be required with a set of health and safety arrangements to manage the process through the essential checks and gateways to ensure stability.

Stability problems can also occur during uncontrolled building works that interface with the structure. The installation of mechanical and electrical systems can involve forming retrospective penetrations with structural consequences. Drilling beams, block walls, concrete and steel frames requires an understanding of the structural performance of the structure and the design and planning to consider the principles of Part A of the building regulation in relation to structural stability.

In conclusion, structural stability is a significant hazard associated with demolition, construction and temporary works. The hazards must be identified early on in the design, planning and risk management process by competent persons to demonstrate compliance with the CDM duty to take all practicable steps to prevent danger to any person, i.e. CDM Regulation 28.

Demolition or dismantling

Due to the potentially high-risk nature of demolition and dismantling and the need for effective planning, the CDM regulations require the arrangements for demolition to be recorded in writing. The regulations do not prescribe any format for the written document but generally based on risk a method statement is the minimum strategy to plan, record, co-ordinate and communicate the demolition arrangements. For higher-risk demolition tasks one could use a demolition plan and guidance on planning and projects from BS6187:2000 the British Standard Code of Practice for demolition. The main plan considerations should include:

- **Effective site knowledge:** e.g. details of isolations and services, knowledge of the structure, extent of demolition and retained structures, ongoing use and client business continuity issues, etc.
- **Legal requirements:** e.g. party wall issues, planning conditions, environmental health conditions, environmental agency conditions and consents, local authority permissions for crushers, burning, etc., site waste management plan, highways and rail infrastructure authority permission, etc.

- **Programme management:** e.g. sequence and method of proposed demolition, identification of exclusion zones on site and timings, details of plant and locations of plant and equipment, site traffic management plan, materials/waste storage and processing areas, temporary works, temporary services, etc.
- **Arrangements for protecting the public:** e.g. site security including fencing/hoarding, access points and guarding where necessary, control of site visitors and other third parties requiring access to site, identification of exclusion zones during critical aspects of demolition programme outside main site, containment of demolished materials, etc.
- **Arrangements for structural stability:** e.g. identification of critical structural elements and strategy to avoid uncontrolled collapse and maintain retained structures, identification of temporary works scope, details of pre-weakening, etc.
- **Environmental management:** e.g. noise assessment at site boundaries, control of dust emissions, waste minimisation and recycling options, bunding arrangements for storage and use of oils and fuels, wheel washing, skip and truck covering/sheeting, asbestos management, contaminated materials and ground management, managing invasive plant species like Japanese knotweed, etc.
- **Occupational health and safety:** e.g. site management staff and risk management planning, e.g. supervisors undertaking risk assessments and producing method statements, briefing workforce on site and task health and safety issues and undertaking safety inspections, welfare arrangements based on risk and numbers of workers, workface access platforms and their maintenance, e.g. scaffolding design and seven-day inspections, definition of working and exclusion zones, site safety, safe systems of work – daily planning, access control, permits to work for access and isolations, etc., hazardous substance management, health surveillance arrangements, induction training and information on health and safety including changes, etc.

The main hazards associated with demolition and dismantling should be managed at the start of a project by the client, designers and CDM co-ordinator (when the project is notifiable) considering what information is available or required to best plan the project to avoid or reduce the risks associated with demolition. If a design or project requires demolition then the contractors should be provided with supporting information, e.g. asbestos, services and conditional structural surveys, on the structure and hazards that are difficult to manage or that are unusual. From this information the demolition contractor can start to plan for safety.

The main hazards that can be associated with demolition that should be subject to a risk assessment process include uncontrolled collapse, falling objects, asbestos, existing services, confined spaces, interface with highways and the public, falls from height, noise and vibration, contamination including zoonoses (diseases communicated from animals, e.g. Weil's disease), hot works and fire/explosion, e.g. when removing redundant fuel storage tanks or pipes and so on.

In conclusion, demolition and dismantling, based on the nature and condition of the structure, can be an inherently hazardous operation. To demonstrate compliance with the CDM Regulations and prevent accidents and ill health, effective planning by competent persons from the very start of the project is essential and the planning must be in writing, in the form of a demolition plan or suitable method statement.

Explosives

The use of explosives is a specialised activity and as such the subject is covered by British Standards, the primary being BS 5607 'Code of practice for the safe use of explosives in the construction industry' and many regulations and HSE guidance documents for manufacture, transportation and use. Explosives are used in demolition of structures, tunnelling and occasionally for ground preparation/works.

The principles of health and safety with explosives are:

- A suitable and sufficient risk assessment and method statement is produced to manage the risk and communicate the health and safety arrangements to control risks to the other contractors and workforce undertaking the work.
- The acquisition and storage of explosives is licensed by the police and an explosives certificate used as formal documentation to demonstrate authorisation. Also the person ordering or taking delivery of the explosives must have a 'recipient competent authority' obtained from the Health and Safety Executive.
- The main contractor or principal contractor must identify a competent contractor or person or persons to be responsible for managing the activity.
- The specialist contractor or competent person ensures that the supervisors and shot firers (persons responsible for detonation) are competent.
- Checks are made by the main contractor or principal contractor regarding notification to the local authority, utilities companies, transport infrastructure companies, local police, airports – in fact, any business or body affected by the activity.
- The transportation arrangements for public roads complies with Carriage of Explosives by Road Regulations 1996, which requires a suitable vehicle, restrictions of carriage of mixed explosives, the marking of the vehicle, written information of explosives to be maintained on the vehicle, and reasonable steps to ensure safe and secure carriage. On site the transportation vehicle must be clean and carry a red flag to highlight the presence of explosives.

- The competence of the driver is identified, certificated and complies with the Transportation of Dangerous Good (Driver Training) Regulations 1999.
- Adequate communication, generally called a 'Code of signals' arrangement, is established to control risks. These arrangements must co-ordinate access via appointed sentries to the site firing warnings, all clear, emergency situation, etc.
- Operation and emergency arrangements for problems associated with explosives also cover:
  - shot firer ensuring safety zone is clear;
  - banning of any means of any unauthorised ignition within 10 m of the explosives or detonators;
  - the prohibition of drilling into old sockets containing explosives or detonators, which may cause an uncontrolled explosion;
  - that explosives are not subject to any localised impact or shock;
  - that explosives and detonators are separated until needed;
  - records are kept of any misfires;
  - all explosive are disposed of by returning back to suppliers.

In conclusion, the use of explosives and all associated activities, requires the use of competent and, where necessary, licensed personnel. The risks associated with explosives are not just associated with the direct activity and must be controlled through the planning and development of safety arrangements via the risk assessment process. Other related hazards also need consideration in this process and the risk assessment must involve co-operation of the explosives and onsite management teams to be suitable and sufficient.

Excavations

The types of hazard associated with excavation are many and the control of these risks are necessary to prevent serious injury or damage to plant and structures. The pre-planning and risk assessment process must consider the pre-construction information issued to the construction team. Ground water, geography, topography and location of excavations in relation to existing services must be part of the risk assessment. The main hazards associated with excavations include:

- no or limited ground information
- falls from height and falling objects
- site plant vehicles (falling in and causing trench collapse)
- confined and restricted spaces
- surface and ground water
- trench or structural collapse of adjacent buildings or structures

- contaminated ground and ordinance
- buried services.

As with the management of all risks on site and compliance with the CDM Regulations there is a requirement for competent personnel with the experience to plan and undertake the work safety. The skills of the competent person, which covers the safe system of work and inspection of excavations, require knowledge of the hazards and the safe construction method to excavate safely. Excavations, based on ground conditions, location, size and depth, can involve the following methods to control the risk of collapse and entrapment:

- battered sides – employing first principles by removing the materials that could fall into the excavation and level of risk associated with the confined space and falling into an excavation;
- double-sided support – can be employed using a trench box or by designed trench sheeting;
- single-sided support – utilising raking supports, a cantilever support (with or without anchors) and piling supports including secant piling, driven sheet piling and H, or soldier, piling with infill sections generally made of timber.

Most excavation support is classified as temporary works and must be managed by adequate CDM design arrangements. This will involve the engagement of a temporary works designer and onsite co-ordinator who should have a safe system of work that promotes checks and authorisations/ permits to work on site, generally called a temporary works register.

All excavations must be formally inspected every seven days and, additionally for excavations with supports or battering, a pre-shift start and post-incident inspection is required to comply with the CDM Regulations and to ensure that no work is undertaken in an unsafe excavation.

In conclusion, to comply with the CDM Regulations and manage risks associated with excavations, the competent contractor must initially assess the nature of the excavations, site/ground information and location in relation to all interfaces as part of the risk assessment and method statement development. They then must make adequate proactive arrangements for avoiding and controlling risks associated with trench collapse/entrapment, falling materials, falling from height and also establish necessary inspections and emergency arrangements. The design and installation of constructed trench support systems must be undertaken by a competent designer and installation overseen by a competent onsite co-ordinator.

Cofferdams and caissons

Cofferdams and caissons are structures designed for persons to work in rivers and the sea and, by the nature of the environment, all associated activities have a high-risk profile. The construction process of a cofferdam, which is fundamentally a dam, can involve sheet piling or loose materials deposited to stop or divert water from the work area. A caisson is a retaining watertight structure generally used to work underwater on foundations of walls and bridges which can be open or enclosed.

Both operations are specialised and require specialist contractors to design and undertake the work.

The main risk associated with both activities are:

- unknown/limited site and environmental knowledge;
- working over and near water;
- lifting operations;
- structural collapse associated with design, collision and changing unplanned natural forces, e.g. flooding and extreme weather;
- working at height and falling objects;
- decompression sickness (caissons);
- confined space and difficult rescue arrangements.

The main onsite health and safety arrangements to manage risks associated with cofferdams and caissons when developing a risk assessment and method statement are:

- environmental and geological surveys and conditions;
- consideration of design identified residual risks and health-and-safety-related instructions;
- site/workplace access, delivery and storage of materials and access control;
- competence of workforce and emergency teams, including medical conditions and checks;
- lifting plan to comply with LOLER requirements;
- emergency plan covering liaison with emergency services, training, communication, fire, explosion, illness, ingress of water/escape route, structural collapse/defect and recovery arrangements;
- physical and management methods of communication, liaison and feedback with and from the workforce;
- statutory inspections of structures involving pre-shift inspections, health and safety monitoring and arrangements to stop work and remedy defects;
- monitoring water and weather conditions;
- occupational hazards associated with piling, working in compressed-air environments and working in water and health monitoring.

In conclusion, cofferdams and caissons are highly specialised activities requiring competence to plan, design, construct, inspect and work in them. The main hazards require the contractor to apply a co-ordinated approach to manage the activities in a manner that addresses the ever-changing risk profile associated with working so directly with water and the forces of nature.

Reports of inspections

The CDM Regulations define the mandatory requirements for reports and inspections of two particularly high-risk environments on construction sites, namely cofferdams and caissons. As the robustness of these structures – most of which are temporary, to prevent collapse and water ingress – are critical to safety it is good risk management and engineering practice to properly inspect the structures. The dynamics of risk are furthermore complicated by changes in the imposed forces and the nature of construction potentially causing damage.

The regulations define in Schedule 3 the particulars to be included in a report of inspection. They include:

1. Name and address of the person on whose behalf the inspection was carried out.
2. Location of the place of work inspected.
3. Description of the place of work or part of that place inspected (including any work equipment and materials).
4. Date and time of the inspection.
5. Details of any matter identified that could give rise to a risk to the health and safety of any person.
6. Details of any action taken as a result of any matter identified in paragraph 5 above.
7. Details of any further action considered necessary.
8. Name and position of the person making the report.

All inspections must be undertaken by competent persons with the knowledge of the structure's dynamics, potential defects and associated risks. They must also be aware of the principal contractor's arrangements to act appropriately in reporting defects and advising the site manager or person in control.

Site safety management systems and arrangements should include inspection pro forma schedules and inspection regimes from temporary works designers where necessary for complex structures to ensure all key structural elements and potential defects have been examined and reported.

The person undertaking the inspections must do so every seven days and, where it is deemed not safe to work, provide the person for whom the inspection is being carried out a report within 24 hours of the inspection.

Site safety management systems must also ensure all supervisors and foremen putting people to work undertake daily/shift workplace inspections and stop work or call the inspector to undertake an inspection as part of their safe systems of work.

The site manager or person responsible for the inspector's service must maintain the inspection report on site for three months and be available for an HSE inspector to inspect.

In conclusion, the CDM Regulations require inspection of cofferdams and caissons at a minimum of every seven days. Certain designs, including temporary works, may require specific and more frequent inspections by a competent inspector. Inspection reports, the details of which are listed in Schedule 3 of the CDM regulations, must be provided to the person/contractor in control of the work within 24 hours, but the inspector has a duty under CDM Regulation 5 to co-operate with the site team and, therefore, inform the persons in control of the works as soon as is reasonably practicable based on the level of risk.

Note: The requirement for inspecting and reporting on scaffolding and work platforms is covered in Regulation 12 for work equipment and 13 for workplace of the Work at Height Regulations 1995 (see Appendix 2).

Energy distribution installations

Energy distribution installations include gas and electric and the risk of contact or damage to these systems requires managing to comply with the CDM Regulations. The arrangements for avoiding or reducing onsite health and safety risks associated with energy distribution installations starts with the client providing information to the designer, the designer designing to manage the risk and the designer and CDM co-ordinator communicating the residual risk to the contractor for health and safety planning.

The onsite arrangements for avoiding accidents associated with these systems includes the following:

- Mark up site plan to identify services above and below ground.
- Undertake any enabling works to deviate or temporarily move services.
- Highlight services on site with appropriate safety signs, physical barriers and overhead warning barriers to avoid contact.
- Liaise with utilities companies, transport infrastructure companies and, where necessary, clients to identify and check locations of services and also to ensure any specific safety standards or restrictions are implemented.
- Adopt a permit to dig that requires all pre-checks to be in place and a safe digging procedure is adopted when digging near or over services.
- Induction training and site toolbox talks include the site plan highlighting the location of the services.
- All site activities are co-ordinated by the principal or main contractor and all risk assessments and method statements are assessed for compliance and health and safety management of the risks associated with energy distribution installations.

In conclusion, the contractor's early planning of work/development of the construction programme, site-safe management system, site set-up arrangements and risk assessment and review process must identify the interfaces and strategies to avoid interface with these systems to comply with the CDM Regulations and prevent serious accidents.

Prevention of drowning

This regulation is designed to set and promote minimum health and safety standards for contractors or persons working over or near water or liquid where there is a risk of drowning. The regulation requires suitable and sufficient steps to be taken to prevent falling, minimise the risk of drowning in the event of such a fall and ensure suitable equipment is provided, maintained and used promptly to undertake a rescue.

As with all health and safety management the risk assessment process undertaken by a competent person is key and the main consideration for managing the risks are:

- managing the work to avoid or reduce the need to be exposed to such risks;
- understanding the risk profile and dynamics of the water or liquid, e.g. tidal, subject to uncontrolled releases of pressure, contaminated/ hazardous, etc.;
- identifying the areas where someone may fall into water or a liquid that can't be avoided;
- establishment of adequate access control to regulate who can enter the higher-risk area and define rules for additional PPE, e.g. life jacket, throw line, life buoys and additional induction and emergency training where necessary;
- use of barriers/leading edge protection and safety signage to control the risk of falling;
- use of fall arrest or fall restraint equipment where using barriers, etc., is not practicable;
- provision and application of a co-ordinated rescue plan to:
  - raise the alarm for a response team, emergency services or both;
  - stop work activities that may affect the rescue;
  - recover someone or persons suspended from a harness;
  - recover someone or persons from a safety/fall protection net;
  - recover someone or persons from the water;
  - apply appropriate first aid;
  - call the emergency services.

The regulations also set standards for the health and safety of any person transported on a boat or other method on water to or from any workplace and to prevent overcrowding of such a vessel. The risk assessment and arrangement to address this duty should consider the following:

- the arrangement for safe access onto and off the vessel;
- the recognised competence of the persons in control of the vessel including local knowledge;
- the suitability of the craft or vessel to transport persons by water, e.g. suitable BS EN (British Standard European Norm) reference, fit for purpose as defined by the Provision and Use of Work Equipment Regulations 1998, i.e. industrial construction designed for transporting the correct number of site workers with adequate controls, communications and safety features to initiate a rescue;
- the transportation is supervised at all times to ensure the craft is subject to pre-use and daily checks based on the manufacturer's requirements and the control measures specified in the risk assessment, e.g. safety equipment checks, supervisor's radio checks, etc.;
- the supervisor has regulated the number of persons and equipment that can safely use the vessel at one time and where persons and equipment can be stowed during use.

In conclusion, the regulations require the risk of drowning to be managed to prevent falling and avoid drowning when a person or persons enter the water accidentally. They also require arrangements to be in place to ensure a vessel used for transporting workers is not to be overloaded with persons, materials or equipment.

Traffic routes

The provision of organised traffic management routes and facilities is covered in this regulation. The principles of the regulations require the traffic routes to:

- be laid out, suitable and sufficient for their intended use, i.e. size, location, construction, etc.;
- promote the segregation and protection of vehicles and pedestrians;
- have gates of access to routes, which are protected/separated to allow pedestrians to see oncoming traffic from a place of safety;
- provide loading bays with at least one exit point exclusively for pedestrians;
- have suitable signage, e.g. traffic management and hazard warning;
- be inspected and maintained;
- be free from obstruction.

Traffic management and the provision of safe routes should be an output of a site risk assessment and to communicate clearly to the workforce where it is deemed necessary a traffic management plan is produced. The plan can have an illustrated drawing and should consider the following:

- key roles and responsibilities for implementing the traffic management plan;

- access points and access control/security;
- road layout indicating primary routes and secondary task-specific routes/areas, one-way and two-way systems and turning points where applicable;
- pedestrian routes and crossing points;
- lighting and signage requirements;
- obstructions and 'pinch points' including overhead services, structures, temporary works including scaffolding, etc.;
- locations of key plant, process areas, fuel storage, construction materials storage, waste storage, lay down areas, etc.;
- location of parking and welfare provision;
- traffic rules, e.g. speed limits, mandatory banksman, flashing beacons, high-visibility clothing, sheeting requirements, gantry locations for working at height off lorries, etc.;
- supervision and enforcement of site rules.

In conclusion, the provision of clearly defined traffic routes with appropriate traffic rules that promote segregation from pedestrians will significantly reduce risks on site and demonstrate compliance with the CDM Regulations.

Vehicles

This regulation focuses on the vehicles on building sites and defines the high-level standards for health and safety. The regulations require arrangements for:

- avoiding unintended movement of vehicles and operator's ability to give warning to others, which can be achieved with:
  - well-maintained vehicles
  - 'no key left in vehicles' policy/use of key-safe system
  - using timber or constructed baulk wheel stops
  - level temporary plant parking area
  - reversing mirrors and audible alarm, reversing cameras, audible horn and competent drivers;
- vehicles driven, loaded, operated and towed in a safe manner, with persons only riding on vehicles in provided places, which can be achieved with:
  - accreditation competent drivers and plant operators
  - rules for securing loads that as an output of a risk assessment require suitable plant and equipment used for securing loads to comply with the Provision and Use of Work Equipment Regulations 1998 and be fit for purpose and maintained in a safe condition;
- avoiding injury to persons on vehicles being loaded by loose materials. The arrangements for controlling this risk should consider:

- o site rules requiring dumper drivers to leave the vehicle when being loaded and having a safe place for the operator
- o selecting plant that allows drivers to stay in a secure cab during loading;

- preventing vehicles from falling into excavations, pits, water or over-running the edge of an embankment or earthworks. The arrangements for controlling these risk should consider:

- o the provision of barriers, baulk wheel stops and safety banks
- o the erection of suitable safety signage to warn the driver/operator.

The safe use of vehicles is a combination of selecting suitable plant, the maintenance of a suitable traffic management environment and the competence of the drivers and operatives.

In conclusion, the dynamic nature of construction sites requires the site management to monitor and review these three criteria to reduce the risks associated with vehicles and mobile plant and demonstrate compliance with this CDM regulation.

Prevention of risks from fire etc.

This regulation covers fire and also risk associated with flooding and any substance liable to cause asphyxiation. All three hazards should be subject to a risk assessment and the implement of adequate controls. Significant residual risk associated with existing plant and redundant plant and environment that have fire and explosion risks should be communicated from the client, designer or CDM co-ordinator. However, it is not always practicable to identify these hazards and the contractors should cover what actions to take when a fire or explosion hazard is identified onsite so work can stop and a risk assessment undertaken to assess the level of risk and what control measures or construction action is needed.

The control of risks associated with fire and explosion must consider:

- development of a fire plan covering site rules for housekeeping, waste management, hot works, means of escape and location of muster points and fire points, etc.;
- development of compartmented areas in a structure by early installation in structures that form part of the engineered fire strategy;
- emergency arrangements and equipment to detect and extinguish small fires, raise the alarm, evacuate the site, contact and provide safety-critical information, e.g. location of LPG cylinders, number of persons not accounted for, etc. to the emergency services
- key appointments, training and competence including:

- o appointments of fire marshals
- o fire plan training at induction.

In respect of flooding and substances likely to cause asphyxiation, the contractor's review of the pre-construction information and initial site audit should provide sufficient information, combined with knowledge of the construction activities, to undertake a suitable and sufficient risk assessment.

The issues to consider in developing controls for these hazards could include:

- suitability of site information and construction options to avoid or reduce need to access a certain environment;
- permit to work systems to control use of plant and check isolation of systems that control water and chemicals;
- competence of the workforce and persons with responsibility for rescue or first aid;
- confined space risks;
- environmental monitoring;
- emergency plan.

In conclusion, the risks of fire, flooding and asphyxiation are significant and a suitable and sufficient risk assessment undertaken by a competent person with knowledge of the construction activities, the site environment and associated hazards. For all these risks emergency plans will be needed that provide, in their development, a secondary and somewhat more detailed assessment to ensure compliance with this CDM regulation.

Emergency procedures

The identification and establishment of emergency procedures on a construction site is fundamental to effective health and safety. This CDM regulation defines the criteria to support the development of suitable and sufficient procedures, which may be developed in the form of an emergency plan, and requires the contractor to consider:

- identification of foreseeable emergencies and procedures for any necessary site evacuation or evacuation from part of a site;
- assessing the type of work and its associated risk profile;
- the characteristics, size and number of locations on the site or sites;
- the number of persons likely to be present on site at any one time;
- the risk profile of any substances on site;
- induction and ongoing training to ensure the site workforce and visitors are aware of the emergency procedures;
- arrangements for testing the emergency procedures.

Owing to the dynamic nature of construction work, procedures may only be applicable for certain types of work, e.g. scaffold recovery during scaffolding erection, but this issue should be managed by the site representative as part of the site safety co-ordination process.

Emergency plans should cover what is reasonably foreseeable and the main emergency procedures on construction sites should include:

- fire and explosion
- first aid and significant accident
- confined space rescue (covered in Regulation 5 of the Confined Spaces Regulations 1997)
- scaffolding rescue plan
- safety net recovery plan
- recovery/rescue from water
- tower crane rescue plan
- rope access operative rescue plan
- chemical/hazardous substances accident
- bomb threat
- recovery from flooding
- emergency response to collapse structure/entrapment
- violence and aggression
- power out/cut.

The development of emergency procedures for reasonably foreseeable issues requires a co-ordinated response and the co-operation of the relevant contractors and site team. Proactive production, training and testing of the procedures is then essential to demonstrate compliance with this regulation and ensure the effectiveness of the arrangements.

Emergency routes and exits

The provision of suitable emergency routes and exits are covered by this regulation and the requirements include the following:

- Provide suitable emergency routes and exits to enable any person to reach a place of safety quickly in the event of danger. The contractor in planning the construction site temporary fire strategy must define the routes based on the shortest practicable travel distances and must consider the changes to the site throughout construction.
- Traffic and emergency routes must be kept clear and where necessary provided with emergency lighting when the site involves working during the hours of darkness.
- In planning the routes the regulations require the following to be considered to ensure suitability and sufficiency as in Regulation 39:

  ○ assessing the type or work and its associated risk profile
  ○ the characteristics, size and number of locations on the site or sites
  ○ the number of persons likely to be present on site at any one time
  ○ the risk profile of any substances on site

- all emergency routes and exits must be indicated by suitable safety signs that comply with the Safety Signs and Signals Regulations 1996.

In conclusion, the provision of suitable emergency routes that provide workers with the opportunity to quickly avoid danger is fundamental to health and safety on site. The routes must be planned to ensure they cover all points of work and are maintained through the changes of the construction programme.

Fire detection and fire-fighting

The identification and establishment of fire-detection and fire-fighting arrangements on a construction site is fundamental to effective health and safety and the effectiveness of the fire safety plan. This CDM regulation requires the contractor to consider and implement the following.

- The provision of suitable and sufficient fire-fighting equipment must be the output of a fire risk assessment to establish the types of extinguishers, their location and the number needed to provide quick access in the event of an emergency. For specific task risk assessment the contractor may be required to provide work area fire-fighting equipment, e.g. for hot works.
- Fire detection and alarm systems, the location, type and number based again on risk. These systems will need to be tested and inspected periodically to ensure they work or to undertake repairs or replacements to ensure the integrity of the holistic fire strategy. Detection and alarm systems on low-risk open buildings can simply be by inspection and word of mouth, but for large enclosed structures a wired-in system will be required for effective detection and alarm.
- The location of fire-fighting equipment should be in a readily accessible location and housekeeping rules must prevent materials and equipment being stored anywhere that would prevent emergency access.
- All persons on site should be trained in the use of fire-fighting equipment and fire safety. The training should cover the selection and effective use of fire-fighting equipment to ensure the fire is extinguished effectively and the operative is not harmed by the fire or hazards associated with selecting the wrong extinguisher and not using it properly. Note: The regulations require a site rule where only instructed/trained persons in using fire-fighting equipment are used for tasks where there is a risk of fire, e.g. hot work plumbing.
- Fire-fighting equipment requires highlighting by suitable health and safety signage that must comply with the Safety Signs and Signals Regulations 1996. To ensure the provision of all fire safety facilities the establishment of fire points is good practice that contain:

- a means of raising the alarm;
- a fire plan illustrating the location of all fire points, means of escape and muster points;
- suitable fire-fighting equipment;
- suitable fire-point/extinguisher signage.

In conclusion, the provision of suitable fire detection and fire-fighting equipment is fundamental to health and safety on site and the implementation of the fire plan. The equipment and arrangements must be planned to ensure they cover the site and are maintained through the changes of the construction programme. Task-specific fire-fighting equipment must also be identified through the risk assessment production and approval process and co-ordinated with the relevant contractor on site.

Fresh air

The provision of fresh air in undertaking a risk assessment is critical for certain tasks. The task and environmental conditions both contribute to the risk factor. Activities involving cutting, grinding, welding, spraying, treating and blasting can all displace and affect the quality of the air. The environmental issues can be obvious, e.g. a restricted or confined space, but they can also be more obscure, e.g. an inversion layer can trap contaminated air in a working area.

To control these risks the principles of prevention can be applied to consider avoiding the work or environment or, if this is not practicable, the use of local ventilation and air monitoring is required where the risks require controls.

Where no such risks are identified, site health and safety arrangements should still require a competent site health and safety representative to assess air quality and receive feedback from the workforce.

Any plant fresh air make-up system should have an appropriate audible and visual alarm to highlight any system failure.

In conclusion this CDM regulation requires persons in control of the site and work activities to ensure all workers have a suitable supply of fresh air.

Temperature and weather protection

This regulation for working environmental temperatures and weather protection is not prescriptive but requires the persons in control of putting people to work indoors to consider what is a safe temperature and what steps can be taken to manage any risk associated with high and low temperatures. In undertaking the assessment, the nature of the work, the duration of the work, the environment and the physical health of the employee must be considered. A person working in low temperatures but undertaking physical work will find it easier to maintain their core body temperature.

A person working in a high temperature undertaking physical work will have problems reducing their core temperature and is at risk of heat exhaustion if adequate controls are not established, e.g. regular breaks in cool room, cooling PPE and so on.

For outside workers exposed to adverse weather the general risk assessment should first consider the design of the environment and assess if the work can be undertaken under cover or in a building. For persons that must work outside, the assessment of suitable PPE again must be based on the nature of the weather, the nature and duration of the work and the physical health of the employee. A surveyor has a very different job from a ground worker but they both need to work in wet weather. The ground worker may be working longer hours and have more physical tasks requiring his PPE to cover all his body and have a stronger construction to maintain its performance.

In conclusion, the assessment of workers' health and safety in relation to the temperatures they must work in and the provision of suitable personal protective equipment is required to demonstrate compliance with this regulation and to ensure health and safety on site.

Lighting

The provision of adequate natural or artificial lighting is an essential health and safety factor. These regulations require the contractor to take reasonable steps to provide suitable and sufficient lighting to workplaces and routes to workplaces primarily with natural lighting. The regulation also requires that the colour of any artificial lighting does not adversely affect or change the perception of any sign or signal provided for the purposes of health and safety. The regulation, in addressing the requirement for lighting, requires secondary lighting to be provided where there would be a risk of the primary lighting failing. Such risks could include problems in exiting the building in an emergency and health and safety associated with using plant and equipment that would need to be shut down safely.

In conclusion, this regulation addresses the need for adequate lighting on site to ensure the health and safety of the workforce and avoid accidents associated with poor lighting that can occur when using plant, accessing work and in emergency conditions.

8 CDM toolkit

CDM Policy Ref	Description	Issue	Date
Client section			
C1	Client CDM checklist		
C2	CDM co-ordinator competence assessment		
C3	Designer competence assessment		
C4	Principal contractor competence assessment		
C5	Initial Health and safety survey		
C6	Health and safety file: certificate of handing over CDM Reg 14(f)		
C7	Client PCI checklist		
PC02	Contractor competence assessment		
Designer section			
D1	Designer CDM/H&S management record		
D2	Designer CDM competence assessment		
CDM co-ordinator section			
CDM01	CDM co-ordination schedule and checklist		
C3	Designer competence assessment		
C4	Principal contractor competence assessment		
CDM02	Construction phase plan appraisal report		
CDM03	Certificate for work to commence CDM Reg 16 (a) and (b)		
CDM04	Project H&S risk register		

CDM Policy Ref	Description	Issue	Date
Principal contractor section			
PC01	Construction (design and management) regulations 2007		
PC02	Contractor competence assessment		
D2	Designer CDM competence assessment		
PC03	Construction phase plan checklist		
PC05	Site H&S co-ordination register		
Contractor section			
PC02	Contractor competence assessment		
D2	Designer CDM competence assessment		
C01	Site induction		
C02	Site H&S co-ordination register		

Form C1

Client CDM Checklist

Project Name:

Project Ref No:

Ref	Project Stage	CDM Requirement	Considerations
1.	Project start notification	Ascertain whether the project is notifiable or not. If the project satisfies either of the criteria below notification is necessary. *Is the project likely to last longer than:* 30 *working days* ☐ *Yes* ☐ *No* 500 *person days* ☐ *Yes* ☐ *No*	Note that notifiable projects carry additional statutory duties. These are also included in the checklist.
2.	Feasibility (early design stage)	**Appoint CDM co-ordinator (CDM-C)** **Establish competence.**	Only necessary for a notifiable project. This is a key appointment which must be made prior to moving beyond initial design work. The CDM co-ordinator potentially makes their largest contribution at the initial / early design stages. They will advise the client on their duties and will be able to assist with the health and safety management arrangements throughout. Note that until the appointment is made of a competent CDM-C the client assumes all their statutory responsibilities.

continued overleaf

3.	Feasibility (early design stage)	Establish a service level agreement with the CDM co-ordinator	This is important to clarify the extent of the appointment and define what services the CDM-C will and will not carry out for the project. It is perfectly reasonable to split the respective duties of the CDM-C as long as competence is established for each statutory duty.
4.	Pre-design / design	**Provision of relevant health and safety information about the existing structure and the site**	The design team requires information to consider the relevant health and safety implications. This must be provided from the earliest design stages. The client can make a significant contribution to the project by providing accurate information in good time. Examples include information on asbestos, contaminated ground, the location of buried and overhead services, structural survey. If the project is notifiable this information is to be provided to the CDM-C. The advice of the CDM-C should be sought as to the extent of information to be collated for the project.
5.	Design	**Appoint designer(s)** – *only if appropriate*	Designers must be able to address the health and safety implications likely to be involved with their designs. The client must ensure this is the case. If appointments are in-house competence still needs to be satisfied. CDM-C will be available to advise if notifiable.
		Establish competence	

6.	Project start and throughout project duration	Ensure there are suitable management arrangements for the project (including welfare facilities). For example:	When deciding on the extent of the management arrangements you will be required to make a judgement based on the nature of the project and the risks associated with the work.
		• Defining roles and responsibilities of the project team. □ *Yes* □ *No*	If you do not feel competent to make this judgement seek the advice of the project manager. For a notifiable project the CDM-C will assist you in detailing suitable management arrangements.
		• Ensuring those with CDM duties have sufficient time and resource to comply. □ *Yes* □ *No*	These arrangements should be documented and communicated to all relevant parties.
		• Ensure good communications, co-ordination and co-operation. □ *Yes* □ *No*	
		• Ensure designers confirm their designs comply with CDM 2007 and ensure design elements work together. □ *Yes* □ *No*	
		• Ensure contractors are provided with pre-construction information. □ *Yes* □ *No*	
		• Have contractors confirmed that health, safety and welfare standards on site will be controlled and monitored throughout. □ *Yes* □ *No*	

continued overleaf

7.	Design	Appoint principal contractor	Only necessary for a notifiable project. Regardless of the procurement route or the scale of the project, if the project is notifiable the client must appoint a principal contractor. They must be both competent and adequately resourced to undertake the project. There can only be one principal contractor but it is possible to change the principal contractor as the project moves on. For example, for any initial demolition works it is possible to appoint the demolition contractor as principal contractor. The CDM-C will be able to advise on the competence of the principal contractor.
		Establish competence	
8.	Pre-construction	Ensure that the construction phase plan is suitably developed for construction work to start	Only necessary for a notifiable project. The CDM-C will be able to advise on the suitability of the plan at this stage. Note, however, the legal responsibility remains with the client to satisfy this regulation. *Note that a breach of this regulation carries no exclusion of civil liability.* This does not mean that the client must actually provide the welfare; rather, they must ensure it is in place. However, if certain constraints exist the client may assist if appropriate.
		Ensure suitable welfare arrangements are in place from the start of the construction phase	
		Ensure that suitable management arrangements for the project are maintained throughout	

| 9. | Throughout | Ensure that the health and safety file is prepared, reviewed (or updated if existing) | Only necessary for a notifiable project. The client should discuss with the CDM-C and agree upon a suitable, user-friendly format for the file. The extent of data to be included should also be agreed. |
| 10. | During construction and throughout operation and maintenance | Ensure that the health and safety file is available for inspection and accurately maintained | Consider that the file may be required at an earlier stage (e.g. at partial occupation, phased handover or for maintenance work prior to completion of project). Note that the file is a valuable source of information for future work and if properly maintained can assist with reducing costs. |

CDM co-ordinator competence assessment

Company	Project Details
Name: Address: Contact: Telephone: e-mail:	Project Name: Project Location: Client:

Note: A response must be submitted for each of the following elements.

Stage 1 Assessment (See appendix 4 of the ACoP to the new CDM Regulations 2007, L144 – Managing Health and Safety in Construction. For larger schemes consider appendix 5 of the ACoP.)

	Elements	Standard to be achieved	Response submitted (✓/✗)	Please identify the page of your submission relating to the respective questions
1.	Health and Safety Policy	If more than five people are employed, please provide a copy of your organisation's safety policy statement, as required by s.2(3) of the Health and Safety at Work etc. Act 1974. The policy must be relevant to the nature and scale of the project and set out the responsibilities for health and safety management at all levels within the organisation.		
2.	Arrangements	Should set out the arrangements for health and safety management within the organisation and should be relevant to the nature and scale of the work. They should set out how the company will discharge their duties under CDM 2007. There should be a clear indication of how these arrangements are communicated to the workforce.		

continued overleaf

3.	Competent advice – corporate and construction-related	Your organisation and your employees must have ready access to competent health and safety advice, preferably from within your own organisation. Please provide details of your source of general health and safety advice.			
4.	Training and information	Please provide details of training arrangements to ensure your employees have the skills and understanding to discharge their duties under CDM 2007. This includes refresher courses, CPD and learning programmes to keep skills and knowledge up to date.			
5.	Individual qualifications and experience	Please provide documentation demonstrating employees holding the appropriate qualifications and experience for the assigned tasks, unless they are under controlled and competent supervision.			
6.	Monitoring, audit and review	Please provide details of how you monitor your procedures, for auditing them at periodic intervals and for reviewing them on an ongoing basis.			
7.	Workforce involvement	Please provide details for procedures you have to implement and establish means of consulting with your workforce on health and safety matters.			

8.	Accident reporting and enforcement action; follow-up investigation	Please provide details of any criminal prosecutions or civil claims against your company relating to health and safety matters that have occurred within as a result of reportable events under RIDDOR for the last three years. Please provide details of any enforcement action taken against your company over the last five years, and actions taken to remedy such matters.	
9.	Sub-contracting / consulting procedures	Please provide details of arrangements in place for appointing competent subcontractors / consultants, and details of how you ensure any subcontractors / consultants appointed by them are competent. What arrangement do you have for monitoring sub-contractor performance?	
10.	Hazard elimination and risk control (for designers only)	Demonstrate procedures and arrangements for meeting your duties under regulation 11 of the CDM Regulations 2007.	
11.	Risk assessment leading to a safe method of work (for contractors)	Please provide details of procedures in place for carrying out risk assessments and for developing and implementing safe systems of work / method statements. (This should include identification of health issues.)	

continued overleaf

12.	Co-operating with others and co-ordinating your work with that of other contractors (for contractors)	Please illustrate how co-operation and co-ordination of your work is achieved in practice, and how you involve the workforce in drawing up method statements / safe systems of work.	
13.	Welfare provisions (for contractors)	Please provide details of how you would ensure that appropriate welfare facilities will be in place before people start work on site.	
14.	CDM – Co-ordinators Duties (for CDM co-ordinators)	Please provide details to demonstrate how you go about encouraging co-operation, co-ordination and communications between designers.	

Stage 2 Assessment (See appendix 4 of the ACoP to the new CDM Regulations 2007, L144 – Managing Health and Safety in Construction.)

1.	Work experience	Please provide details of relevant experience in the chosen field for which you are applying.

Stage 3 Assessment – Supplementary Project Questions

	Elements	Response submitted (✓/✗)	Please identify the page of your submission relating to the respective questions	S/U
1.	Please provide examples of work carried out previously that is comparable in size and nature to this project.			
2.	Who in your organisation has day-to-day responsibility for health and safety matters? Please provide details of their experience and qualifications and a copy of their curriculum vitae.			
3.	Who will be providing advice on health and safety issues on this project? Please provide details of their experience and qualifications and a copy of their curriculum vitae.			
4.	How many professional staff does your office employ? Please provide a percentage breakdown by discipline.			
5.	Please provide details of the experience, qualifications, membership of professional bodies, etc., and arrangements for continuing professional development of key staff who would be employed on the project. Please enclose curricula vitae.			

continued overleaf

6.	Please provide details of your arrangements for ensuring continuing health and safety training.					
7.	What methods do you employ to ensure compliance with your duties under Regulation 11 of the Construction (Design and Management) Regulations 2007?					
8.	Please provide details of how you will co-operate with the CDM co-ordinator and other designers to ensure that health and safety problems can be suitably addressed and overcome?					
9.	Please provide details of any formal notices issued or legal proceedings having been taken against your organisation by the Health and Safety Executive in the last three years.					
10.	Please provide details of the other resources (including equipment and technical facilities) that your organisation will allocate to ensure that health and safety is incorporated into your design work on this project.					
11.	Please illustrate how you would prepare design programmes and allocate resources for each project.					
12.	Please describe your hazard identification methods and procedures and how this information is presented. If possible, please provide an example from a current project.					

13.	Please confirm that your company holds an appropriate amount of insurances (including professional indemnity insurance where appropriate) for the nature of the project.	

Overall Rating	
Comments (for client use)	

Submitted by:	Designation:	Date:	Assessed by:	Designation:	Date:

Designer competence assessment

Company	Project Details
Name: Address: Contact: Telephone: e-mail:	Project Name: Project Location: Client:

Note: A response must be submitted for each of the following elements.

Stage 1 Assessment (See Appendix 4 of the ACoP to the new CDM Regulations 2007, L144 – Managing Health and safety in Construction)

	Elements	Standard to be achieved	Response submitted (✓/✗)	Please identify the page of your submission relating to the respective questions
1.	Health and safety Policy	If more than five people are employed, please provide a copy of your organisation's safety policy statement, as required by s.2(3) of the Health and Safety at Work etc Act 1974. The Policy must be relevant to the nature and scale of the project and set out the responsibilities for health and safety management at all levels within the organisation		
2.	Arrangements	Set out the arrangements for health and safety management within the organisation and should be relevant to the nature and scale of the work. They should set out how the company will discharge their duties under CDM 2007. There should be a clear indication of how these arrangements are communicated to the workforce.		

continued overleaf

3.	Competent advice – corporate and construction-related	Your organisation and your employees must have ready access to competent health and safety advice, preferably from within your own organisation. Please provide details of your source of general health and safety advice.		
4.	Training and information	Please provide details of training arrangements to ensure your employees have the skills and understanding to discharge their duties under CDM 2007. This includes refresher courses, CPD and learning programmes to keep skills and knowledge up to date.		
5.	Individual qualifications and experience	Please provide documentation demonstrating employees holding the appropriate qualifications and experience for the assigned tasks, unless they are under controlled and competent supervision.		
6.	Monitoring, audit and review	Please provide details of how you monitor your procedures, for auditing them at periodic intervals, and for reviewing them on an ongoing basis.		
7.	Workforce involvement	Please provide details for procedures you have to implement and establish means of consulting with your workforce on health and safety matters.		

8.	Accident reporting and enforcement action; follow up investigation	Please provide details of any Criminal Prosecutions, or Civil Claims against your Company relating to Health and Safety matters that have occurred within as a result of reportable events under RIDDOR for the last three years. Please provide details of any enforcement action taken against your company over the last five years, and actions taken to remedy such matters.		
9.	Sub-contracting / Consulting procedures	Please provide details of arrangements in place for appointing competent sub-contractors / consultants, and details of how you ensure any sub-contractors /consultants appointed by them are competent. What arrangement do you have for monitoring sub-contractor performance?		
10.	Hazard Elimination and Risk Control (For designers only)	Demonstrate procedures and arrangements for meeting your duties under regulation 11 of the CDM Regs 2007.		
11.	Risk assessment leading to a safe method of work (for contractors)	Please provide details of procedures in place for carrying out risk assessments and for developing and implementing safe systems of work / method statements. (This should include identification of health issues.)		

continued overleaf

12.	Co-operating with others and co-ordinating your work with that of other contractors (for contractors)	Please illustrate how co-operation and co-ordination of your work is achieved in practice, and how you involve the workforce in drawing up method statements / safe systems of work.		
13.	Welfare provisions (for contractors)	Please provide details of how you would ensure that appropriate welfare facilities will be in place before people start work on site.		
14.	CDM – Co-ordinators Duties (For CDM Co-ordinators)	Please provide details to demonstrate how you go about encouraging co-operation, co-ordination and communications between designers.		

Stage 2 Assessment (See Appendix 4 of the ACoP to the new CDM Regulations 2007, L144 – Managing Health and safety in Construction)

1	Work Experience	Please provide details of relevant experience in the chosen field for which you are applying.	

Stage 3 Assessment – Supplementary Project Questions

	Elements	Response submitted (✓/✗)	Please identify the page of your submission relating to the respective questions	S/U
1.	Please provide examples of work carried out previously, which is comparable in size and nature to this project.			
2.	Who in your organisation has day to day responsibility for health and safety matters? Please provide details of their experience and qualifications and a copy of their curriculum vitae.			
3.	Who will be providing advice on health and safety issues on this project? Please provide details of their experience and qualifications and a copy of their curriculum vitae.			
4.	How many professional staff does your office employ? Please provide a percentage breakdown by discipline.			
5.	Please provide details of the experience, qualifications, membership of professional bodies etc and arrangements for continuing professional development of key staff who would be employed on the project. Please enclose curricula vitae.			

continued overleaf

6.	Please provide details of your arrangements for ensuring continuing health and safety training.				
7.	What methods do you employ to ensure compliance with your duties under Regulation 11 of the Construction (Design and Management) Regulations 2007?				
8.	Please provide details of how you will co-operate with the CDM Co-ordinator and other designers to ensure that health and safety problems can be suitably addressed and overcome?				
9.	Please provide details of any formal notices issued or legal proceedings been taken against your organisation by the Health and Safety Executive in the last three years.				
10.	Please provide details of the other resources (including equipment and technical facilities) that your organisation will allocate to ensure that health and safety is incorporated into your design work on this project.				
11.	Please illustrate how you would prepare design programmes and allocate resources for each project.				
12.	Please describe your hazard identification methods and procedures and how this information is presented. If possible, please provide an example from a current project.				

13.	Please provide confirmation of procedures for assessing the health and safety competence and resource of those companies / Designers who will be employed by you on a subcontractor basis.		
14.	Please confirm that your Company holds an appropriate amount of insurances (including Professional Indemnity Insurance where appropriate) for the nature of the project.		

Comments (for client / CDM co-ordinator use)	Overall Rating

Submitted by:	Designation:	Date:	Assessed by:	Designation:	Date:

Principal contractor competence assessment

Company	Project Details
Name: Address: Contact: Telephone: e-mail:	Project Name: Project Location: Client:

Note: A response must be submitted for each of the following elements.

Stage 1 Assessment (See Appendix 4 of the ACoP to the new CDM Regulations 2007, L144 – Managing Health and safety in Construction. For larger schemes consider Appendix 5 of the ACoP)

	Elements	Standard to be achieved	Response submitted (✓/✗)	Please identify the page of your submission relating to the respective questions
1.	Health and safety Policy	If more than five people are employed, please provide a copy of your organisation's safety policy statement, as required by s.2(3) of the Health and Safety at Work etc Act 1974. The Policy must be relevant to the nature and scale of the project and set out the responsibilities for health and safety management at all levels within the organisation		
2.	Arrangements	Set out the arrangements for health and safety management within the organisation and should be relevant to the nature and scale of the work. They should set out how the company will discharge their duties under CDM 2007. There should be a clear indication of how these arrangements are communicated to the workforce.		
3.	Competent advice – corporate and construction-related	Your organisation and your employees must have ready access to competent health and safety advice, preferably from within your own organisation. Please provide details of your source of general health and safety advice.		

continued overleaf

4.	Training and information	Please provide details of training arrangements to ensure your employees have the skills and understanding to discharge their duties under CDM 2007. This includes refresher courses, CPD and learning programmes to keep skills and knowledge up to date.			
5.	Individual qualifications and experience	Please provide documentation demonstrating employees holding the appropriate qualifications and experience for the assigned tasks, unless they are under controlled and competent supervision.			
6.	Monitoring, audit and review	Please provide details of how you monitor your procedures, for auditing them at periodic intervals, and for reviewing them on an ongoing basis.			
7.	Workforce involvement	Please provide details for procedures you have to implement and establish means of consulting with your workforce on health and safety matters.			
8.	Accident reporting and enforcement action; follow up investigation	Please provide details of any Criminal Prosecutions, or Civil Claims against your Company relating to Health and Safety matters that have occurred within as a result of reportable events under RIDDOR for the last three years. Please provide details of any enforcement action taken against your company over the last five years, and actions taken to remedy such matters.			

9.	Sub-contracting / Consulting procedures	Please provide details of arrangements in place for appointing competent sub-contractors / consultants, and details of how you ensure any sub-contractors /consultants appointed by them are competent. What arrangement do you have for monitoring sub-contractor performance?			
10.	Hazard Elimination and Risk Control (For designers only)	Demonstrate procedures and arrangements for meeting your duties under regulation 11 of the CDM Regs 2007.			
11.	Risk assessment leading to a safe method of work (for contractors)	Please provide details of procedures in place for carrying out risk assessments and for developing and implementing safe systems of work / method statements. (This should include identification of health issues.)			
12.	Co-operating with others and co-ordinating your work with that of other contractors (for contractors)	Please illustrate how co-operation and co-ordination of your work is achieved in practice, and how you involve the workforce in drawing up method statements / safe systems of work.			
13.	Welfare provisions (for contractors)	Please provide details of how you would ensure that appropriate welfare facilities will be in place before people start work on site.			
14.	CDM – Co-ordinators Duties (For CDM Co-ordinators)	Please provide details to demonstrate how you go about encouraging co-operation, co-ordination and communications between designers.			

continued overleaf

Stage 2 Assessment (See Appendix 4 of the ACoP to the new CDM Regulations 2007, L144 – Managing Health and safety in Construction)

1	Work Experience	Please provide details of relevant experience in the chosen field for which you are applying.		

Stage 3 Assessment – Supplementary Project Questions

	Elements	Response submitted (✓/✗)	Please identify the page of your submission relating to the respective questions	S/U
1.	Please provide examples of work carried out previously, which is comparable in size and nature to this project.			
2.	Who in your organisation has day to day responsibility for health and safety matters? Please provide details of their experience and qualifications and a copy of their curriculum vitae.			
3.	Who will be providing advice on health and safety issues on this project? Please provide details of their experience and qualifications and a copy of their curriculum vitae.			
4.	How many professional staff does your office employ? Please provide a percentage breakdown by discipline.			

No.	Question					
5.	Please provide details of the experience, qualifications, membership of professional bodies etc and arrangements for continuing professional development of key staff who would be employed on the project. Please enclose curricula vitae.					
6.	Please provide details of your arrangements for ensuring continuing health and safety training.					
7.	What methods do you employ to ensure compliance with your duties under Regulation 11 of the Construction (Design and Management) Regulations 2007?					
8.	Please provide details of how you will co-operate with the CDM Co-ordinator and other designers to ensure that health and safety problems can be suitably addressed and overcome?					
9.	Please provide details of any formal notices issued or legal proceedings been taken against your organisation by the Health and Safety Executive in the last three years.					
10.	Please provide details of the other resources (including equipment and technical facilities) that your organisation will allocate to ensure that health and safety is incorporated into your design work on this project.					
11.	Please illustrate how you would prepare design programmes and allocate resources for each project.					

continued overleaf

No.	Question			
12.	Please describe your hazard identification methods and procedures and how this information is presented. If possible, please provide an example from a current project.			
13.	Please confirm that your Company holds an appropriate amount of insurances (including Professional Indemnity Insurance where appropriate) for the nature of the project.			

Overall Rating	
Comments (for client use)	

Submitted by:	Designation:	Date:	Assessed by:	Designation:	Date:

Initial Health and Safety Survey

Note: Suitable for clients and CDM co-ordinators assessing pre-construction information.

Project .... Date ....

Client details	
Site Address	

Nature of Construction work (Brief Description)

Time scale	Start:	Finish:

Existing Drawings

Drawing No	Scale	By	Description

Existing H&S File- Yes/No	Location and Access Details

Existing Environment

Subject	Details	Dwg Ref	Doc Ref
Land Use/Other construction etc			
Services Gas: Water: Sewage: TV Cable: Electricity: Telecoms: Fire alarm: Other:			

Traffic restrictions:			
Ground Conditions:			
Construction Materials:			
Site wide considerations: Schools: Shops: Other Construction:			
Client's existing operations			
Site Rules:			
Continuing Liaison:			

General Project Safety Checklist

Existing Hazards	Findings	Method Statement Required	Photo/ Info Required
Falls Roof access: Holes in floors: Balconies: High-level Plant: Low windows: Low (Below 910 mm) ballast rails: Fixing Points: Access Equipment:			
Access (general) Car Parking: Loading/ Unloading: Security Arrangements: Materials Storage: Time restrictions:			

continued overleaf

Structure Stability Loose Materials: Structural Cracks: Supporting Scaffold: Subsidence:			
Confined Spaces Basements: Attic Voids: Manhole access: Silos: Boiler Rooms: Risers: Lift Shafts: Ducting: Cooling Tower:			
Plant and Equipment Boiler: Cooking Equipment: Air Conditioning: Lifts:			

Asbestos ACMs	Yes/No	Date	Details
Has an asbestos survey been commissioned? Lab analyses: Air monitoring: Results:			
Radon Is premises situated in high-risk radon area? Air Testing: Results:			
Legionellosis Surveyed: Cooling Tower: Evaporative Condensers: Spray Humidifiers: HW System +300 litres Showers: Fountains: Maintenance contract:			

Lead LCMs Lead Paintwork: Roof Flashing: Damp-proof Courses: Has an assessment been undertaken:			
Damp/Rot Treatment Chemical Injection: Chemicals sprayed: Paint-on Chemicals: Dry rot spores:			
Electrical Installation Current test certificate: Lift Certificate:			
COSHH Assessments Existing: Chemicals: Processes:			

Signed-		**Date**	
Comment			

Form C6

Health and Safety File:

Certificate Of Handing Over
CDM Reg 14(f)

Project:

....

Client:

....

This certificate is signed in acknowledgement of handling over of the Health and Safety File for the above project.

The Health and Safety File has been compiled in accordance with the requirements of the Construction (Design and Management) Regulations 2007 and is completed within the terms of Regulation 20 (2) (f) with the exception of the following information which has not been received by the planning supervisor:

Outstanding

.... due

from ....

.... due

from ....

.... due

from ....

This information will be added to the file by the client when received.

Signed .... For .... (CDM Co-ordinator)

Date of file handover ....

Signed .... For .... (Client)

Please keep for record

Client PCI checklist

Client Information
Non-notifiable – to be provided to designer/contractor

Notifiable – to be provided to CDM co-ordinator

Note:- The CDM regulations require that clients make available relevant health and safety information about existing structures and the site.

Information Description	Location (if not available)	Tick Where Applicable✓
o Existing site surveys		
o Existing geology		
o Structure surveys		
o Construction history		
o Contamination		
o Site services		
o Other buried services		
o Overhead services		
o Underground chambers, wells, water courses, etc.		
o Existing building drawings		
o Structure		
o Previous structural alterations		
o Fire damage		
o Anchorage points		
o Fragile materials		
o Hazardous construction materials		
o Use of pre-stressed or post-tensioned structures		

continued overleaf

o Existing building services surveys		
o Asbestos survey/management plan		
o Other hazardous materials		
o Hazards from adjoining property		
o Hazards from existing operations		
o Existing O&M or building manuals		
o Existing H&S files		
o Existing drawings		
o Client rules, emergency procedures, requirements or restrictions		
o Access restrictions		
Other persons on site: Children / disabled / tenants / shoppers / maintenance workers / deliveries / other Please specify below		
Other (please specify)		
Copy to		Date
Comments		

Note: Alternatively it may in some instances be beneficial to commission surveys to determine some of the detail in the list above, e.g. asbestos or geological surveys.

Contractor competence assessment

Company	Project Details
Name: Address: Contact: Telephone: e-mail:	Project Name: Project Location: Client:

Note: A response must be submitted for each of the following elements.

Stage 1 Assessment (See Appendix 4 of the ACoP to the new CDM Regulations 2007, L144 – Managing Health and safety in Construction. For larger schemes consider Appendix 5 of the ACoP)

	Elements	Standard to be achieved	Response submitted (✓/✗)	Please identify the page of your submission relating to the respective questions
1.	Health and safety Policy	If more than five people are employed, please provide a copy of your organisation's safety policy statement, as required by s.2(3) of the Health and Safety at Work etc Act 1974. The Policy must be relevant to the nature and scale of the project and set out the responsibilities for health and safety management at all levels within the organisation		
2.	Arrangements	Set out the arrangements for health and safety management within the organisation and should be relevant to the nature and scale of the work. They should set out how the company will discharge their duties under CDM 2007. There should be a clear indication of how these arrangements are communicated to the workforce.		

continued overleaf

3.	Competent advice – corporate and construction-related	Your organisation and your employees must have ready access to competent health and safety advice, preferably from within your own organisation. Please provide details of your source of general health and safety advice.			
4.	Training and information	Please provide details of training arrangements to ensure your employees have the skills and understanding to discharge their duties under CDM 2007. This includes refresher courses, CPD and learning programmes to keep skills and knowledge up to date.			
5.	Individual qualifications and experience	Please provide documentation demonstrating employees holding the appropriate qualifications and experience for the assigned tasks, unless they are under controlled and competent supervision.			
6.	Monitoring, audit and review	Please provide details of how you monitor your procedures, for auditing them at periodic intervals, and for reviewing them on an ongoing basis.			
7.	Workforce involvement	Please provide details for procedures you have to implement and establish means of consulting with your workforce on health and safety matters.			

8.	Accident reporting and enforcement action; follow up investigation	Please provide details of any Criminal Prosecutions, or Civil Claims against your Company relating to Health and Safety matters that have occurred within as a result of reportable events under RIDDOR for the last three years. Please provide details of any enforcement action taken against your company over the last five years, and actions taken to remedy such matters.		
9.	Sub-contracting / Consulting procedures	Please provide details of arrangements in place for appointing competent sub-contractors / consultants, and details of how you ensure any sub-contractors /consultants appointed by them are competent. What arrangement do you have for monitoring sub-contractor performance?		
10.	Hazard Elimination and Risk Control (For designers only)	Demonstrate procedures and arrangements for meeting your duties under regulation 11 of the CDM Regs 2007.		
11.	Risk assessment leading to a safe method of work (for contractors)	Please provide details of procedures in place for carrying out risk assessments and for developing and implementing safe systems of work / method statements. (This should include identification of health issues.)		

continued overleaf

12.	Co-operating with others and co-ordinating your work with that of other contractors (for contractors)	Please illustrate how co-operation and co-ordination of your work is achieved in practice, and how you involve the workforce in drawing up method statements / safe systems of work.	
13.	Welfare provisions	Please provide details of how you would ensure that appropriate welfare facilities will be in place before people start work on site.	
14.	CDM – Co-ordinators Duties (For CDM Co-ordinators)	Please provide details to demonstrate how you go about encouraging co-operation, co-ordination and communications between designers.	

Stage 2 Assessment (See Appendix 4 of the ACoP to the new CDM Regulations 2007, L144 – Managing Health and safety in Construction)

1	Work Experience	Please provide details of relevant experience in the chosen field for which you are applying.

Stage 3 Assessment – Supplementary Project Questions

	Elements	Response submitted (✓/✗)	Please identify the page of your submission relating to the respective questions	S/U
1.	Please provide examples of work carried out previously, which is comparable in size and nature to this project.			
2.	Who in your organisation has day to day responsibility for health and safety matters? Please provide details of their experience and qualifications and a copy of their curriculum vitae.			
3.	Who will be providing advice on health and safety issues on this project? Please provide details of their experience and qualifications and a copy of their curriculum vitae.			
4.	How many professional staff does your office employ? Please provide a percentage breakdown by discipline.			
5.	Please provide details of the experience, qualifications, membership of professional bodies etc and arrangements for continuing professional development of key staff who would be employed on the project. Please enclose curricula vitae.			

continued overleaf

6.	Please provide details of your arrangements for ensuring continuing health and safety training.				
7.	What methods do you employ to ensure compliance with your duties under Regulation 11 of the Construction (Design and Management) Regulations 2007?				
8.	Please provide details of how you will co-operate with the CDM Co-ordinator and other designers to ensure that health and safety problems can be suitably addressed and overcome?				
9.	Please provide details of any formal notices issued or legal proceedings been taken against your organisation by the Health and Safety Executive in the last three years.				
10.	Please provide details of the other resources (including equipment and technical facilities) that your organisation will allocate to ensure that health and safety is incorporated into your design work on this project.				
11.	Please illustrate how you would prepare design programmes and allocate resources for each project.				
12.	Please describe your hazard identification methods and procedures and how this information is presented. If possible, please provide an example from a current project.				

13.	Please confirm that your Company holds an appropriate amount of insurances (including Professional Indemnity Insurance where appropriate) for the nature of the project.		

Comments (for client use)	Overall Rating

Submitted by:	Designation:	Date:	Assessed by:	Designation:	Date:

Form D1

Designer CDM/H&S Management Record

Project . . . .

Lead Designer/Architect . . . .

Significant Hazards and Designer's Action ➡		Significant Hazards Identified *During Design*													
Design Areas and Construction/ Maintenance Activities ⬇		← *Guidance – Design Best practice*	Hazardous Substances	Contamination	Fall From Height	Falling Objects	Site Plant Vehicles	Collapsing Structure	Manual Handling	Lifting Operations	Buried/Overhead Services	Interface With Others	Cut/Drilling Concrete	Noise and Vibration	Deep Excavations	Asbestos and MM Minerals
Supporting Guidance Notes ➜		1	2	3	4	5	6	7	8	9	10	11	12	13	14
Site Set Up and Logistics															
Access To Site	1														
Site Offices and Compound	2														
Surveys	3														
Temp Services	4														
Enabling Works	5														
Public/Highway Traffic Safety	6														
Demolition and Dismantling	7														
Design Areas and Associated Construction Activities	8														
Ground Excavation Works	9														
Piling	10														
Concrete Substructure	11														
Slabs	12														
Interfaces	13														
Drainage and Utility Services	14														
Superstructure Frame	15														
Superstructure Flooring	16														
Roofing System	17														

Design Stage . . . . Date . . . .

Designer . . . .

														Designers' Actions
Fire Means of Escape	Highway Traffic	Restricted Access to Workface	Access for Maintenance	Component Replacement	Confined Spaces	Working Over or Near Water	Temporary Works Required	Workplace Regulation Addressed	Supporting Info Required (RFI)	DTM Agenda /Ent on Risk Reg	Initials of Designer(s) Responsible	Industry Guidance Considered	Design Co-ordination Issue	**Key** **C**=Comments/Qualification; **H**=Other Hazards; **CR**=Cross Reference to drawing/specification: **DA**=Summary of Design Action Where Complex **I**= Information Required to assist design **Guidance**- Summary of Principles of Prevention that MUST be applied to a significant risk when designing- **Avoidance** (Design to avoid identified hazards but beware of introducing others) **Reduction** (Design to reduce identifiable hazards but beware of increasing others) **Control and Transfer** (Design to provide acceptable safeguards or transfer the hazard with information)
15	16	17	18	19	20	21	22	23	24	25	26	27	28	

continued overleaf

Supporting Guidance Notes →		1	2	3	4	5	6	7	8	9	10	11	12	13	14
Windows and Curtain Walling	18														
Brick Blockwork	19														
Cladding	20														
RW System	21														
Mechanical -Heating	22														
Mechanical-Lifts	23														
Mechanical- Extraction	24														
Mechanical- AHU	25														
Mechanical -General	26														
Mechanical- AC Units	27														
Mechanical- Attenuation	28														
Mechanical- Chimney/ Flue	29														
Mechanical- Water Treatment	30														
Electrical- Power and Lts (Int)	31														
Electrical- Power and Lts (Ext)	32														
Electrical- Em/ Lighting	33														
Electrical- Lightning Protection	34														
Electrical- CHP Plant	35														
Electrical-HV	36														
Electrical- Alarms	37														
Internal Walls	38														
Internal Ceilings	39														
Floor Screed	39														
Painting	40														
Tiling	41														
Plastering	42														
	43														
	44														
	45														
Maintenance															
Roof Insp and Cleaning Gutters	46														
M&E Lighting	47														
Window Cleaning	48														
Component Replacement	49														

15	16	17	18	19	20	21	22	23	24	25	26	27	28	

Designer CDM competence assessment

Company	Project Details
Name: Address: Contact: Telephone: e-mail:	Project Name: Project Location: Client:

Note: A response must be submitted for each of the following elements.

Stage 1 Assessment (See Appendix 4 of the ACoP to the new CDM Regulations 2007, L144 – Managing Health and safety in Construction)

	Elements	Standard to be achieved	Response submitted (✓/✗)	Please identify the page of your submission relating to the respective questions
1.	Health and safety Policy	If more than five people are employed, please provide a copy of your organisation's safety policy statement, as required by s.2(3) of the Health and Safety at Work etc Act 1974. The Policy must be relevant to the nature and scale of the project and set out the responsibilities for health and safety management at all levels within the organisation		
2.	Arrangements	Set out the arrangements for health and safety management within the organisation and should be relevant to the nature and scale of the work. They should set out how the company will discharge their duties under CDM 2007. There should be a clear indication of how these arrangements are communicated to the workforce.		

#					
3.	Competent advice – corporate and construction-related	Your organisation and your employees must have ready access to competent health and safety advice, preferably from within your own organisation. Please provide details of your source of general health and safety advice.			
4.	Training and information	Please provide details of training arrangements to ensure your employees have the skills and understanding to discharge their duties under CDM 2007. This includes refresher courses, CPD and learning programmes to keep skills and knowledge up to date.			
5.	Individual qualifications and experience	Please provide documentation demonstrating employees holding the appropriate qualifications and experience for the assigned tasks, unless they are under controlled and competent supervision.			
6.	Monitoring, audit and review	Please provide details of how you monitor your procedures, for auditing them at periodic intervals, and for reviewing them on an ongoing basis.			
7.	Workforce involvement	Please provide details for procedures you have to implement and establish means of consulting with your workforce on health and safety matters.			

8.	Accident reporting and enforcement action; follow up investigation	Please provide details of any Criminal Prosecutions, or Civil Claims against your Company relating to Health and Safety matters that have occurred within as a result of reportable events under RIDDOR for the last three years. Please provide details of any enforcement action taken against your company over the last five years, and actions taken to remedy such matters.	
9.	Sub-contracting / Consulting procedures	Please provide details of arrangements in place for appointing competent sub-contractors / consultants, and details of how you ensure any sub-contractors / consultants appointed by them are competent. What arrangement do you have for monitoring sub-contractor performance?	
10.	Hazard Elimination and Risk Control (For designers only)	Demonstrate procedures and arrangements for meeting your duties under regulation 11 of the CDM Regs 2007.	
11.	Risk assessment leading to a safe method of work (for contractors)	Please provide details of procedures in place for carrying out risk assessments and for developing and implementing safe systems of work / method statements. (This should include identification of health issues.)	

continued overleaf

12.	Co-operating with others and co-ordinating your work with that of other contractors (for contractors)	Please illustrate how co-operation and co-ordination of your work is achieved in practice, and how you involve the workforce in drawing up method statements / safe systems of work.	
13.	Welfare provisions (for contractors)	Please provide details of how you would ensure that appropriate welfare facilities will be in place before people start work on site.	
14.	CDM – Co-ordinators Duties (For CDM Co-ordinators)	Please provide details to demonstrate how you go about encouraging co-operation, co-ordination and communications between designers.	

Stage 2 Assessment (See Appendix 4 of the ACoP to the new CDM Regulations 2007, L144 – Managing Health and safety in Construction)

1	Work Experience	Please provide details of relevant experience in the chosen field for which you are applying.	

Stage 3 Assessment – Supplementary Project Questions

	Elements	Response submitted (✓/✗)	Please identify the page of your submission relating to the respective questions	S/U
1.	Please provide examples of work carried out previously, which is comparable in size and nature to this project.			
2.	Who in your organisation has day to day responsibility for health and safety matters? Please provide details of their experience and qualifications and a copy of their curriculum vitae.			
3.	Who will be providing advice on health and safety issues on this project? Please provide details of their experience and qualifications and a copy of their curriculum vitae.			
4.	How many professional staff does your office employ? Please provide a percentage breakdown by discipline.			
5.	Please provide details of the experience, qualifications, membership of professional bodies etc and arrangements for continuing professional development of key staff who would be employed on the project. Please enclose curricula vitae.			

continued overleaf

6.	Please provide details of your arrangements for ensuring continuing health and safety training.				
7.	What methods do you employ to ensure compliance with your duties under Regulation 11 of the Construction (Design and Management) Regulations 2007?				
8.	Please provide details of how you will co-operate with the CDM Co-ordinator and other designers to ensure that health and safety problems can be suitably addressed and overcome?				
9.	Please provide details of any formal notices issued or legal proceedings been taken against your organisation by the Health and Safety Executive in the last three years.				
10.	Please provide details of the other resources (including equipment and technical facilities) that your organisation will allocate to ensure that health and safety is incorporated into your design work on this project.				
11.	Please illustrate how you would prepare design programmes and allocate resources for each project.				

12.	Please describe your hazard identification methods and procedures and how this information is presented. If possible, please provide an example from a current project.		
13.	Please provide confirmation of procedures for assessing the health and safety competence and resource of those companies / Designers who will be employed by you on a subcontractor basis.		
14.	Please confirm that your Company holds an appropriate amount of insurances (including Professional Indemnity Insurance where appropriate) for the nature of the project.		

Comments (for client / CDM co-ordinator use)			Overall Rating

Submitted by:	Designation:	Date:	Assessed by:	Designation:	Date:

CDM Co-ordination Schedule and Checklist

Regulation #	Regulation	Practical Application	Sign off / Notes
20 (1) (a)	*Provide suitable and sufficient advice and assistance to the client on the measures to be undertaken for him to comply to Regulations 9 and 16 of the CDM Regulations*	Development of project H&S management arrangements and minimum standards.	
		Define roles and responsibilities	
		Establish good communication, co-ordination and co-operation between team.	
		Communicate arrangements to team.	
		Pre-qualify design team for CDM competence. Secure declaration of CDM competence.	
		Ensure all designers are able to confirm they are complying with Regulation 11 throughout design.	
		Ensure design elements work together without creating risk.	
		Ensure contractor is provided with pre-construction information as and when required.	
		Ensure contractors confirm that H&S standards on site will be controlled and monitored and welfare is adequate from the start of construction work.	
		Establish and communicate the requirements for the H&S file.	

21 (1,2,3 and 4)	*Notify the particulars of the project (as specified in Schedule 1) to the Health and Safety Executive*
	Complete F10 as soon as appointed and secure client signature. Forward to HSE. Additional notification necessary when more detail becomes available, e.g. principal contractor details.
20 (1) (b)	*Ensure that suitable arrangements are made and implemented for the co-ordination of health and safety measures during planning and preparation for the construction phase, including the facilitation of:*
	Development and management of project specific H&S risk register. Attendance at selected design team meetings. Design team workshop looking at H&S implications at relevant stages. Emphasis on the hierarchy of risk control / principles of prevention throughout. Review individual designs / drawings and discuss approach to eliminate / reduce risks as appropriate.
(i)	*Co-operation and co-ordination between persons concerned in the project in pursuance of Regulations 5 and 6.*
(ii)	*The application of the general principles of prevention (referred to in Regulation 7).*
20 (2) (c)	*Take reasonable steps to ensure that designers comply with their duties under Regulations 11 and 12.*

continued overleaf

20 (2) (a)	Take reasonable steps to identify and collect the pre-construction information	Develop schedule of information necessary for client to provide to team. This includes existing information or information which is reasonably obtainable.
20 (2) (b)	Provide pre-construction information to:	
(i)	Designers	Ensure this information is made available to those who may require it.
(ii)	Contractors appointed by the client	
20 (1) (c)	Liaise with the principal contractor regarding:	This will be established in the project arrangements document and monitored throughout the construction phase.
(i)	The contents of the health and safety file	
(ii)	The information which the principal contractor needs to prepare the construction stage plan	We work with the principal contractor to ensure all necessary information is received and the construction phase plan is suitably developed for work to begin.
(iii)	Design development which may affect planning and management of construction work	Ensure that they are aware of designer duties and the project arrangements for safe design.
20 (2) (d)	Ensure co-operation between designers and the principal contractor during the construction stage in relation to any design or design change	Attendance at project meetings.
20 (2) (e)	Prepare (where none exists) and otherwise review and update a record (the health and safety file) containing information relating to the project which is likely to be needed during any subsequent construction work	

Designer competence assessment

Company	Project Details
Name: Address: Contact: Telephone: e-mail:	Project Name: Project Location: Client:

Note: A response must be submitted for each of the following elements.

Stage 1 Assessment (See Appendix 4 of the ACoP to the new CDM Regulations 2007, L144 – Managing Health and safety in Construction)

	Elements	Standard to be achieved	Response submitted (✓/✗)	Please identify the page of your submission relating to the respective questions
1.	Health and safety Policy	If more than five people are employed, please provide a copy of your organisation's safety policy statement, as required by s.2(3) of the Health and Safety at Work etc Act 1974. The Policy must be relevant to the nature and scale of the project and set out the responsibilities for health and safety management at all levels within the organisation		
2.	Arrangements	Set out the arrangements for health and safety management within the organisation and should be relevant to the nature and scale of the work. They should set out how the company will discharge their duties under CDM 2007. There should be a clear indication of how these arrangements are communicated to the workforce.		

3.	Competent advice – corporate and construction-related	Your organisation and your employees must have ready access to competent health and safety advice, preferably from within your own organisation. Please provide details of your source of general health and safety advice.			
4.	Training and information	Please provide details of training arrangements to ensure your employees have the skills and understanding to discharge their duties under CDM 2007. This includes refresher courses, CPD and learning programmes to keep skills and knowledge up to date.			
5.	Individual qualifications and experience	Please provide documentation demonstrating employees holding the appropriate qualifications and experience for the assigned tasks, unless they are under controlled and competent supervision.			
6.	Monitoring, audit and review	Please provide details of how you monitor your procedures, for auditing them at periodic intervals, and for reviewing them on an ongoing basis.			
7.	Workforce involvement	Please provide details for procedures you have to implement and establish means of consulting with your workforce on health and safety matters.			

continued overleaf

8.	Accident reporting and enforcement action; follow up investigation	Please provide details of any Criminal Prosecutions, or Civil Claims against your Company relating to Health and Safety matters that have occurred within as a result of reportable events under RIDDOR for the last three years. Please provide details of any enforcement action taken against your company over the last five years, and actions taken to remedy such matters.			
9.	Sub-contracting / Consulting procedures	Please provide details of arrangements in place for appointing competent sub-contractors / consultants, and details of how you ensure any sub-contractors /consultants appointed by them are competent. What arrangement do you have for monitoring sub-contractor performance?			
10.	Hazard Elimination and Risk Control (For designers only)	Demonstrate procedures and arrangements for meeting your duties under regulation 11 of the CDM Regs 2007.			
11.	Risk assessment leading to a safe method of work (for contractors)	Please provide details of procedures in place for carrying out risk assessments and for developing and implementing safe systems of work / method statements. (This should include identification of health issues.)			

12.	Co-operating with others and co-ordinating your work with that of other contractors (for contractors)	Please illustrate how co-operation and co-ordination of your work is achieved in practice, and how you involve the workforce in drawing up method statements / safe systems of work.			
13.	Welfare provisions (for contractors)	Please provide details of how you would ensure that appropriate welfare facilities will be in place before people start work on site.			
14.	CDM – Co-ordinators Duties (For CDM Co-ordinators)	Please provide details to demonstrate how you go about encouraging co-operation, co-ordination and communications between designers.			

Stage 2 Assessment (See Appendix 4 of the ACoP to the new CDM Regulations 2007, L144 – Managing Health and safety in Construction)

| 1 | Work Experience | Please provide details of relevant experience in the chosen field for which you are applying. | | |

Stage 3 Assessment – Supplementary Project Questions

	Elements	Response submitted (✓/✗)	Please identify the page of your submission relating to the respective questions	S/U
1.	Please provide examples of work carried out previously, which is comparable in size and nature to this project.			
2.	Who in your organisation has day to day responsibility for health and safety matters? Please provide details of their experience and qualifications and a copy of their curriculum vitae.			
3.	Who will be providing advice on health and safety issues on this project? Please provide details of their experience and qualifications and a copy of their curriculum vitae.			
4.	How many professional staff does your office employ? Please provide a percentage breakdown by discipline.			
5.	Please provide details of the experience, qualifications, membership of professional bodies etc and arrangements for continuing professional development of key staff who would be employed on the project. Please enclose curricula vitae.			

6.	Please provide details of your arrangements for ensuring continuing health and safety training.					
7.	What methods do you employ to ensure compliance with your duties under Regulation 11 of the Construction (Design and Management) Regulations 2007?					
8.	Please provide details of how you will co-operate with the CDM Co-ordinator and other designers to ensure that health and safety problems can be suitably addressed and overcome?					
9.	Please provide details of any formal notices issued or legal proceedings been taken against your organisation by the Health and Safety Executive in the last three years.					
10.	Please provide details of the other resources (including equipment and technical facilities) that your organisation will allocate to ensure that health and safety is incorporated into your design work on this project.					
11.	Please illustrate how you would prepare design programmes and allocate resources for each project.					
12.	Please describe your hazard identification methods and procedures and how this information is presented. If possible, please provide an example from a current project.					

continued overleaf

No.	Question			
13.	Please provide confirmation of procedures for assessing the health and safety competence and resource of those companies / Designers who will be employed by you on a subcontractor basis.			
14.	Please confirm that your Company holds an appropriate amount of insurances (including Professional Indemnity Insurance where appropriate) for the nature of the project.			

Comments (for client / CDM co-ordinator use)	Overall Rating

Submitted by:	Designation:	Date:	Assessed by:	Designation:	Date:

Principal contractor competence assessment

Company	Project Details
Name: Address: Contact: Telephone: e-mail:	Project Name: Project Location: Client:

Note: A response must be submitted for each of the following elements.

Stage 1 Assessment (See Appendix 4 of the ACoP to the new CDM Regulations 2007, L144 – Managing Health and safety in Construction. For larger schemes consider Appendix 5 of the ACoP)

	Elements	Standard to be achieved	Response submitted (✓/✗)	Please identify the page of your submission relating to the respective questions
1.	Health and safety Policy	If more than five people are employed, please provide a copy of your organisation's safety policy statement, as required by s.2(3) of the Health and Safety at Work etc Act 1974. The Policy must be relevant to the nature and scale of the project and set out the responsibilities for health and safety management at all levels within the organisation		
2.	Arrangements	Set out the arrangements for health and safety management within the organisation and should be relevant to the nature and scale of the work. They should set out how the company will discharge their duties under CDM 2007. There should be a clear indication of how these arrangements are communicated to the workforce.		

3.	Competent advice – corporate and construction-related	Your organisation and your employees must have ready access to competent health and safety advice, preferably from within your own organisation. Please provide details of your source of general health and safety advice.			
4.	Training and information	Please provide details of training arrangements to ensure your employees have the skills and understanding to discharge their duties under CDM 2007. This includes refresher courses, CPD and learning programmes to keep skills and knowledge up to date.			
5.	Individual qualifications and experience	Please provide documentation demonstrating employees holding the appropriate qualifications and experience for the assigned tasks, unless they are under controlled and competent supervision.			
6.	Monitoring, audit and review	Please provide details of how you monitor your procedures, for auditing them at periodic intervals, and for reviewing them on an ongoing basis.			
7.	Workforce involvement	Please provide details for procedures you have to implement and establish means of consulting with your workforce on health and safety matters.			

continued overleaf

8.	Accident reporting and enforcement action; follow up investigation	Please provide details of any Criminal Prosecutions, or Civil Claims against your Company relating to Health and Safety matters that have occurred within as a result of reportable events under RIDDOR for the last three years. Please provide details of any enforcement action taken against your company over the last five years, and actions taken to remedy such matters.	
9.	Sub-contracting / Consulting procedures	Please provide details of arrangements in place for appointing competent sub-contractors / consultants, and details of how you ensure any sub-contractors /consultants appointed by them are competent. What arrangement do you have for monitoring sub-contractor performance?	
10.	Hazard Elimination and Risk Control (For designers only)	Demonstrate procedures and arrangements for meeting your duties under regulation 11 of the CDM Regs 2007.	
11.	Risk assessment leading to a safe method of work (for contractors)	Please provide details of procedures in place for carrying out risk assessments and for developing and implementing safe systems of work / method statements. (This should include identification of health issues.)	

12.	Co-operating with others and co-ordinating your work with that of other contractors (for contractors)	Please illustrate how co-operation and co-ordination of your work is achieved in practice, and how you involve the workforce in drawing up method statements / safe systems of work.
13.	Welfare provisions (for contractors)	Please provide details of how you would ensure that appropriate welfare facilities will be in place before people start work on site.
14.	CDM – Co-ordinators Duties (For CDM Co-ordinators)	Please provide details to demonstrate how you go about encouraging co-operation, co-ordination and communications between designers.

Stage 2 Assessment (See Appendix 4 of the ACoP to the new CDM Regulations 2007, L144 – Managing Health and safety in Construction)

1	Work Experience	Please provide details of relevant experience in the chosen field for which you are applying.

continued overleaf

Stage 3 Assessment – Supplementary Project Questions

	Elements	Response submitted (✓/✗)	Please identify the page of your submission relating to the respective questions	S/U
1.	Please provide examples of work carried out previously, which is comparable in size and nature to this project.			
2.	Who in your organisation has day to day responsibility for health and safety matters? Please provide details of their experience and qualifications and a copy of their curriculum vitae.			
3.	Who will be providing advice on health and safety issues on this project? Please provide details of their experience and qualifications and a copy of their curriculum vitae.			
4.	How many professional staff does your office employ? Please provide a percentage breakdown by discipline.			
5.	Please provide details of the experience, qualifications, membership of professional bodies etc and arrangements for continuing professional development of key staff who would be employed on the project. Please enclose curricula vitae.			

6.	Please provide details of your arrangements for ensuring continuing health and safety training.					
7.	What methods do you employ to ensure compliance with your duties under Regulation 11 of the Construction (Design and Management) Regulations 2007?					
8.	Please provide details of how you will co-operate with the CDM Co-ordinator and other designers to ensure that health and safety problems can be suitably addressed and overcome?					
9.	Please provide details of any formal notices issued or legal proceedings been taken against your organisation by the Health and Safety Executive in the last three years.					
10.	Please provide details of the other resources (including equipment and technical facilities) that your organisation will allocate to ensure that health and safety is incorporated into your design work on this project.					
11.	Please illustrate how you would prepare design programmes and allocate resources for each project.					
12.	Please describe your hazard identification methods and procedures and how this information is presented. If possible, please provide an example from a current project.					

continued overleaf

13.	Please confirm that your Company holds an appropriate amount of insurances (including Professional Indemnity Insurance where appropriate) for the nature of the project.		

Comments (for client use)	Overall Rating

Submitted by:	Designation:	Date:	Assessed by:	Designation:	Date:

Construction Phase Plan Appraisal Report

Project Name:	
Principal Contractor:	
Address:	
Contact for further information and Tel No:	
E-mail Address:	

Note: Under Regulation 16 of the Construction (Design and Management) Regulations 2007 the client must ensure that a suitably developed construction phase plan is developed before work commences. The CDM co-ordinator will offer advice to the client on this matter.

The plan has been assessed by _____, and the following status allocated:

(Please enter status A, B or C clearly in the box adjacent.)

 A = Works May Proceed

 B = Works May Proceed Subject To Comments Below
    and Submission of Revised Plan/Method Statement/Risk
    Assessment(s) within 24hours

 C = Rejection Do Not Proceed With The Works, Please Contact ....

No.	Does the construction phase plan include?	Yes/ No	Critical Yes/No
1.	A project description that includes the activities.		
2.	Contact details of CDM duty holders.		
3.	Construction programme.		

continued overleaf

4.	Details of management structure and arrangements for health and safety.		
5.	Extent and location of existing plans and records relating to the site/structure. The position of all known services has been indicated on the contract drawings.		
6.	Arrangements (where appropriate) for: • regular liaison between parties on site; • consultation with the workforce; • exchange of design information; • handling design changes; • selection and control of contractors; • exchange of health and safety information between contractors; • security, site induction and on-site training; HSE Guidance Note GS 7 – Accidents to Children on Construction Sites. • welfare facilities and first aid (NB: first aider yet TBC); • reporting and investigation of accidents; • production and approval of risk assessments and method statements.		
7.	Clear site health and safety rules.		
8.	Fire and emergency procedures. To be developed with CDM co-ordinator and client as discussed Don / Kevin.		

| 9. | Arrangements (where appropriate) for controlling significant site risks for:

    • delivery and removal of materials (including waste);

    • services, including temporary services/installations;

    • preventing falls;

Only states that PC will comply with The Work at Height Regulations

    • working with or near fragile materials;

TBC

    • control of lifting operations;

    • maintenance of plant and equipment;

Addressed in site rules

    • poor ground conditions;

    • traffic routes and segregation of vehicles and pedestrians;

    • storage of hazardous materials;

To be addressed in COSHH assessment

    • accommodating adjacent land use;

    • entry into confined spaces;

Only states that PC will comply with Confined Spaces Regulations

    • dealing with/removal of asbestos

TBC – client permit to be adopted
Has ACM awareness training been undertaken by contractors?

    • dealing with lead;

    • manual handling;

    • use of hazardous substances;

    • reducing noise and vibration | | |

continued overleaf

10.	The health and safety file arrangements for: • layout and format; • collection and gathering of information; • storage of information.		
11.	Initial method statements and supporting info *(Required to deem Construction Phase Plan (CPP) suitably developed – client or CDM co-ordinator to tick if required ☑)* • Site set-up (*covering welfare facilities*) ☐ • Enabling Works (*services re-direction, demolition, temp road/access, etc.*) ☐ • Holistic MS Covering All works (*small project*) ☐ • Site Traffic Management Plan (*highlighting pedestrian and traffic routes*) ☐ • Site Fire Safety Plan (*highlighting means of escape, muster points, fire points, etc.*) ☐		

Summary of necessary development to deem the plan suitably developed for construction work to commence:

Signed: **Position:**

Date:

Form CDM03

We hereby confirm that .... as project CDM co-ordinators have assessed the construction phase plan prepared

by...

dated ....

For

Project...

The project was initially notified to the Health and Safety Executive under Regulation 21 of the Construction (Design and Management) Regulations 2007 on the .... A copy of the notice is attached for signature.

*I/we hereby advise the client that the construction plan has been developed sufficiently by the principal contractor in compliance with Regulation 23 and there are adequate welfare facilities on site in compliance with CDM Schedule 2. Therefore, we can advise you that the **construction phase of the project may commence.***

Signed..

For...(CDM co-ordinator)

Date...

Please keep for record

Form CDM04

Project H&S Risk Register

Project		Risk Register Co-ordinator		Tel and e-mail			

Item Ref No.	Date Entered	Process/ Location	Hazards	Action Taken and Date	Further Action and Date	By	Date	Completed

Construction (Design and Management) Regulations 2007

Principal contractor project checklist

Project name:

CDM Duty	Compliant Yes / No	Actions	Comments
(a) plan, manage and monitor the construction phase in a way which ensures that, so far as is reasonably practicable, it is carried out without risks to health or safety, including facilitating—			
(i) co-operation and co-ordination between persons concerned in the project in pursuance of regulations 5 and 6, and			
(ii) the application of the general principles of prevention in pursuance of regulation 7;			
(b) liaise with the CDM co-ordinator in performing his duties in regulation 20(2) (d) during the construction phase in relation to any design or change to a design;			
(c) ensure that welfare facilities sufficient to comply with the requirements of Schedule 2 are provided throughout the construction phase;			
(d) where necessary for health and safety, draw up rules which are appropriate to the construction site and the activities on it (referred to in these Regulations as "site rules");			
(e) give reasonable directions to any contractor so far as is necessary to enable the principal contractor to comply with his duties under these Regulations;			
(f) ensure that every contractor is informed of the minimum amount of time which will be allowed to him for planning and preparation before he begins construction work;			

continued overleaf

(g) where necessary, consult a contractor before finalising such part of the construction phase plan as is relevant to the work to be performed by him;

(h) ensure that every contractor is given, before he begins construction work and in sufficient time to enable him to prepare properly for that work, access to such part of the construction phase plan as is relevant to the work to be performed by him;

(i) ensure that every contractor is given, before he begins construction work and in sufficient time to enable him to prepare properly for that work, such further information as he needs—

(i) to comply punctually with the duty under regulation 13(7), and

(ii) to carry out the work to be performed by him without risk, so far as is reasonably practicable, to the health and safety of any person;

(j) identify to each contractor the information relating to the contractor's activity which is likely to be required by the CDM co-ordinator for inclusion in the health and safety file in pursuance of regulation 20(2)(e) and ensure that such information is promptly provided to the CDM co-ordinator;

(k) ensure that the particulars required to be in the notice given under regulation 21 are displayed in a readable condition in a position where they can be read by any worker engaged in the construction work; and

(l) take reasonable steps to prevent access by unauthorised persons to the construction site.

(2) The principal contractor shall take all reasonable steps to ensure that every worker carrying out the construction work is provided with—

(a) a suitable site induction;

(b) the information and training referred to in regulation 13(4) by a contractor on whom a duty is placed by that regulation; and

(c) any further information and training which he needs for the particular work to be carried out without undue risk to health or safety.

Contractor competence assessment

Company	Project Details
Name:	Project Name:
Address:	
	Project Location:
Contact:	
Telephone:	Client:
e-mail:	

Note: A response must be submitted for each of the following elements.

Stage 1 Assessment (See Appendix 4 of the ACoP to the new CDM Regulations 2007, L144 – Managing Health and safety in Construction. For larger schemes consider Appendix 5 of the ACoP)

	Elements	Standard to be achieved	Response submitted (✓/✗)	Please identify the page of your submission relating to the respective questions
1.	Health and safety Policy	If more than five people are employed, please provide a copy of your organisation's safety policy statement, as required by s.2(3) of the Health and Safety at Work etc Act 1974. The Policy must be relevant to the nature and scale of the project and set out the responsibilities for health and safety management at all levels within the organisation		
2.	Arrangements	Set out the arrangements for health and safety management within the organisation and should be relevant to the nature and scale of the work. They should set out how the company will discharge their duties under CDM 2007. There should be a clear indication of how these arrangements are communicated to the workforce.		

3.	Competent advice – corporate and construction-related	Your organisation and your employees must have ready access to competent health and safety advice, preferably from within your own organisation. Please provide details of your source of general health and safety advice.		
4.	Training and information	Please provide details of training arrangements to ensure your employees have the skills and understanding to discharge their duties under CDM 2007. This includes refresher courses, CPD and learning programmes to keep skills and knowledge up to date.		
5.	Individual qualifications and experience	Please provide documentation demonstrating employees holding the appropriate qualifications and experience for the assigned tasks, unless they are under controlled and competent supervision.		
6.	Monitoring, audit and review	Please provide details of how you monitor your procedures, for auditing them at periodic intervals, and for reviewing them on an ongoing basis.		
7.	Workforce involvement	Please provide details for procedures you have to implement and establish means of consulting with your workforce on health and safety matters.		

continued overleaf

8.	Accident reporting and enforcement action; follow up investigation	Please provide details of any Criminal Prosecutions, or Civil Claims against your Company relating to Health and Safety matters that have occurred within as a result of reportable events under RIDDOR for the last three years. Please provide details of any enforcement action taken against your company over the last five years, and actions taken to remedy such matters.		
9.	Sub-contracting / Consulting procedures	Please provide details of arrangements in place for appointing competent sub-contractors / consultants, and details of how you ensure any sub-contractors /consultants appointed by them are competent. What arrangement do you have for monitoring sub-contractor performance?		
10.	Hazard Elimination and Risk Control (For designers only)	Demonstrate procedures and arrangements for meeting your duties under regulation 11 of the CDM Regs 2007.		
11.	Risk assessment leading to a safe method of work (for contractors)	Please provide details of procedures in place for carrying out risk assessments and for developing and implementing safe systems of work / method statements. (This should include identification of health issues.)		

12.	Co-operating with others and co-ordinating your work with that of other contractors (for contractors)	Please illustrate how co-operation and co-ordination of your work is achieved in practice, and how you involve the workforce in drawing up method statements / safe systems of work.	
13.	Welfare provisions (for contractors)	Please provide details of how you would ensure that appropriate welfare facilities will be in place before people start work on site.	
14.	CDM – Co-ordinators Duties **(For CDM Co-ordinators)**	Please provide details to demonstrate how you go about encouraging co-operation, co-ordination and communications between designers.	

Stage 2 Assessment (See Appendix 4 of the ACoP to the new CDM Regulations 2007, L144 – Managing Health and safety in Construction)

1	Work Experience	Please provide details of relevant experience in the chosen field for which you are applying.

Stage 3 Assessment – Supplementary Project Questions

	Elements	Response submitted (✓/✗)	Please identify the page of your submission relating to the respective questions	S/U
1.	Please provide examples of work carried out previously, which is comparable in size and nature to this project.			
2.	Who in your organisation has day to day responsibility for health and safety matters? Please provide details of their experience and qualifications and a copy of their curriculum vitae.			
3.	Who will be providing advice on health and safety issues on this project? Please provide details of their experience and qualifications and a copy of their curriculum vitae.			
4.	How many professional staff does your office employ? Please provide a percentage breakdown by discipline.			
5.	Please provide details of the experience, qualifications, membership of professional bodies etc and arrangements for continuing professional development of key staff who would be employed on the project. Please enclose curricula vitae.			

6.	Please provide details of your arrangements for ensuring continuing health and safety training.		
7.	What methods do you employ to ensure compliance with your duties under Regulation 11 of the Construction (Design and Management) Regulations 2007?		
8.	Please provide details of how you will co-operate with the CDM Co-ordinator and other designers to ensure that health and safety problems can be suitably addressed and overcome?		
9.	Please provide details of any formal notices issued or legal proceedings been taken against your organisation by the Health and Safety Executive in the last three years.		
10.	Please provide details of the other resources (including equipment and technical facilities) that your organisation will allocate to ensure that health and safety is incorporated into your design work on this project.		
11.	Please illustrate how you would prepare design programmes and allocate resources for each project.		

continued overleaf

12.	Please describe your hazard identification methods and procedures and how this information is presented. If possible, please provide an example from a current project.		
13.	Please confirm that your Company holds an appropriate amount of insurances (including Professional Indemnity Insurance where appropriate) for the nature of the project.		

Overall Rating

Comments (for client use)

Submitted by:	Designation:	Date:

Assessed by:	Designation:	Date:

Designer CDM competence assessment

Company	Project Details
Name: Address: Contact: Telephone: e-mail:	Project Name: Project Location: Client:

Note: A response must be submitted for each of the following elements.

Stage 1 Assessment (See Appendix 4 of the ACoP to the new CDM Regulations 2007, L144 – Managing Health and safety in Construction)

	Elements	Standard to be achieved	Response submitted (✓/✗)	Please identify the page of your submission relating to the respective questions	
1.	Health and safety Policy	If more than five people are employed, please provide a copy of your organisation's safety policy statement, as required by s.2(3) of the Health and Safety at Work etc Act 1974. The Policy must be relevant to the nature and scale of the project and set out the responsibilities for health and safety management at all levels within the organisation			
2.	Arrangements	Set out the arrangements for health and safety management within the organisation and should be relevant to the nature and scale of the work. They should set out how the company will discharge their duties under CDM 2007. There should be a clear indication of how these arrangements are communicated to the workforce.			

3.	Competent advice – corporate and construction-related	Your organisation and your employees must have ready access to competent health and safety advice, preferably from within your own organisation. Please provide details of your source of general health and safety advice.		
4.	Training and information	Please provide details of training arrangements to ensure your employees have the skills and understanding to discharge their duties under CDM 2007. This includes refresher courses, CPD and learning programmes to keep skills and knowledge up to date.		
5.	Individual qualifications and experience	Please provide documentation demonstrating employees holding the appropriate qualifications and experience for the assigned tasks, unless they are under controlled and competent supervision.		
6.	Monitoring, audit and review	Please provide details of how you monitor your procedures, for auditing them at periodic intervals, and for reviewing them on an ongoing basis.		
7.	Workforce involvement	Please provide details for procedures you have to implement and establish means of consulting with your workforce on health and safety matters.		

continued overleaf

8.	Accident reporting and enforcement action; follow up investigation	Please provide details of any Criminal Prosecutions, or Civil Claims against your Company relating to Health and Safety matters that have occurred within as a result of reportable events under RIDDOR for the last three years. Please provide details of any enforcement action taken against your company over the last five years, and actions taken to remedy such matters.		
9.	Sub-contracting / Consulting procedures	Please provide details of arrangements in place for appointing competent sub-contractors / consultants, and details of how you ensure any sub-contractors /consultants appointed by them are competent. What arrangement do you have for monitoring sub-contractor performance?		
10.	Hazard Elimination and Risk Control (For designers only)	Demonstrate procedures and arrangements for meeting your duties under regulation 11 of the CDM Regs 2007.		
11.	Risk assessment leading to a safe method of work (for contractors)	Please provide details of procedures in place for carrying out risk assessments and for developing and implementing safe systems of work / method statements. (This should include identification of health issues.)		

12.	Co-operating with others and co-ordinating your work with that of other contractors (for contractors)	Please illustrate how co-operation and co-ordination of your work is achieved in practice, and how you involve the workforce in drawing up method statements / safe systems of work.		
13.	Welfare provisions (for contractors)	Please provide details of how you would ensure that appropriate welfare facilities will be in place before people start work on site.		
14.	CDM – Co-ordinators Duties (For CDM Co-ordinators)	Please provide details to demonstrate how you go about encouraging co-operation, co-ordination and communications between designers.		

Stage 2 Assessment (See Appendix 4 of the ACoP to the new CDM Regulations 2007, L144 – Managing Health and safety in Construction)

| 1 | Work Experience | Please provide details of relevant experience in the chosen field for which you are applying. | |

Stage 3 Assessment – Supplementary Project Questions

	Elements	Response submitted (✓/✗)	Please identify the page of your submission relating to the respective questions	S/U
1.	Please provide examples of work carried out previously, which is comparable in size and nature to this project.			
2.	Who in your organisation has day to day responsibility for health and safety matters? Please provide details of their experience and qualifications and a copy of their curriculum vitae.			
3.	Who will be providing advice on health and safety issues on this project? Please provide details of their experience and qualifications and a copy of their curriculum vitae.			
4.	How many professional staff does your office employ? Please provide a percentage breakdown by discipline.			
5.	Please provide details of the experience, qualifications, membership of professional bodies etc and arrangements for continuing professional development of key staff who would be employed on the project. Please enclose curricula vitae.			

6.	Please provide details of your arrangements for ensuring continuing health and safety training.					
7.	What methods do you employ to ensure compliance with your duties under Regulation 11 of the Construction (Design and Management) Regulations 2007?					
8.	Please provide details of how you will co-operate with the CDM Co-ordinator and other designers to ensure that health and safety problems can be suitably addressed and overcome?					
9.	Please provide details of any formal notices issued or legal proceedings been taken against your organisation by the Health and Safety Executive in the last three years.					
10.	Please provide details of the other resources (including equipment and technical facilities) that your organisation will allocate to ensure that health and safety is incorporated into your design work on this project.					
11.	Please illustrate how you would prepare design programmes and allocate resources for each project.					
12.	Please describe your hazard identification methods and procedures and how this information is presented. If possible, please provide an example from a current project.					

continued overleaf

13.	Please provide confirmation of procedures for assessing the health and safety competence and resource of those companies / Designers who will be employed by you on a subcontractor basis.	
14.	Please confirm that your Company holds an appropriate amount of insurances (including Professional Indemnity Insurance where appropriate) for the nature of the project.	

Comments (for client / CDM co-ordinator use)	Overall Rating

Submitted by:	Designation:	Date:	Assessed by:	Designation:	Date:

Construction Phase Plan Checklist

Project:		Date:	
Checked by (principal contractor representative)-			
NOTE: *Please check the construction phase plan against the checklist below before submitting to the Client or Planning supervisor for approval. Please amend the plan if necessary.*			
No.	Does the construction phase H&S plan include?	Yes/No	Plan Changed
1.	A project description that includes the activities.		
2.	Contact details of CDM duty holders.		
3.	Details of time scales including shut-down periods or different phases.		
4.	Details of management structure and arrangements for health and safety.		
5.	Named individuals and responsibilities for hazard/construction activities.		
6.	Arrangements (where appropriate) for: • regular liaison between parties on site; • consultation with the workforce; • exchange of design information; • handling design changes; • selection and control of contractors; • exchange of health and safety information between contractors; • security, site induction and on-site training; • welfare facilities and first aid; • reporting and investigation of accidents; • production and approval of risk assessments and method statements.		
7.	Clear site health and safety rules.		
8.	Fire and emergency procedures.		

9.	Arrangements (where appropriate) for controlling significant site risks for: • services, including temporary services/installations; • preventing falls; • working with or near fragile materials; • control of lifting operations; • maintenance of plant and equipment; • poor ground conditions; • traffic routes and segregation of vehicles and pedestrians; • storage of hazardous materials; • dealing with existing unstable structures; • accommodating adjacent land use; • entry into confined spaces; • dealing with/removal of asbestos • dealing with lead; • manual handling; • use of hazardous substances; • dealing with contaminated land; • working over or near water; • reducing noise and vibration • other(s) specify . . . . • . . . . • other(s) specify . . . . •		
10.	The health and safety file arrangements for: • layout and format; • collection and gathering of information; • storage of information.		
Is the plan suitably developed for submission to the client/CDM co-ordinator? Y/N			
Signed:			Date:
Note: COPY on project file			
H&S risk assessment and method appraisal:			

Form PC05

Site H&S Co-ordination Register-

Project						Ref No		Contracts Manager								
Construction Activity and Reference No.	Contractor(s)	Start Date	Pre-Qualification Questionnaire		Initial Induction Training Given	Contractors Briefed on Specific Activities and Arrangements	Risk Assessments/Method Statement Approval (Initials)			Safety Information Given By PC to Contractors			Authorised To Start (Sign)
			Sent	Received and Accepted			By	Ref No.	Approved	Risk Ass.	Drawings	Method State.	

Contractor competence assessment

Company	Project Details
Name: Address: Contact: Telephone: e-mail:	Project Name: Project Location: Client:

Note: A response must be submitted for each of the following elements.

Stage 1 Assessment (See Appendix 4 of the ACoP to the new CDM Regulations 2007, L144 – Managing Health and safety in Construction. For larger schemes consider Appendix 5 of the ACoP)

	Elements	Standard to be achieved	Response submitted (✓/✗)	Please identify the page of your submission relating to the respective questions
1.	Health and safety Policy	If more than five people are employed, please provide a copy of your organisation's safety policy statement, as required by s.2(3) of the Health and Safety at Work etc Act 1974. The Policy must be relevant to the nature and scale of the project and set out the responsibilities for health and safety management at all levels within the organisation		
2.	Arrangements	Set out the arrangements for health and safety management within the organisation and should be relevant to the nature and scale of the work. They should set out how the company will discharge their duties under CDM 2007. There should be a clear indication of how these arrangements are communicated to the workforce.		

continued overleaf

3.	Competent advice – corporate and construction-related	Your organisation and your employees must have ready access to competent health and safety advice, preferably from within your own organisation. Please provide details of your source of general health and safety advice.			
4.	Training and information	Please provide details of training arrangements to ensure your employees have the skills and understanding to discharge their duties under CDM 2007. This includes refresher courses, CPD and learning programmes to keep skills and knowledge up to date.			
5.	Individual qualifications and experience	Please provide documentation demonstrating employees holding the appropriate qualifications and experience for the assigned tasks, unless they are under controlled and competent supervision.			
6.	Monitoring, audit and review	Please provide details of how you monitor your procedures, for auditing them at periodic intervals, and for reviewing them on an ongoing basis.			
7.	Workforce involvement	Please provide details for procedures you have to implement and establish means of consulting with your workforce on health and safety matters.			

8.	Accident reporting and enforcement action; follow up investigation	Please provide details of any Criminal Prosecutions, or Civil Claims against your Company relating to Health and Safety matters that have occurred within as a result of reportable events under RIDDOR for the last three years. Please provide details of any enforcement action taken against your company over the last five years, and actions taken to remedy such matters.	
9.	Sub-contracting / Consulting procedures	Please provide details of arrangements in place for appointing competent sub-contractors / consultants, and details of how you ensure any sub-contractors /consultants appointed by them are competent. What arrangement do you have for monitoring sub-contractor performance?	
10.	Hazard Elimination and Risk Control (For designers only)	Demonstrate procedures and arrangements for meeting your duties under regulation 11 of the CDM Regs 2007.	
11.	Risk assessment leading to a safe method of work (for contractors)	Please provide details of procedures in place for carrying out risk assessments and for developing and implementing safe systems of work / method statements. (This should include identification of health issues.)	

continued overleaf

12.	Co-operating with others and co-ordinating your work with that of other contractors (for contractors)	Please illustrate how co-operation and co-ordination of your work is achieved in practice, and how you involve the workforce in drawing up method statements / safe systems of work.		
13.	Welfare provisions (for contractors)	Please provide details of how you would ensure that appropriate welfare facilities will be in place before people start work on site.		
14.	CDM – Co-ordinators Duties (For CDM Co-ordinators)	Please provide details to demonstrate how you go about encouraging co-operation, co-ordination and communications between designers.		

Stage 2 Assessment (See Appendix 4 of the ACoP to the new CDM Regulations 2007, L144 – Managing Health and safety in Construction)

| 1 | Work Experience | Please provide details of relevant experience in the chosen field for which you are applying. | |

Stage 3 Assessment – Supplementary Project Questions

	Elements	Response submitted (✓/×)	Please identify the page of your submission relating to the respective questions	S/U
1.	Please provide examples of work carried out previously, which is comparable in size and nature to this project.			
2.	Who in your organisation has day to day responsibility for health and safety matters? Please provide details of their experience and qualifications and a copy of their curriculum vitae.			
3.	Who will be providing advice on health and safety issues on this project? Please provide details of their experience and qualifications and a copy of their curriculum vitae.			
4.	How many professional staff does your office employ? Please provide a percentage breakdown by discipline.			
5.	Please provide details of the experience, qualifications, membership of professional bodies etc and arrangements for continuing professional development of key staff who would be employed on the project. Please enclose curricula vitae.			

continued overleaf

6.	Please provide details of your arrangements for ensuring continuing health and safety training.					
7.	What methods do you employ to ensure compliance with your duties under Regulation 11 of the Construction (Design and Management) Regulations 2007?					
8.	Please provide details of how you will co-operate with the CDM Co-ordinator and other designers to ensure that health and safety problems can be suitably addressed and overcome?					
9.	Please provide details of any formal notices issued or legal proceedings been taken against your organisation by the Health and Safety Executive in the last three years.					
10.	Please provide details of the other resources (including equipment and technical facilities) that your organisation will allocate to ensure that health and safety is incorporated into your design work on this project.					
11.	Please illustrate how you would prepare design programmes and allocate resources for each project.					
12.	Please describe your hazard identification methods and procedures and how this information is presented. If possible, please provide an example from a current project.					

13.	Please confirm that your Company holds an appropriate amount of insurances (including Professional Indemnity Insurance where appropriate) for the nature of the project.		

Comments (for client use)	Overall Rating

Submitted by:	Designation:	Date:	Assessed by:	Designation:	Date:

Designer CDM competence assessment

Company	Project Details
Name: Address: Contact: Telephone: e-mail:	Project Name: Project Location: Client:

Note: A response must be submitted for each of the following elements.

Stage 1 Assessment (See Appendix 4 of the ACoP to the new CDM Regulations 2007, L144 – Managing Health and safety in Construction)

	Elements	Standard to be achieved	Response submitted (✓/✗)	Please identify the page of your submission relating to the respective questions
1.	Health and safety Policy	If more than five people are employed, please provide a copy of your organisation's safety policy statement, as required by s.2(3) of the Health and Safety at Work etc Act 1974. The Policy must be relevant to the nature and scale of the project and set out the responsibilities for health and safety management at all levels within the organisation		
2.	Arrangements	Set out the arrangements for health and safety management within the organisation and should be relevant to the nature and scale of the work. They should set out how the company will discharge their duties under CDM 2007. There should be a clear indication of how these arrangements are communicated to the workforce.		

continued overleaf

3.	Competent advice – corporate and construction-related	Your organisation and your employees must have ready access to competent health and safety advice, preferably from within your own organisation. Please provide details of your source of general health and safety advice.		
4.	Training and information	Please provide details of training arrangements to ensure your employees have the skills and understanding to discharge their duties under CDM 2007. This includes refresher courses, CPD and learning programmes to keep skills and knowledge up to date.		
5.	Individual qualifications and experience	Please provide documentation demonstrating employees holding the appropriate qualifications and experience for the assigned tasks, unless they are under controlled and competent supervision.		
6.	Monitoring, audit and review	Please provide details of how you monitor your procedures, for auditing them at periodic intervals, and for reviewing them on an ongoing basis.		
7.	Workforce involvement	Please provide details for procedures you have to implement and establish means of consulting with your workforce on health and safety matters.		

8.	Accident reporting and enforcement action; follow up investigation	Please provide details of any Criminal Prosecutions, or Civil Claims against your Company relating to Health and Safety matters that have occurred within as a result of reportable events under RIDDOR for the last three years. Please provide details of any enforcement action taken against your company over the last five years, and actions taken to remedy such matters.		
9.	Sub-contracting / Consulting procedures	Please provide details of arrangements in place for appointing competent sub-contractors / consultants, and details of how you ensure any sub-contractors /consultants appointed by them are competent. What arrangement do you have for monitoring sub-contractor performance?		
10.	Hazard Elimination and Risk Control (For designers only)	Demonstrate procedures and arrangements for meeting your duties under regulation 11 of the CDM Regs 2007.		
11.	Risk assessment leading to a safe method of work (for contractors)	Please provide details of procedures in place for carrying out risk assessments and for developing and implementing safe systems of work / method statements. (This should include identification of health issues.)		

continued overleaf

12.	Co-operating with others and co-ordinating your work with that of other contractors (for contractors)	Please illustrate how co-operation and co-ordination of your work is achieved in practice, and how you involve the workforce in drawing up method statements / safe systems of work.	
13.	Welfare provisions (for contractors)	Please provide details of how you would ensure that appropriate welfare facilities will be in place before people start work on site.	
14.	CDM – Co-ordinators Duties (**For CDM Co-ordinators**)	Please provide details to demonstrate how you go about encouraging co-operation, co-ordination and communications between designers.	

Stage 2 Assessment (See Appendix 4 of the ACoP to the new CDM Regulations 2007, L144 – Managing Health and safety in Construction)

1	Work Experience	Please provide details of relevant experience in the chosen field for which you are applying.	

Stage 3 Assessment – Supplementary Project Questions

	Elements	Response submitted (✓/✗)	Please identify the page of your submission relating to the respective questions	S/U
1.	Please provide examples of work carried out previously, which is comparable in size and nature to this project.			
2.	Who in your organisation has day to day responsibility for health and safety matters? Please provide details of their experience and qualifications and a copy of their curriculum vitae.			
3.	Who will be providing advice on health and safety issues on this project? Please provide details of their experience and qualifications and a copy of their curriculum vitae.			
4.	How many professional staff does your office employ? Please provide a percentage breakdown by discipline.			
5.	Please provide details of the experience, qualifications, membership of professional bodies etc and arrangements for continuing professional development of key staff who would be employed on the project. Please enclose curricula vitae.			

continued overleaf

6.	Please provide details of your arrangements for ensuring continuing health and safety training.					
7.	What methods do you employ to ensure compliance with your duties under Regulation 11 of the Construction (Design and Management) Regulations 2007?					
8.	Please provide details of how you will co-operate with the CDM Co-ordinator and other designers to ensure that health and safety problems can be suitably addressed and overcome?					
9.	Please provide details of any formal notices issued or legal proceedings been taken against your organisation by the Health and Safety Executive in the last three years.					
10.	Please provide details of the other resources (including equipment and technical facilities) that your organisation will allocate to ensure that health and safety is incorporated into your design work on this project.					
11.	Please illustrate how you would prepare design programmes and allocate resources for each project.					
12.	Please describe your hazard identification methods and procedures and how this information is presented. If possible, please provide an example from a current project.					

13.	Please provide confirmation of procedures for assessing the health and safety competence and resource of those companies / Designers who will be employed by you on a subcontractor basis.		
14.	Please confirm that your Company holds an appropriate amount of insurances (including Professional Indemnity Insurance where appropriate) for the nature of the project.		

Overall Rating

Comments (for client / CDM co-ordinator use)

Submitted by:	**Designation:**	**Date:**	**Assessed by:**	**Designation:**	**Date:**

SAFETY INDUCTION

PROJECT TITLE:	
Ref:sc/sms/005	

The site is managed by: .... Tel:

and in his absence by: .... Tel:

Your contribution is necessary to ensure the satisfactory completion of the works. As you will have seen by now, our works are in and around a closed facility. However, you will also note that the public interface closely with some of our activities

We request that you respect the entire neighbouring environment and that you cause the minimum disruption inside and outside the confines of the site. It is our policy to maintain a high standard in all works and all site personnel/contractors shall conduct their activities so that conditions and methods of work are safe for themselves, their own employees and members of the public, visitors and other persons who may be affected by the work. Please do not discuss the work or argue with any personnel either neighbouring the site or on the site. Please convey any disagreements or complaints to the site manager.

Do not 'catcall' or whistle at any persons passing by the site.

General Information

- Plant and machine operators **MUST** be fully trained and able to produce a current relevant certificate prior to commencing work. HSE registers for plant and machinery to be maintained on site at all times.
- Agreed risk assessments and control measures must be adhered to and work will not commence until this information is in place and all operatives briefed on the details by their supervisor.
- Agreed method statements must not be deviated from and any changes made to the way in which the work is to be carried out will only be permitted with the written agreement of the contractor supervisor and changes made to the method statement.
- Site rules for this site are as detailed on the attached sheet and generally the remaining safety rules for this site are as outlined below.

WELFARE LOCATIONS

Toilets and wash facilities

Canteen

Drying room

Drinking water

SMOKING

Smoking is not permitted anywhere on site.

ALCOHOL AND DRUGS

Principal contractor does not allow any drugs (apart from prescription drugs) or alcohol to be brought on or consumed on site. Should anyone be suspected of being under the influence of alcohol or drugs then they will not be permitted on site. Should you consume any alcohol off site during the day then please do not return to site.

YOU HAVE BEEN WARNED

SAFETY

.... are acting as the main contractor for the work you are undertaking on this site.

Before working on this site you must attend this induction and during which we will be reviewing the health and safety documentation for your work and issuing the appropriate permits before entering the area.

Use of any scaffold must be by prior agreement with the supervisor and there must be no alteration carried out by anyone other than the trained scaffolders who erected the structure.

Erection of any scaffold towers can only be carried out by trained personnel (proof of training will be required).

It is your responsibility to ensure that you are working safely. If you do not then you will be stopped. You must not interfere with or misuse anything provided in the interest of health, safety and welfare. All operatives must work in accordance with an approved risk assessment which details the control measures to be adopted in order to reduce the risk to an acceptable level. Where high-risk activities are carried out then a specific method statement must be produced and attached to the risk assessment/control measures.

You must wear a **safety helmet** at all times on site.

You must wear **safety footwear** at all times on site.

You must wear a **high-visibility vest**.

You must wear **personal protective equipment** when the need arises, i.e. ear defenders, goggles, etc.

NO SAFETY CLOTHING OR EQUIPMENT, NO WORK!

FIRST AID

.... is a trained first aider. **If you are not first aid trained and you witness an accident then get help!** <u>A first aid box is located in the site office.</u>

All accidents and incidents must be reported to the site supervisor and if necessary recorded in the first aid book.

GENERAL CONDUCT

All **visitors** must **report to the site office** on arrival and **sign the visitors book.** They must also record their time of departure. Each subcontractor foreman is to maintain a register of their operatives on site. The numbers present each day is to be reported to the site supervisor by 10.00 a.m.

PARKING

You should park your car (or transport to site) in the contractor's car park.

GENERAL

- Food and drink must only be consumed in the designated mess room or off site.
- The playing of radios, cassette recorders, CD players, etc., is forbidden.
- Plant and machinery operators <u>**MUST**</u> be fully trained and able to produce a current relevant certificate prior to commencing work. HSE registers for machinery to be maintained at all times.

PERMITS

A permit to work must be obtained from the site manager before any of the following activities are commenced:

- Hot works involving naked flames, radiant heat, spark-producing, etc.
- Electrical permit to work
- Confined space permit to work

The risk assessment will tell you if you need a permit or not. Ensure you read and understand the safety documents produced for the work you are doing

- Agreed risk assessments/control measures and method statements must not be deviated from.

WASTE AND TIDINESS

It is your responsibility to minimise waste. If the principal contractor is supplying your materials your company may be charged for excess waste. If your company is supplying materials it is in your own interest to control waste.

KEEP YOUR WORK AREA AND THE SITE TIDY.

It is your responsibility to clear your debris to a designated point. All works and debris produced by the works must be placed in the rubbish skips as soon as possible as and by no later than the end of each day. If you don't clear up when instructed by the principal contractor your company will be charged for others to do it.

FIRE
If you discover a fire:

- Do not take risks. Do not put yourself in danger. Do not attack the fire unless trained to do so.
- Raise the alarm by operating the nearest break glass or klaxon alarm.
- Please familiarise yourself with all the exits and the alarm call points in your work areas.

PLEASE FAMILIARISE YOURSELF WITH THE SITE FIRE SAFETY PLAN AND BE AWARE OF THE EMERGENCY MUSTER POINT

PERMITTED SITE HOURS

Monday to Friday ....
Saturday/Sunday ....

PERSONAL ABILITIES

If you have or develop a physical or medical condition which could affect your personal safety on site or the safety of other persons you must report such conditions to the principal contractor site manager so that a risk assessment can be made to reflect these conditions. This information will be kept strictly confidential.

YOUNG PERSONS

If you are under 18 years of age you must inform the site manager so that the appropriate risk assessment may be completed and control measures put in place.

EMERGENCY CONTACT

You will be asked to complete the emergency contact list for employees. This will be kept confidential.

You will be asked to sign the induction register form to show that you received induction training and **have read and understood** the contents of these safety induction notes.

SITE SAFETY RULES

YOU ARE REQUIRED TO:

- Take reasonable care of your own health and safety
- Ensure that you do not put the health or safety of any other person at risk
- Co-operate with the site management to comply with their health and safety responsibilities

YOU MUST:

- Wear a safety helmet at all times in construction areas
- Wear appropriate eye protection as required by the risk assessment. Close fitting safety glasses are the minimum acceptable protection. Specific tasks, such as grinding or opening up process equipment will require the use of goggles or full-face visor.
- Wear a high visibility vest
- Wear safety protective footwear, incorporating steel toecaps and reinforced mid soles
- Wear ear defenders or ear plugs where required to do so by the risk assessment
- Carry a pair of gloves at all times and wear them when there is any risk of hand injury
- Wash your hands frequently and thoroughly
- Wear the protective clothing (PPE) provided as detailed in your company risk assessment
- Keep works/storage areas tidy
- Put all debris into waste skips/rubbish areas
- Obey all warning and hazard signs
- Observe the site speed limit
- Comply with all permit-to-work systems
- Report all accidents, incidents, which could have had serious consequences (near misses) and unsafe work conditions to your immediate supervisor or the site manager. Also report injuries and dangerous occurrences.
- Inform the site manager/supervisor if you are under eighteen
- Tie ladders securely at all times
- Evacuate to your designated muster point if the site alarm sounds

YOU MUST NOT:

- Alter scaffolds and scaffold towers. Remove boards or handrails from any scaffolding.

- Climb scaffolding
- Attach lifting equipment to any part of the existing building unless instructed to do so by the site manager
- Leave tools or materials lying about at height
- Use a step ladder without first having undertaken a specific risk assessment with the Carreg site manager
- Use damaged access equipment/tools
- Remove guards from tools/machines
- Throw tools or any others materials/equipment from scaffolding or from height
- Change abrasive wheels unless trained
- Operate any plant unless trained/competent to do so
- Ride as a passenger on any forklift, dumper or other mobile plant, unless it is specially equipped to do so
- Leave vehicles unattended with the engine running
- Tamper with electricity
- Reverse any vehicle on site, unless you are being directed by a competent person/banksman
- Drive any vehicle on site unless you hold a full driving license and are over 18 years old
- Use potentially hazardous materials without proper instruction
- Drink alcohol or take un-prescribed drugs
- Work alone outside normal working hours
- Create tripping hazards for yourself or others with electrical leads, hoses or discarded materials
- Eat or drink outside the facilities provided
- Urinate or defecate anywhere but in the toilets

NOTE: The above rules are not exhaustive. They have been extracted from the company safety policy, which MUST be complied with at all times.

<u>REMEMBER: DON'T WALK BY – REPORT ALL UNSAFE CONDITIONS IMMEDIATELY</u>

<u>IF IN DOUBT, ASK!!</u>

Form C02

Site H&S Co-ordination Register

Health and Safety Management System   Sheet No .... of ....

Project							Ref No.		Contracts Manager						
Construction Activity and Reference No.	Contractor(s)	Start Date	Pre-Qualification Questionnaire		Initial Induction Training Given	Toolbox Talks and Training Planned	Risk Assessments/Method Statement Approval (Initials)			Safety Information Given By PC to Contractors			Authorised To Start (Sign)
			Sent	Received and Accepted			By	Ref No.	Approved	Risk Ass..	Draw ings	Method State..	

Site Contractor H&S Co-ordination Register

NOTE: TO BE COMPLETED BY SITE MANAGER

Appendix 1

The Construction (Design and Management) Regulations 2007

Statutory instruments

2007 No. 320

Health and Safety

The Construction (Design and Management) Regulations 2007

Made	*7th February 2007*
Laid before Parliament	*15th February 2007*
Coming into force	*6 April 2007*

Contents

The Secretary of State makes the following Regulations in the exercise of the powers conferred upon him by sections 15(1), (2), (3)(a) and (c), 5(a), (6)(a) and (b), (8) and (9), 47(2) and (3), 80(1) and (2) and 82(3)(a) of, and paragraphs 1(1) and (2), 6, 7, 8(1), 9 to 12, 14, 15(1), 16, 18, 20 and 21 of Schedule 3 to, the Health and Safety at Work etc. Act 1974(1) ("the 1974 Act").

In doing so he gives effect without modifications to proposals submitted to him by the Health and Safety Commission under section 11(2)(d) of the 1974 Act after the carrying out by the said Commission of consultations in accordance with section 50(3) of that Act, and it appearing expedient to him after consulting such bodies as appear to him to be appropriate in accordance with section 80(4) of that Act(2).

(1) 1974 c.37; sections 11(2), 15(1) and 50(3) were amended by the Employment Protection Act 1975 c.71, Schedule 15, paragraphs 4, 6 and 16(3) respectively. Back [1]

(2) As regards Scotland, see also section 57(1) of the Scotland Act 1998 (1998 c.46) which provides that, despite the transfer to the Scottish Ministers by virtue of that Act of functions in relation to observing and implementing obligations under Community law, any function of a Minister of the Crown in relation to any matter shall continue to be exercisable by him as regards Scotland for the purposes specified in section 2(2) of the European Communities Act 1972 (1972 c.68). Back [2]

Part 1 Introduction

Citation and commencement

1. These Regulations may be cited as the Construction (Design and Management) Regulations 2007 and shall come into force on 6th April 2007.

Interpretation

2.—(1) In these Regulations, unless the context otherwise requires—
   "business" means a trade, business or other undertaking (whether for profit or not);

"client" means a person who in the course or furtherance of a business—

(a) seeks or accepts the services of another which may be used in the carrying out of a project for him; or
(b) carries out a project himself;

"CDM co-ordinator" means the person appointed as the CDM co-ordinator under regulation 14(1);

"construction site" includes any place where construction work is being carried out or to which the workers have access, but does not include a workplace within it which is set aside for purposes other than construction work;

"construction phase" means the period of time starting when construction work in any project starts and ending when construction work in that project is completed;

"construction phase plan" means a document recording the health and safety arrangements, site rules and any special measures for construction work;

"construction work" means the carrying out of any building, civil engineering or engineering construction work and includes—

(a) the construction, alteration, conversion, fitting out, commissioning, renovation, repair, upkeep, redecoration or other maintenance (including cleaning which involves the use of water or an abrasive at high pressure or the use of corrosive or toxic substances), de-commissioning, demolition or dismantling of a structure;
(b) the preparation for an intended structure, including site clearance, exploration, investigation (but not site survey) and excavation, and the clearance or preparation of the site or structure for use or occupation at its conclusion;
(c) the assembly on site of prefabricated elements to form a structure or the disassembly on site of prefabricated elements which, immediately before such disassembly, formed a structure;
(d) the removal of a structure or of any product or waste resulting from demolition or dismantling of a structure or from disassembly of prefabricated elements which immediately before such disassembly formed such a structure; and
(e) the installation, commissioning, maintenance, repair or removal of mechanical, electrical, gas, compressed air, hydraulic, telecommunications, computer or similar services which are normally fixed within or to a structure,

but does not include the exploration for or extraction of mineral resources or activities preparatory thereto carried out at a place where such exploration or extraction is carried out;

"contractor" means any person (including a client, principal contractor or other person referred to in these Regulations) who, in the course or furtherance of a business, carries out or manages construction work;

"design" includes drawings, design details, specification and bill of quantities (including specification of articles or substances) relating to a structure, and calculations prepared for the purpose of a design;

"designer" means any person (including a client, contractor or other person referred to in these Regulations) who in the course or furtherance of a business—

(a) prepares or modifies a design; or

(b) arranges for or instructs any person under his control to do so,

relating to a structure or to a product or mechanical or electrical system intended for a particular structure, and a person is deemed to prepare a design where a design is prepared by a person under his control;

"excavation" includes any earthwork, trench, well, shaft, tunnel or underground working;

"the Executive" means the Health and Safety Executive;

"the general principles of prevention" means the general principles of prevention specified in Schedule 1 to the Management of Health and Safety at Work Regulations 1999(3)

"health and safety file"—

(a) means the record referred to in regulation 20(2)(e); and

(b) includes a health and safety file prepared under regulation 14(d) of the Construction (Design and Management) Regulations 1994(4);

"loading bay" means any facility for loading or unloading;

"place of work" means any place which is used by any person at work for the purposes of construction work or for the purposes of any activity arising out of or in connection with construction work;

"pre-construction information" means the information described in regulation 10 and, where the project is notifiable, regulation 15.

"principal contractor" means the person appointed as the principal contractor under regulation 14(2);

"project" means a project which includes or is intended to include construction work and includes all planning, design, management or other work involved in a project until the end of the construction phase;

"site rules" means the rules described in regulation 22(1)(d);

"structure" means—

(a) any building, timber, masonry, metal or reinforced concrete structure, railway line or siding, tramway line, dock, harbour, inland navigation, tunnel, shaft, bridge, viaduct, waterworks, reservoir, pipe or pipe-line, cable, aqueduct, sewer, sewage works, gasholder, road, airfield, sea defence works, river works, drainage works, earthworks, lagoon, dam, wall, caisson, mast, tower, pylon, underground tank, earth retaining structure or structure designed to preserve or alter any natural feature, fixed plant and any structure similar to the foregoing; or

(b) any formwork, falsework, scaffold or other structure designed or used to provide support or means of access during construction work,

and any reference to a structure includes a part of a structure.
"traffic route" means a route for pedestrian traffic or for vehicles and includes any doorway, gateway, loading bay or ramp;
"vehicle" includes any mobile work equipment;
"work equipment" means any machinery, appliance, apparatus, tool or installation for use at work (whether exclusively or not);
"workplace" means a workplace within the meaning of regulation 2(1) of the Workplace (Health, Safety and Welfare) Regulations 1992(5) other than a construction site; and
"writing" includes writing which is kept in electronic form and which can be printed.

(2) Any reference in these Regulations to a plan, rules, document, report or copy includes a plan, rules, document, report or copy which is kept in a form—

(a) in which it is capable of being reproduced as a printed copy when required; and
(b) which is secure from loss or unauthorised interference.

(3) For the purposes of these Regulations, a project is notifiable if the construction phase is likely to involve more than—

(a) 30 days; or
(b) 500 person days,

of construction work.

Application

3.—(1) These Regulations shall apply—

(a) in Great Britain; and
(b) outside Great Britain as sections 1 to 59 and 80 to 82 of the 1974 Act apply by virtue of article 8(1)(a) of the Health and Safety at Work etc. Act 1974 (Application outside Great Britain) Order 2001(6).

(2) Subject to the following paragraphs of this regulation, these Regulations shall apply to and in relation to construction work.

(3) The duties under Part 3 shall apply only where a project—

(a) is notifiable; and
(b) is carried out for or on behalf of, or by, a client.

(4) Part 4 shall apply only in relation to a construction site.

(5) Regulations 9(1)(b), 13(7), 22(1)(c), and Schedule 2 shall apply only in relation to persons at work who are carrying out construction work.

Part 2 General management duties applying to construction projects

Competence

4.—(1) No person on whom these Regulations place a duty shall—

(a) appoint or engage a CDM co-ordinator, designer, principal contractor or contractor unless he has taken reasonable steps to ensure that the person to be appointed or engaged is competent;
(b) accept such an appointment or engagement unless he is competent;
(c) arrange for or instruct a worker to carry out or manage design or construction work unless the worker is—
  (i) competent, or
  (ii) under the supervision of a competent person.

(2) Any reference in this regulation to a person being competent shall extend only to his being competent to—

(a) perform any requirement; and
(b) avoid contravening any prohibition,

imposed on him by or under any of the relevant statutory provisions.

Co-operation

5.—(1) Every person concerned in a project on whom a duty is placed by these Regulations, including paragraph (2), shall—

(a) seek the co-operation of any other person concerned in any project involving construction work at the same or an adjoining site so far as is necessary to enable himself to perform any duty or function under these Regulations; and
(b) co-operate with any other person concerned in any project involving construction work at the same or an adjoining site so far as is necessary to enable that person to perform any duty or function under these Regulations.

(2) Every person concerned in a project who is working under the control of another person shall report to that person anything which he is aware is likely to endanger the health or safety of himself or others.

Co-ordination

6. All persons concerned in a project on whom a duty is placed by these Regulations shall co-ordinate their activities with one another in a manner which ensures, so far as is reasonably practicable, the health and safety of persons—

(a) carrying out the construction work; and
(b) affected by the construction work.

General principles of prevention

7.—(1) Every person on whom a duty is placed by these Regulations in relation to the design, planning and preparation of a project shall take account of the general principles of prevention in the performance of those duties during all the stages of the project.

(2) Every person on whom a duty is placed by these Regulations in relation to the construction phase of a project shall ensure so far as is reasonably practicable that the general principles of prevention are applied in the carrying out of the construction work.

Election by clients

8. Where there is more than one client in relation to a project, if one or more of such clients elect in writing to be treated for the purposes of these Regulations as the only client or clients, no other client who has agreed in writing to such election shall be subject after such election and consent to any duty owed by a client under these Regulations save the duties in regulations 5(1)(b), 10(1), 15 and 17(1) insofar as those duties relate to information in his possession.

Client's duty in relation to arrangements for managing projects

9.—(1) Every client shall take reasonable steps to ensure that the arrangements made for managing the project (including the allocation of sufficient time and other resources) by persons with a duty under these Regulations (including the client himself) are suitable to ensure that—

(a) the construction work can be carried out so far as is reasonably practicable without risk to the health and safety of any person;

(b) the requirements of Schedule 2 are complied with in respect of any person carrying out the construction work; and

(c) any structure designed for use as a workplace has been designed taking account of the provisions of the Workplace (Health, Safety and Welfare) Regulations 1992 which relate to the design of, and materials used in, the structure.

(2) The client shall take reasonable steps to ensure that the arrangements referred to in paragraph (1) are maintained and reviewed throughout the project.

Client's duty in relation to information

10.—(1) Every client shall ensure that

(a) every person designing the structure; and

(b) every contractor who has been or may be appointed by the client, is promptly provided with pre-construction information in accordance with paragraph (2).

(2) The pre-construction information shall consist of all the information in the client's possession (or which is reasonably obtainable), including—

(a) any information about or affecting the site or the construction work;

(b) any information concerning the proposed use of the structure as a workplace;

(c) the minimum amount of time before the construction phase which will be allowed to the contractors appointed by the client for planning and preparation for construction work; and

(d) any information in any existing health and safety file,

which is relevant to the person to whom the client provides it for the purposes specified in paragraph (3).

(3) The purposes referred to in paragraph (2) are—

(a) to ensure so far as is reasonably practicable the health and safety of persons—
    (i) engaged in the construction work,
    (ii) liable to be affected by the way in which it is carried out, and
    (iii) who will use the structure as a workplace; and

(b) without prejudice to sub-paragraph (a), to assist the persons to whom information is provided under this regulation—
    (i) to perform their duties under these Regulations, and
    (ii) to determine the resources referred to in regulation 9(1) which they are to allocate for managing the project.

Duties of designers

11.—(1) No designer shall commence work in relation to a project unless any client for the project is aware of his duties under these Regulations.

(2) The duties in paragraphs (3) and (4) shall be performed so far as is reasonably practicable, taking due account of other relevant design considerations.
(3) Every designer shall in preparing or modifying a design which may be used in construction work in Great Britain avoid foreseeable risks to the health and safety of any person—

  (a) carrying out construction work;
  (b) liable to be affected by such construction work;
  (c) cleaning any window or any transparent or translucent wall, ceiling or roof in or on a structure;
  (d) maintaining the permanent fixtures and fittings of a structure; or
  (e) using a structure designed as a workplace.

(4) In discharging the duty in paragraph (3), the designer shall—

  (a) eliminate hazards which may give rise to risks; and
  (b) reduce risks from any remaining hazards,

and in so doing shall give collective measures priority over individual measures.
(5) In designing any structure for use as a workplace the designer shall take account of the provisions of the Workplace (Health, Safety and Welfare) Regulations 1992 which relate to the design of, and materials used in, the structure.
(6) The designer shall take all reasonable steps to provide with his design sufficient information about aspects of the design of the structure or its construction or maintenance as will adequately assist—

  (a) clients;
  (b) other designers; and
  (c) contractors,

to comply with their duties under these Regulations.

Designs prepared or modified outside Great Britain

12. Where a design is prepared or modified outside Great Britain for use in construction work to which these Regulations apply—

  (a) the person who commissions it, if he is established within Great Britain; or
  (b) if that person is not so established, any client for the project,

shall ensure that regulation 11 is complied with.

Duties of contractors

13.—(1) No contractor shall carry out construction work in relation to a project unless any client for the project is aware of his duties under these Regulations.

(2) Every contractor shall plan, manage and monitor construction work carried out by him or under his control in a way which ensures that, so far as is reasonably practicable, it is carried out without risks to health and safety.

(3) Every contractor shall ensure that any contractor whom he appoints or engages in his turn in connection with a project is informed of the minimum amount of time which will be allowed to him for planning and preparation before he begins construction work.

(4) Every contractor shall provide every worker carrying out the construction work under his control with any information and training which he needs for the particular work to be carried out safely and without risk to health, including—

(a) suitable site induction, where not provided by any principal contractor;

(b) information on the risks to their health and safety—
  (i) identified by his risk assessment under regulation 3 of the Management of Health and Safety at Work Regulations 1999, or
  (ii) arising out of the conduct by another contractor of his undertaking and of which he is or ought reasonably to be aware;

(c) the measures which have been identified by the contractor in consequence of the risk assessment as the measures he needs to take to comply with the requirements and prohibitions imposed upon him by or under the relevant statutory provisions;

(d) any site rules;

(e) the procedures to be followed in the event of serious and imminent danger to such workers; and

(f) the identity of the persons nominated to implement those procedures.

(5) Without prejudice to paragraph (4), every contractor shall in the case of any of his employees provide those employees with any health and safety training which he is required to provide to them in respect of the construction work by virtue of regulation 13(2)(b) of the Management of Health and Safety at Work Regulations 1999.

(6) No contractor shall begin work on a construction site unless reasonable steps have been taken to prevent access by unauthorised persons to that site.

(7) Every contractor shall ensure, so far as is reasonably practicable, that the requirements of Schedule 2 are complied with throughout the construction phase in respect of any person at work who is under his control.

Part 3 Additional duties where project is notifiable

Appointments by the client where a project is notifiable

14.—(1) Where a project is notifiable, the client shall appoint a person ("the CDM co-ordinator") to perform the duties specified in regulations 20 and 21 as soon as is practicable after initial design work or other preparation for construction work has begun.

(2) After appointing a CDM co-ordinator under paragraph (1), the client shall appoint a person ("the principal contractor") to perform the duties specified in regulations 22 to 24 as soon as is practicable after the client knows enough about the project to be able to select a suitable person for such appointment.

(3) The client shall ensure that appointments under paragraphs (1) and (2) are changed or renewed as necessary to ensure that there is at all times until the end of the construction phase a CDM co-ordinator and principal contractor.

(4) The client shall—

    (a) be deemed for the purposes of these Regulations, save paragraphs (1) and (2) and regulations 18(1) and 19(1)(a) to have been appointed as the CDM co-ordinator or principal contractor, or both, for any period for which no person (including himself) has been so appointed; and

    (b) accordingly be subject to the duties imposed by regulations 20 and 21 on a CDM co-ordinator or, as the case may be, the duties imposed by regulations 22 to 24 on a principal contractor, or both sets of duties.

(5) Any reference in this regulation to appointment is to appointment in writing.

Client's duty in relation to information where a project is notifiable

15. Where the project is notifiable, the client shall promptly provide the CDM co-ordinator with pre-construction information consisting of—

    (a) all the information described in regulation 10(2) to be provided to any person in pursuance of regulation 10(1);

    (b) any further information as described in regulation 10(2) in the client's possession (or which is reasonably obtainable) which is relevant to the CDM co-ordinator for the purposes specified in regulation 10(3), including the minimum amount of time before the construction phase which will be allowed to the principal contractor for planning and preparation for construction work.

The client's duty in relation to the start of the construction phase where a project is notifiable

16. Where the project is notifiable, the client shall ensure that the construction phase does not start unless—

- (a) the principal contractor has prepared a construction phase plan which complies with regulations 23(1)(a) and 23(2); and
- (b) he is satisfied that the requirements of regulation 22(1)(c) (provision of welfare facilities) will be complied with during the construction phase.

The client's duty in relation to the health and safety file

17.—(1) The client shall ensure that the CDM co-ordinator is provided with all the health and safety information in the client's possession (or which is reasonably obtainable) relating to the project which is likely to be needed for inclusion in the health and safety file, including information specified in regulation 4(9)(c) of the Control of Asbestos Regulations 2006(a).

(2) Where a single health and safety file relates to more than one project, site or structure, or where it includes other related information, the client shall ensure that the information relating to each site or structure can be easily identified.

(3) The client shall take reasonable steps to ensure that after the construction phase the information in the health and safety file—

- (a) is kept available for inspection by any person who may need it to comply with the relevant statutory provisions; and
- (b) is revised as often as may be appropriate to incorporate any relevant new information.

(4) It shall be sufficient compliance with paragraph (3)(a) by a client who disposes of his entire interest in the structure if he delivers the health and safety file to the person who acquires his interest in it and ensures that he is aware of the nature and purpose of the file.

Additional duties of designers

18.—(1) Where a project is notifiable, no designer shall commence work (other than initial design work) in relation to the project unless a CDM co-ordinator has been appointed for the project.

(2) The designer shall take all reasonable steps to provide with his design sufficient information about aspects of the design of the structure or its construction or maintenance as will adequately assist the CDM co-ordinator to comply with his duties under these Regulations, including his duties in relation to the health and safety file.

Additional duties of contractors

19.—(1) Where a project is notifiable, no contractor shall carry out construction work in relation to the project unless—

(a) he has been provided with the names of the CDM co-ordinator and principal contractor;

(b) he has been given access to such part of the construction phase plan as is relevant to the work to be performed by him, containing sufficient detail in relation to such work; and

(c) notice of the project has been given to the Executive, or as the case may be the Office of Rail Regulation, under regulation 21.

(2) Every contractor shall—

(a) promptly provide the principal contractor with any information (including any relevant part of any risk assessment in his possession or control) which—

(i) might affect the health or safety of any person carrying out the construction work or of any person who may be affected by it,

(ii) might justify a review of the construction phase plan, or

(iii) has been identified for inclusion in the health and safety file in pursuance of regulation 22(1)(j);

(b) promptly identify any contractor whom he appoints or engages in his turn in connection with the project to the principal contractor;

(c) comply with—

(i) any directions of the principal contractor given to him under regulation 22(1)(e), and

(ii) any site rules;

(d) promptly provide the principal contractor with the information in relation to any death, injury, condition or dangerous occurrence which the contractor is required to notify or report under the Reporting of Injuries, Diseases and Dangerous Occurrences Regulations 1995(8).

(3) Every contractor shall—

(a) in complying with his duty under regulation 13(2) take all reasonable steps to ensure that the construction work is carried out in accordance with the construction phase plan;

(b) take appropriate action to ensure health and safety where it is not possible to comply with the construction phase plan in any particular case; and

(c) notify the principal contractor of any significant finding which requires the construction phase plan to be altered or added to.

General duties of CDM co-ordinators

20.—(1) The CDM co-ordinator shall—

(a) give suitable and sufficient advice and assistance to the client on undertaking the measures he needs to take to comply with these Regulations during the project (including, in particular, assisting the client in complying with regulations 9 and 16);

(b) ensure that suitable arrangements are made and implemented for the co-ordination of health and safety measures during planning and preparation for the construction phase, including facilitating—
   (i) co-operation and co-ordination between persons concerned in the project in pursuance of regulations 5 and 6, and
   (ii) the application of the general principles of prevention in pursuance of regulation 7; and

(c) liaise with the principal contractor regarding—
   (i) the contents of the health and safety file,
   (ii) the information which the principal contractor needs to prepare the construction phase plan, and
   (iii) any design development which may affect planning and management of the construction work.

(2) Without prejudice to paragraph (1) the CDM co-ordinator shall—

(a) take all reasonable steps to identify and collect the pre-construction information;

(b) promptly provide in a convenient form to—
   (i) every person designing the structure, and
   (ii) every contractor who has been or may be appointed by the client (including the principal contractor),

such of the pre-construction information in his possession as is relevant to each;

(c) take all reasonable steps to ensure that designers comply with their duties under regulations 11 and 18(2);

(d) take all reasonable steps to ensure co-operation between designers and the principal contractor during the construction phase in relation to any design or change to a design;

(e) prepare, where none exists, and otherwise review and update a record ("the health and safety file") containing information relating to the project which is likely to be needed during any subsequent construction work to ensure the health and safety of any person, including the information provided in pursuance of regulations 17(1), 18(2) and 22(1)(j); and

(f) at the end of the construction phase, pass the health and safety file to the client.

Notification of project by the CDM co-ordinator

21.—(1) The CDM co-ordinator shall as soon as is practicable after his appointment ensure that notice is given to the Executive containing such of the particulars specified in Schedule 1 as are available.

(2) Where any particulars specified in Schedule 1 have not been notified under paragraph (1) because a principal contractor has not yet been appointed, notice of such particulars shall be given to the Executive as soon as is practicable after the appointment of the principal contractor, and in any event before the start of the construction work.

(3) Any notice under paragraph (1) or (2) shall be signed by or on behalf of the client or, if sent by electronic means, shall otherwise show that he has approved it.

(4) Insofar as the project includes construction work of a description for which the Office of Rail Regulation is made the enforcing authority by regulation 3(1) of the Health and Safety (Enforcing Authority for Railways and Other Guided Transport Systems) Regulations 2006(9), paragraphs (1) and (2) shall have effect as if any reference to the Executive were a reference to the Office of Rail Regulation.

Duties of the principal contractor

22.—(1) The principal contractor for a project shall—

(a) plan, manage and monitor the construction phase in a way which ensures that, so far as is reasonably practicable, it is carried out without risks to health or safety, including facilitating—
  (i) co-operation and co-ordination between persons concerned in the project in pursuance of regulations 5 and 6, and
  (ii) the application of the general principles of prevention in pursuance of regulation 7;

(b) liaise with the CDM co-ordinator in performing his duties in regulation 20(2)(d) during the construction phase in relation to any design or change to a design;

(c) ensure that welfare facilities sufficient to comply with the requirements of Schedule 2 are provided throughout the construction phase;

(d) where necessary for health and safety, draw up rules which are appropriate to the construction site and the activities on it (referred to in these Regulations as "site rules");

(e) give reasonable directions to any contractor so far as is necessary to enable the principal contractor to comply with his duties under these Regulations;

(f) ensure that every contractor is informed of the minimum amount of time which will be allowed to him for planning and preparation before he begins construction work;

(g) where necessary, consult a contractor before finalising such part of the construction phase plan as is relevant to the work to be performed by him;

(h) ensure that every contractor is given, before he begins construction work and in sufficient time to enable him to prepare properly for that work, access to such part of the construction phase plan as is relevant to the work to be performed by him;

(i) ensure that every contractor is given, before he begins construction work and in sufficient time to enable him to prepare properly for that work, such further information as he needs—

   (i) to comply punctually with the duty under regulation 13(7), and

   (ii) to carry out the work to be performed by him without risk, so far as is reasonably practicable, to the health and safety of any person;

(j) identify to each contractor the information relating to the contractor's activity which is likely to be required by the CDM co-ordinator for inclusion in the health and safety file in pursuance of regulation 20(2)(e) and ensure that such information is promptly provided to the CDM co-ordinator;

(k) ensure that the particulars required to be in the notice given under regulation 21 are displayed in a readable condition in a position where they can be read by any worker engaged in the construction work; and

(l) take reasonable steps to prevent access by unauthorised persons to the construction site.

(2) The principal contractor shall take all reasonable steps to ensure that every worker carrying out the construction work is provided with—

(a) a suitable site induction;

(b) the information and training referred to in regulation 13(4) by a contractor on whom a duty is placed by that regulation; and

(c) any further information and training which he needs for the particular work to be carried out without undue risk to health or safety.

The principal contractor's duty in relation to the construction phase plan

23.—(1) The principal contractor shall—

  (a) before the start of the construction phase, prepare a construction phase plan which is sufficient to ensure that the construction phase is planned, managed and monitored in a way which enables the construction work to be started so far as is reasonably practicable without risk to health or safety, paying adequate regard to the information provided by the designer under regulations 11(6) and 18(2) and the pre-construction information provided under regulation 20(2)(b);

  (b) from time to time and as often as may be appropriate throughout the project update, review, revise and refine the construction phase plan so that it continues to be sufficient to ensure that the construction phase is planned, managed and monitored in a way which enables the construction work to be carried out so far as is reasonably practicable without risk to health or safety; and

  (c) arrange for the construction phase plan to be implemented in a way which will ensure so far as is reasonably practicable the health and safety of all persons carrying out the construction work and all persons who may be affected by the work.

(2) The principal contractor shall take all reasonable steps to ensure that the construction phase plan identifies the risks to health and safety arising from the construction work (including the risks specific to the particular type of construction work concerned) and includes suitable and sufficient measures to address such risks, including any site rules.

The principal contractor's duty in relation to co-operation and consultation with workers

24. The principal contractor shall—

  (a) make and maintain arrangements which will enable him and the workers engaged in the construction work to co-operate effectively in promoting and developing measures to ensure the health, safety and welfare of the workers and in checking the effectiveness of such measures;

  (b) consult those workers or their representatives in good time on matters connected with the project which may affect their health, safety or welfare, so far as they or their representatives are not so consulted on those matters by any employer of theirs;

  (c) ensure that such workers or their representatives can inspect and take copies of any information which the principal contractor has, or which these Regulations require to be provided to him, which relates to the planning and management of the project, or which otherwise may affect their health, safety or welfare at the site, except any information—

(i) the disclosure of which would be against the interests of national security,

(ii) which he could not disclose without contravening a prohibition imposed by or under an enactment,

(iii) relating specifically to an individual, unless he has consented to its being disclosed,

(iv) the disclosure of which would, for reasons other than its effect on health, safety or welfare at work, cause substantial injury to his undertaking or, where the information was supplied to him by some other person, to the undertaking of that other person, or

(v) obtained by him for the purpose of bringing, prosecuting or defending any legal proceedings.

Part 4 Duties relating to health and safety on construction sites

Application of Regulations 26 to 44

25.—(1) Every contractor carrying out construction work shall comply with the requirements of regulations 26 to 44 insofar as they affect him or any person carrying out construction work under his control or relate to matters within his control.

(2) Every person (other than a contractor carrying out construction work) who controls the way in which any construction work is carried out by a person at work shall comply with the requirements of regulations 26 to 44 insofar as they relate to matters which are within his control.

(3) Every person at work on construction work under the control of another person shall report to that person any defect which he is aware may endanger the health and safety of himself or another person.

(4) Paragraphs (1) and (2) shall not apply to regulation 33, which expressly says on whom the duties in that regulation are imposed.

Safe places of work

26.—(1) There shall, so far as is reasonably practicable, be suitable and sufficient safe access to and egress from every place of work and to and from every other place provided for the use of any person while at work, which access and egress shall be properly maintained.

(2) Every place of work shall, so far as is reasonably practicable, be made and kept safe for, and without risks to health to, any person at work there.

(3) Suitable and sufficient steps shall be taken to ensure, so far as is reasonably practicable, that no person uses access or egress, or gains access to any place, which does not comply with the requirements of paragraph (1) or (2) respectively.

(4) Every place of work shall, so far as is reasonably practicable, have sufficient working space and be so arranged that it is suitable for any person who is working or who is likely to work there, taking account of any necessary work equipment present.

Good order and site security

27.—(1) Every part of a construction site shall, so far as is reasonably practicable, be kept in good order and every part of a construction site which is used as a place of work shall be kept in a reasonable state of cleanliness.

(2) Where necessary in the interests of health and safety, a construction site shall, so far as is reasonably practicable and in accordance with the level of risk posed, either—

   (a) have its perimeter identified by suitable signs and be so arranged that its extent is readily identifiable; or
   (b) be fenced off,

   or both.

(3) No timber or other material with projecting nails (or similar sharp object) shall—

   (a) be used in any work; or
   (b) be allowed to remain in any place,

   if the nails (or similar sharp object) may be a source of danger to any person.

Stability of structures

28.—(1) All practicable steps shall be taken, where necessary to prevent danger to any person, to ensure that any new or existing structure or any part of such structure which may become unstable or in a temporary state of weakness or instability due to the carrying out of construction work does not collapse.

(2) Any buttress, temporary support or temporary structure must be of such design and so installed and maintained as to withstand any foreseeable

loads which may be imposed on it, and must only be used for the purposes for which it is so designed, installed and maintained.

(3) No part of a structure shall be so loaded as to render it unsafe to any person.

Demolition or dismantling

29.—(1) The demolition or dismantling of a structure, or part of a structure, shall be planned and carried out in such a manner as to prevent danger or, where it is not practicable to prevent it, to reduce danger to as low a level as is reasonably practicable.

(2) The arrangements for carrying out such demolition or dismantling shall be recorded in writing before the demolition or dismantling work begins.

Explosives

30.—(1) So far as is reasonably practicable, explosives shall be stored, transported and used safely and securely.

(2) Without prejudice to paragraph (1), an explosive charge shall be used or fired only if suitable and sufficient steps have been taken to ensure that no person is exposed to risk of injury from the explosion or from projected or flying material caused thereby.

Excavations

31.—(1) All practicable steps shall be taken, where necessary to prevent danger to any person, including, where necessary, the provision of supports or battering, to ensure that—

(a) any excavation or part of an excavation does not collapse;
(b) no material from a side or roof of, or adjacent to, any excavation is dislodged or falls; and
(c) no person is buried or trapped in an excavation by material which is dislodged or falls.

(2) Suitable and sufficient steps shall be taken to prevent any person, work equipment, or any accumulation of material from falling into any excavation

(3) Without prejudice to paragraphs (1) and (2), suitable and sufficient steps shall be taken, where necessary, to prevent any part of an excavation or ground adjacent to it from being overloaded by work equipment or material;

(4) Construction work shall not be carried out in an excavation where any supports or battering have been provided pursuant to paragraph (1) unless—

  (a) the excavation and any work equipment and materials which affect its safety, have been inspected by a competent person—
    (i) at the start of the shift in which the work is to be carried out,
    (ii) after any event likely to have affected the strength or stability of the excavation, and
    (iii) after any material unintentionally falls or is dislodged; and

  (b) the person who carried out the inspection is satisfied that the work can be carried out there safely.

(5) Where the person who carried out the inspection has under regulation 33(1)(a) informed the person on whose behalf the inspection was carried out of any matter about which he is not satisfied, work shall not be carried out in the excavation until the matters have been satisfactorily remedied.

Cofferdams and caissons

32.—(1) Every cofferdam or caisson shall be—

  (a) of suitable design and construction;
  (b) appropriately equipped so that workers can gain shelter or escape if water or materials enter it; and
  (c) properly maintained.

(2) A cofferdam or caisson shall be used to carry out construction work only if—

  (a) the cofferdam or caisson, and any work equipment and materials which affect its safety, have been inspected by a competent person—
    (i) at the start of the shift in which the work is to be carried out, and
    (ii) after any event likely to have affected the strength or stability of the cofferdam or caisson; and

  (b) the person who carried out the inspection is satisfied that the work can be safely carried out there.

(3) Where the person who carried out the inspection has under regulation 33(1)(a) informed the person on whose behalf the inspection was carried out of any matter about which he is not satisfied, work shall not be carried out in the cofferdam or caisson until the matters have been satisfactorily remedied.

Reports of inspections

33.—(1) Subject to paragraph (5), the person who carries out an inspection under regulation 31 or 32 shall, before the end of the shift within which the inspection is completed—

   (a) where he is not satisfied that the construction work can be carried out safely at the place inspected, inform the person for whom the inspection was carried out of any matters about which he is not satisfied; and

   (b) prepare a report which shall include the particulars set out in Schedule 3.

(2) A person who prepares a report under paragraph (1) shall, within 24 hours of completing the inspection to which the report relates, provide the report or a copy of it to the person on whose behalf the inspection was carried out.

(3) Where the person owing a duty under paragraph (1) or (2) is an employee or works under the control of another, his employer or, as the case may be, the person under whose control he works shall ensure that he performs the duty.

(4) The person on whose behalf the inspection was carried out shall—

   (a) keep the report or a copy of it available for inspection by an inspector appointed under section 19 of the Health and Safety at Work etc. Act 1974(10)—

      (i) at the site of the place of work in respect of which the inspection was carried out until that work is completed, and

      (ii) after that for 3 months,

   and send to the inspector such extracts from or copies of it as the inspector may from time to time require.

(5) Nothing in this regulation shall require as regards an inspection carried out on a place of work for the purposes of regulations 31(4)(a)(i) and 32(2)(a) (i), the preparation of more than one report within a period of 7 days

Energy distribution installations

34.—(1) Where necessary to prevent danger, energy distribution installations shall be suitably located, checked and clearly indicated.

(2) Where there is a risk from electric power cables—

   (a) they shall be directed away from the area of risk; or

   (b) the power shall be isolated and, where necessary, earthed; or

(c) if it is not reasonably practicable to comply with paragraph (a) or (b), suitable warning notices and—
    (i) barriers suitable for excluding work equipment which is not needed, or
    (ii) where vehicles need to pass beneath the cables, suspended protections, or
    (iii) in either case, measures providing an equivalent level of safety, shall be provided or (in the case of measures) taken.

(3) No construction work which is liable to create a risk to health or safety from an underground service, or from damage to or disturbance of it, shall be carried out unless suitable and sufficient steps (including any steps required by this regulation) have been taken to prevent such risk, so far as is reasonably practicable.

Prevention of drowning

35.—(1) Where in the course of construction work any person is liable to fall into water or other liquid with a risk of drowning, suitable and sufficient steps shall be taken—

(a) to prevent, so far as is reasonably practicable, such person from so falling;
(b) to minimise the risk of drowning in the event of such a fall; and
(c) to ensure that suitable rescue equipment is provided, maintained and, when necessary, used so that such person may be promptly rescued in the event of such a fall.

(2) Suitable and sufficient steps shall be taken to ensure the safe transport of any person conveyed by water to or from any place of work.
(3) Any vessel used to convey any person by water to or from a place of work shall not be overcrowded or overloaded.

Traffic routes

36.—(1) Every construction site shall be organised in such a way that, so far as is reasonably practicable, pedestrians and vehicles can move safely and without risks to health.

(2) Traffic routes shall be suitable for the persons or vehicles using them, sufficient in number, in suitable positions and of sufficient size.
(3) A traffic route shall not satisfy sub-paragraph (2) unless suitable and sufficient steps are taken to ensure that—

(a) pedestrians or vehicles may use it without causing danger to the health or safety of persons near it;

(b) any door or gate for pedestrians which leads onto a traffic route is sufficiently separated from that traffic route to enable pedestrians to see any approaching vehicle or plant from a place of safety;

(c) there is sufficient separation between vehicles and pedestrians to ensure safety or, where this is not reasonably practicable—

(i) there are provided other means for the protection of pedestrians, and

(ii) there are effective arrangements for warning any person liable to be crushed or trapped by any vehicle of its approach;

(d) any loading bay has at least one exit point for the exclusive use of pedestrians; and

(e) where it is unsafe for pedestrians to use a gate intended primarily for vehicles, one or more doors for pedestrians is provided in the immediate vicinity of the gate, is clearly marked and is kept free from obstruction.

(4) Every traffic route shall be—

(a) indicated by suitable signs where necessary for reasons of health or safety;

(b) regularly checked; and

(c) properly maintained.

(5) No vehicle shall be driven on a traffic route unless, so far as is reasonably practicable, that traffic route is free from obstruction and permits sufficient clearance.

Vehicles

37.—(1) Suitable and sufficient steps shall be taken to prevent or control the unintended movement of any vehicle.

(2) Suitable and sufficient steps shall be taken to ensure that, where any person may be endangered by the movement of any vehicle, the person having effective control of the vehicle shall give warning to any person who is liable to be at risk from the movement of the vehicle.

(3) Any vehicle being used for the purposes of construction work shall when being driven, operated or towed—

(a) be driven, operated or towed in such a manner as is safe in the circumstances; and

(b) be loaded in such a way that it can be driven, operated or towed safely.

(4) No person shall ride or be required or permitted to ride on any vehicle being used for the purposes of construction work otherwise than in a safe place thereon provided for that purpose.

(5) No person shall remain or be required or permitted to remain on any vehicle during the loading or unloading of any loose material unless a safe place of work is provided and maintained for such person.

(6) Suitable and sufficient measures shall be taken so as to prevent any vehicle from falling into any excavation or pit, or into water, or overrunning the edge of any embankment or earthwork.

Prevention of risk from fire etc.

38. Suitable and sufficient steps shall be taken to prevent, so far as is reasonably practicable, the risk of injury to any person during the carrying out of construction work arising from—

(a) fire or explosion;
(b) flooding; or
(c) any substance liable to cause asphyxiation.

Emergency procedures

39.—(1) Where necessary in the interests of the health and safety of any person on a construction site, there shall be prepared and, where necessary, implemented suitable and sufficient arrangements for dealing with any foreseeable emergency, which arrangements shall include procedures for any necessary evacuation of the site or any part thereof.

(2) In making arrangements under paragraph (1), account shall be taken of—

(a) the type of work for which the construction site is being used;
(b) the characteristics and size of the construction site and the number and location of places of work on that site;
(c) the work equipment being used;
(d) the number of persons likely to be present on the site at any one time; and
(e) the physical and chemical properties of any substances or materials on or likely to be on the site.

(3) Where arrangements are prepared pursuant to paragraph (1), suitable and sufficient steps shall be taken to ensure that—

(a) every person to whom the arrangements extend is familiar with those arrangements; and
(b) the arrangements are tested by being put into effect at suitable intervals.

Emergency routes and exits

40.—(1) Where necessary in the interests of the health and safety of any person on a construction site, a sufficient number of suitable emergency routes and exits shall be provided to enable any person to reach a place of safety quickly in the event of danger.

(2) An emergency route or exit provided pursuant to paragraph (1) shall lead as directly as possible to an identified safe area.

(3) Any emergency route or exit provided in accordance with paragraph (1), and any traffic route giving access thereto, shall be kept clear and free from obstruction and, where necessary, provided with emergency lighting so that such emergency route or exit may be used at any time.

(4) In making provision under paragraph (1), account shall be taken of the matters in regulation 39(2).

(5) All emergency routes or exits shall be indicated by suitable signs.

Fire detection and fire-fighting

41.—(1) Where necessary in the interests of the health and safety of any person at work on a construction site there shall be provided suitable and sufficient—

(a) fire-fighting equipment; and
(b) fire detection and alarm systems,

which shall be suitably located.

(2) In making provision under paragraph (1), account shall be taken of the matters in regulation 39(2).

(3) Any fire-fighting equipment and any fire detection and alarm system provided under paragraph (1) shall be examined and tested at suitable intervals and properly maintained.

(4) Any fire-fighting equipment which is not designed to come into use automatically shall be easily accessible.

(5) Every person at work on a construction site shall, so far as is reasonably practicable, be instructed in the correct use of any fire-fighting equipment which it may be necessary for him to use.

(6) Where a work activity may give rise to a particular risk of fire, a person shall not carry out such work unless he is suitably instructed.

(7) Fire-fighting equipment shall be indicated by suitable signs.

Fresh air

42.—(1) Suitable and sufficient steps shall be taken to ensure, so far as is reasonably practicable, that every place of work or approach thereto has sufficient fresh or purified air to ensure that the place or approach is safe and without risks to health.

(2) Any plant used for the purpose of complying with paragraph (1) shall, where necessary for reasons of health or safety, include an effective device to give visible or audible warning of any failure of the plant.

Temperature and weather protection

43.—(1) Suitable and sufficient steps shall be taken to ensure, so far as is reasonably practicable, that during working hours the temperature at any place of work indoors is reasonable having regard to the purpose for which that place is used.

(2) Every place of work outdoors shall, where necessary to ensure the health and safety of persons at work there, be so arranged that, so far as is reasonably practicable and having regard to the purpose for which that place is used and any protective clothing or work equipment provided for the use of any person at work there, it provides protection from adverse weather.

Lighting

44.—(1) Every place of work and approach thereto and every traffic route shall be provided with suitable and sufficient lighting, which shall be, so far as is reasonably practicable, by natural light.

(2) The colour of any artificial lighting provided shall not adversely affect or change the perception of any sign or signal provided for the purposes of health and safety.
(3) Without prejudice to paragraph (1), suitable and sufficient secondary lighting shall be provided in any place where there would be a risk to the health or safety of any person in the event of failure of primary artificial lighting.

Part 5 General

Civil liability

45. Breach of a duty imposed by the preceding provisions of these Regulations, other than those imposed by regulations 9(1)(b), 13(6) and (7), 16, 22(1) (c) and (l), 25(1), (2) and (4), 26 to 44 and Schedule 2, shall not confer a right of action in any civil proceedings insofar as that duty applies for the protection of a person who is not an employee of the person on whom the duty is placed.

Enforcement in respect of fire

46.—(1) Subject to paragraphs (2) and (3)—

    (a) in England and Wales the enforcing authority within the meaning of article 25 of the Regulatory Reform (Fire Safety) Order 2005(11); or

    (b) in Scotland the enforcing authority within the meaning of section 61 of the Fire (Scotland) Act 2005(12),

shall be the enforcing authority in respect of a construction site which is contained within, or forms part of, premises which are occupied by persons other than those carrying out the construction work or any activity arising from such work as regards regulations 39 and 40, in so far as those regulations relate to fire, and regulation 41.

(2) In England and Wales paragraph (1) only applies in respect of premises to which the Regulatory Reform (Fire Safety) Order 2005 applies.

(3) In Scotland paragraph (1) only applies in respect of premises to which Part 3 of the Fire (Scotland) Act 2005 applies(13).

Transitional provisions

47.—(1) These Regulations shall apply in relation to a project which began before their coming into force, with the following modifications.

(2) Subject to paragraph (3), where the time specified in paragraph (1) or (2) of regulation 14 for the appointment of the CDM co-ordinator or the principal contractor occurred before the coming into force of these Regulations, the client shall appoint the CDM co-ordinator or, as the case may be, the principal contractor, as soon as is practicable.

(3) Where a client appoints any planning supervisor or principal contractor already appointed under regulation 6 of the Construction (Design and Management) Regulations 1994(14) (referred to in this regulation as "the 1994 Regulations") as the CDM co-ordinator or the principal contractor respectively pursuant to paragraph (2), regulation 4(1) shall have effect so that the client shall within twelve months of the coming into force of these Regulations take reasonable steps to ensure that any CDM co-ordinator or principal contractor so appointed is competent within the meaning of regulation 4(2).

(4) Any planning supervisor or principal contractor appointed under regulation 6 of the 1994 Regulations shall, in the absence of an express appointment by the client, be treated for the purposes of paragraph (2) as having been appointed as the CDM co-ordinator, or the principal contractor, respectively.

(5) Any person treated as having been appointed as the CDM co-ordinator or the principal contractor pursuant to paragraph (4) shall within twelve months of the coming into force of these Regulations take such steps as are necessary to ensure that he is competent within the meaning of regulation 4(2).

(6) Any agent appointed by a client under regulation 4 of the 1994 Regulations before the coming into force of these Regulations may, if requested by the client and if he himself consents, continue to act as the agent of that client and shall be subject to such requirements and prohibitions as are placed by these Regulations on that client, unless or until such time as such appointment is revoked by that client, or the project comes to an end, or five years elapse from the coming into force of these Regulations, whichever arises first.

(7) Where notice has been given under regulation 7 of the 1994 Regulations, the references in regulations 19(1)(c) and 22(1)(k) to notice under regulation 21 shall be construed as being to notice under that regulation.

Revocations and amendments

48.—(1) The revocations listed in Schedule 4 shall have effect.

(2) The amendments listed in Schedule 5 shall have effect.

Signed by authority of the Secretary of State for Work and Pensions.

Bill McKenzie

Parliamentary Under Secretary of State,

Department for Work and Pensions

7th February 2007

Regulation 21(1), (2) and (4)

Schedule 1 Particulars to be notified to the Executive (or Office of Rail Regulation)

1. Date of forwarding.
2. Exact address of the construction site.
3. The name of the local authority where the site is located.
4. A brief description of the project and the construction work which it includes.
5. Contact details of the client (name, address, telephone number and any e-mail address).
6. Contact details of the CDM co-ordinator (name, address, telephone number and any e-mail address).
7. Contact details of the principal contractor (name, address, telephone number and any e-mail address).
8. Date planned for the start of the construction phase.
9. The time allowed by the client to the principal contractor referred to in regulation 15(b) for planning and preparation for construction work.
10. Planned duration of the construction phase.
11. Estimated maximum number of people at work on the construction site.
12. Planned number of contractors on the construction site.
13. Name and address of any contractor already appointed.
14. Name and address of any designer already engaged.
15. A declaration signed by or on behalf of the client that he is aware of his duties under these Regulations.

Regulations 9(1)(b), 13(7) and 22(1)(c)

Schedule 2 Welfare facilities

Sanitary conveniences

1. Suitable and sufficient sanitary conveniences shall be provided or made available at readily accessible places. So far as is reasonably practicable, rooms containing sanitary conveniences shall be adequately ventilated and lit.
2. So far as is reasonably practicable, sanitary conveniences and the rooms containing them shall be kept in a clean and orderly condition.
3. Separate rooms containing sanitary conveniences shall be provided for men and women, except where and so far as each convenience is in a separate room, the door of which is capable of being secured from the inside.

Washing facilities

4. Suitable and sufficient washing facilities, including showers if required by the nature of the work or for health reasons, shall so far as is reasonably practicable be provided or made available at readily accessible places.

5. Washing facilities shall be provided—

   (a) in the immediate vicinity of every sanitary convenience, whether or not provided elsewhere; and

   (b) in the vicinity of any changing rooms required by paragraph 14 whether or not provided elsewhere.

6. Washing facilities shall include—

   (a) a supply of clean hot and cold, or warm, water (which shall be running water so far as is reasonably practicable);

   (b) soap or other suitable means of cleaning; and

   (c) towels or other suitable means of drying.

7. Rooms containing washing facilities shall be sufficiently ventilated and lit.

8. Washing facilities and the rooms containing them shall be kept in a clean and orderly condition.

9. Subject to paragraph 10 below, separate washing facilities shall be provided for men and women, except where and so far as they are provided in a room the door of which is capable of being secured from inside and the facilities in each such room are intended to be used by only one person at a time.

10. Paragraph 9 above shall not apply to facilities which are provided for washing hands, forearms and face only.

Drinking water

11. An adequate supply of wholesome drinking water shall be provided or made available at readily accessible and suitable places.

12. Every supply of drinking water shall be conspicuously marked by an appropriate sign where necessary for reasons of health and safety.

13. Where a supply of drinking water is provided, there shall also be provided a sufficient number of suitable cups or other drinking vessels unless the supply of drinking water is in a jet from which persons can drink easily.

Changing rooms and lockers

14.—(1) Suitable and sufficient changing rooms shall be provided or made available at readily accessible places if—

   (a) a worker has to wear special clothing for the purposes of his work; and

(b) he cannot, for reasons of health or propriety, be expected to change elsewhere, being separate rooms for, or separate use of rooms by, men and women where necessary for reasons of propriety.

(2) Changing rooms shall—

(a) be provided with seating; and
(b) include, where necessary, facilities to enable a person to dry any such special clothing and his own clothing and personal effects.

(3) Suitable and sufficient facilities shall, where necessary, be provided or made available at readily accessible places to enable persons to lock away—

(a) any such special clothing which is not taken home;
(b) their own clothing which is not worn during working hours; and
(c) their personal effects.

Facilities for rest

15.—(1) Suitable and sufficient rest rooms or rest areas shall be provided or made available at readily accessible places.

(2) Rest rooms and rest areas shall—

(a) include suitable arrangements to protect non-smokers from discomfort caused by tobacco smoke;
(b) be equipped with an adequate number of tables and adequate seating with backs for the number of persons at work likely to use them at any one time;
(c) where necessary, include suitable facilities for any person at work who is a pregnant woman or nursing mother to rest lying down;
(d) include suitable arrangements to ensure that meals can be prepared and eaten;
(e) include the means for boiling water; and
(f) be maintained at an appropriate temperature.

Regulation 33(1)(b)

Schedule 3 Particulars to be included in a report of inspection

1. Name and address of the person on whose behalf the inspection was carried out.
2. Location of the place of work inspected.
3. Description of the place of work or part of that place inspected (including any work equipment and materials).
4. Date and time of the inspection.

5. Details of any matter identified that could give rise to a risk to the health or safety of any person.
6. Details of any action taken as a result of any matter identified in paragraph 5 above.
7. Details of any further action considered necessary.
8. Name and position of the person making the report.

Regulation 48(1)

Schedule 4 Revocation of instruments

Description of instrument	Reference	Extent of revocation
The Construction (General Provisions) Regulations 1961	S.I. 1961/1580	The whole Regulations
The Health and Safety Information for Employees Regulations 1989	S.I. 1989/682	Regulation 8(3) and part III of the Schedule
The Construction (Design and Management) Regulations 1994	S.I. 1994/3140	The whole Regulations
The Construction (Health, Safety and Welfare) Regulations 1996	S.I. 1996/1592	The whole Regulations
The Health and Safety (Enforcing Authority) Regulations 1998	S.I. 1998/494	In Schedule 3, the entries relating to the Construction (Design and Management) Regulations 1994 and to the Construction (Health, Safety and Welfare) Regulations 1996
The Provision and Use of Work Equipment Regulations 1998	S.I. 1998/2306	In Schedule 4, the entry relating to the Construction (Health, Safety and Welfare) Regulations 1996
The Lifting Operations and Lifting Equipment Regulations 1998	S.I. 1998/2307	In Schedule 2, the entry relating to the Construction (Health, Safety and Welfare) Regulations 1996
The Management of Health and Safety at Work Regulations 1999	S.I. 1999/3242	Regulation 27

continued overleaf

Description of instrument	Reference	Extent of revocation
		In Schedule 2, the entry relating to the Construction (Design and Management) Regulations 1994
The Construction (Design and Management)(Amendment) Regulations 2000	S.I. 2000/2380	The whole Regulations
The Fire and Rescue Services Act 2004 (Consequential Amendments)(England) Order 2004	S.I. 2004/3168	Article 37
The Work at Height Regulations 2005	S.I. 2005/735	In Schedule 8, the entry relating to the Construction (Health, Safety and Welfare) Regulations 1996
The Regulatory Reform (Fire Safety) Order 2005	S.I. 2005/1541	Schedule 3 paragraph 3
The Fire and Rescue Services Act 2004 (Consequential Amendments)(Wales) Order 2005	S.I. 2005/2929	Article 37
The Fire (Scotland) Act 2005 (Consequential Modifications and Amendments)(No.2) Order 2005	S.S.I. 2005/344	Schedule 1 Part 1 paragraph 18
The Fire (Scotland) Act 2005 (Consequential Modifications and Savings)(No.2) Order 2006	S.S.I. 2006/457	Schedule 1 paragraph 4
The Health and Safety (Enforcing Authority for Railways and Other Guided Transport Systems) Regulations 2006	S.I. 2006/557	

Schedule 5 Amendments

Description of instrument	Reference	Extent of amendment
The Factories Act 1961	1961 c.34, as amended by S.I. 1996/1592	In section 176(1) in the definitions "building operation" and "work of engineering construction" for "1994" substitute "2007"
The Fire (Scotland) Act 2005	2005 asp 5, as amended by S.I. 2005/2060	For the words in section 61(9)(za)(iv) substitute "which are a workplace which is, or is on, a construction site (as defined in regulation 2(1) of the Construction (Design and Management) Regulations 2007) and to which those Regulations apply (other than a construction site to which regulation 46(1) of those Regulations applies)"
The Construction (Head Protection) Regulations 1989	S.I. 1989/2209	For the words in regulation 2(1) substitute "Subject to paragraph (2) of this regulation, these Regulations shall apply to construction work within the meaning of regulation 2(1) of the Construction (Design and Management) Regulations 2007"
The Workplace (Health Safety and Welfare) Regulations 1992	S.I. 1992/3004, as amended by S.I. 1996/1592	For the words in regulation 3(1)(b) substitute "a workplace which is a construction site within the meaning of the Construction (Design and Management) Regulations 2007, and in which the only activity being undertaken is construction work within the meaning of those regulations, save that— (i) regulations 18 and 25A apply to such a workplace; and (ii) regulations 7(1A), 12, 14, 15, 16, 18, 19 and 26(1) apply to such a workplace which is indoors"
The Work in Compressed Air Regulations 1996	S.I. 1996/1656	In regulation 2(1) for the words ""the 1996 Regulations" means the Construction (Health, Safety and Welfare) Regulations 1996" substitute ""the 2007 Regulations" means the Construction (Design and Management) Regulations 2007" In regulation 3(1) for "1994" substitute "2007" and for the words "is not excluded by regulation 3(2)" substitute "is carried out in the course of a project which is notifiable within the meaning of regulation 2(3)"

Description of instrument	Reference	Extent of amendment
		In regulation 5(3) for "1994" substitute "2007"
		In regulation 13(2)(a) for the words "19, 20 and 25(3) of the 1996 Regulations" substitute "39, 40 and 44(3) of the 2007 Regulations"
		In regulation 13(2)(d) for the words "20(1) of the 1996 Regulations" substitute "39(1) of the 2007 Regulations"
		In regulation 14(1) for the words "21 of the 1996 Regulations" substitute "41 of the 2007 Regulations"
		In regulation 18(a) for the words "regulation 22 of the 1996 Regulations" substitute "Schedule 2 of the 2007 Regulations"
The Railway Safety (Miscellaneous Provisions) Regulations 1997	S.I. 1997/553	In regulation 2(1) in the definition "construction work" for "1994" substitute "2007"
The Health and Safety (Enforcing Authority) Regulations 1998	S.I. 1998/494	In regulation 2(1) in the definitions "construction work" and "contractor" for "1994" substitute "2007"
		In Schedule 2 for the words in paragraph 4(a)(i) substitute "the project which includes the work is notifiable within the meaning of regulation 2(3) of the Construction (Design and Management) Regulations 2007; or"
The Provision and Use of Work Equipment Regulations 1998	S.I. 1998/2306	In regulation 6(5)(e) for the words "regulation 29 of the Construction (Health, Safety and Welfare) Regulations 1996" substitute "regulations 31(4) or 32(2) of the Construction (Design and Management) Regulations 2007"
The Gas Safety (Installation and Use) Regulations 1998	S.I. 1998/2451	In regulation 2(4)(d) for "1994" substitute "2007"

continued overleaf

Description of instrument	Reference	Extent of amendment
The Work at Height Regulations 2005	S.I. 2005/735	In regulation 2(1) in the definition "construction work" for the words "the Construction (Health, Safety and Welfare) Regulations 1996" substitute "the Construction (Design and Management) Regulations 2007"
The Regulatory Reform (Fire Safety) Order 2005	S.I. 2005/1541	In article 25(b)(iv) for the words "the Construction (Health, Safety and Welfare) Regulations 1996" substitute "the Construction (Design and Management) Regulations 2007" and for "33" substitute "46"
The Health and Safety (Enforcing Authority for Railways and Other Guided Transport Systems) Regulations 2006	S.I. 2006/557	In regulation 2 in the definition "construction work" for "1994" substitute "2007"
		For the words in regulation 5(2)(a)(i) substitute "the project which includes that work is notifiable within the meaning of regulation 2(3) of the Construction (Design and Management) Regulations 2007; and"

Explanatory note

(*This note is not part of the Regulations*)

1. These Regulations revoke and replace the Construction (Design and Management) Regulations 1994 (S.I. 1994/3140) (Parts 2 and 3) and revoke and re-enact, with modifications, the Construction (Health, Safety and Welfare) Regulations 1996 (S.I. 1996/1592) (Part 4). They implement in Great Britain the requirements of Directive 92/57/EEC (OJ No L245, 26.8.92, p.6) ("the Directive") on the implementation of minimum safety and health requirements at temporary or mobile construction sites (eighth individual Directive within the meaning of Article 16(1) of Directive 89/391/EEC), except certain requirements which are implemented in the Work at Height Regulations 2005 (S.I. 2005/735). These Regulations do not apply the client's duties in the Directive to persons who act otherwise than in the course or furtherance of a trade, business, or other undertaking (regulation 2(1)). They apply the client's duties to make appointments and to ensure that a safety and health plan is drawn up only to projects that meet the threshold for notification to the Health and Safety Executive (or to the Office of Rail Regulation (regulation 21(4)).

2. Parts 2 and 3 set out duties in respect of the planning, management and monitoring of health, safety and welfare in construction projects and of the co-ordination of the performance of these duties by dutyholders. Duties applicable to all projects, including duties of clients, designers and contractors, are set out in Part 2. These include a duty on every person working under the control of another to report anything that he is aware is likely to endanger health or safety (regulation 5(2)).

3. Part 3 imposes additional duties on clients, designers and contractors (regulations 14 to 19) where the project is notifiable, defined as likely to involve more than 30 days or 500 person days of construction work (regulation 2(3)). These include the duty of the client to appoint a CDM co-ordinator and a principal contractor (regulation 14), whose particular duties are then set out (regulations 20 to 24).

4. The changes which Parts 2 and 3 make in comparison with the Construction (Design and Management) Regulations 1994 include the following—

   (a) All dutyholders under the Regulations are to co-operate with any other person at work on the same or any adjoining site in enabling one another to perform their duties (regulation 5).

   (b) All dutyholders under the Regulations are to co-ordinate their activities to ensure so far as is reasonably practicable the health and safety of persons carrying out or affected by the construction work (regulation 6).

   (c) All dutyholders under the Regulations are to take account of the general principles of prevention in Schedule 1 to the Management of Health and Safety at Work Regulations 1999 (S.I. 1999/3242) in the performance of their duties and in the carrying out of the construction work (regulation 7).

(d) The client is under a duty to take reasonable steps to ensure that arrangements for managing the project that are suitable to ensure that construction work can be carried out so far as is reasonably practicable without risk to health and safety are made and maintained by dutyholders (regulation 9).

(e) The threshold for notification of a construction project is now also the point at which duties including the making of appointments by the client and the duties of the persons so appointed arise (regulations 14 to 24).

(f) The former appointment of a planning supervisor is now replaced by that of the CDM co-ordinator with enhanced duties, in particular in relation to assisting the client and to the co-ordination of health and safety measures (regulations 20 and 21).

(g) The former duty of the planning supervisor to prepare a health and safety plan has been replaced by that of the principal contractor to prepare a construction phase plan (regulation 23).

5. Part 4 sets out duties applicable to all contractors or to others controlling the way in which construction work is carried out (regulation 25(1) and (2)) in respect of measures to be taken to ensure specified aspects of health and safety and to prevent danger from a number of specified hazards.

6. Civil liability is now restricted under these Regulations only in respect of the Part 2 and 3 duties, for which there is civil liability only to employees, except in respect of the duties concerning welfare facilities and to prevent access by any unauthorised person, and of the client's duty concerning the construction phase plan, for which liability is unrestricted (regulation 45).

7. A copy of the regulatory impact assessment prepared in respect of these Regulations can be obtained from the Health and Safety Executive, Economic Advisers Unit, Rose Court, 2 Southwark Bridge, London SE1 9HS. A copy of the transposition note in relation to implementation of the Directive can be obtained from the Health and Safety Executive, International Branch at the same address. Copies of both these documents have been placed in the Library of each House of Parliament.

Appendix 2
The Work at Height Regulations 2005

Statutory instruments

2005 No. 735

Health and Safety

The Work at Height Regulations 2005

Made	*16th March 2005*
Laid before Parliament	*16th March 2005*
Coming into force	*6th April 2005*

Arrangement of Regulations

The Secretary of State, in the exercise of the powers conferred on him by sections 15(1), (2), (3)(a), (5)(b), (6)(a) and 82(3)(a) of, and paragraphs 1(1), (2) and (3), 9, 11, 14, 15(1) and 16 of Schedule 3 to, the Health and Safety at Work etc. Act 1974[1] ("the 1974 Act") and for the purpose of giving effect without modifications to proposals submitted to him by the Health and Safety Commission under section 11(2)(d) of the 1974 Act, after the carrying out by the said Commission of consultations in accordance with section 50(3) of that Act, hereby makes the following Regulations:

Citation and commencement

1. These Regulations may be cited as the Work at Height Regulations 2005 and shall come into force on 6th April 2005.

Interpretation

2.—(1) In these Regulations, unless the context otherwise requires—

"the 1974 Act" means the Health and Safety at Work etc. Act 1974;

"access" and "egress" include ascent and descent;

"construction work" has the meaning assigned to it by regulation 2(1) of the Construction (Health, Safety and Welfare) Regulations 1996[2];

"fragile surface" means a surface which would be liable to fail if any reasonably foreseeable loading were to be applied to it;

"ladder" includes a fixed ladder and a stepladder;

"line" includes rope, chain or webbing;

"the Management Regulations" means the Management of Health and Safety at Work Regulations 1999[3];

"personal fall protection system" means—

(a) a fall prevention, work restraint, work positioning, fall arrest or rescue system, other than a system in which the only safeguards are collective safeguards; or
(b) rope access and positioning techniques;

"suitable" means suitable in any respect which it is reasonably foreseeable will affect the safety of any person;

"work at height" means—

(a) work in any place, including a place at or below ground level;
(b) obtaining access to or egress from such place while at work, except by a staircase in a permanent workplace,

where, if measures required by these Regulations were not taken, a person could fall a distance liable to cause personal injury;

"work equipment" means any machinery, appliance, apparatus, tool or installation for use at work (whether exclusively or not) and includes anything to which regulation 8 and Schedules 2 to 6 apply;
"working platform"—

(a) means any platform used as a place of work or as a means of access to or egress from a place of work;
(b) includes any scaffold, suspended scaffold, cradle, mobile platform, trestle, gangway, gantry and stairway which is so used.

(2) Any reference in these Regulations to the keeping of a report or copy of a report or plan shall include reference to its being kept in a form—

(a) in which it is capable of being reproduced as a printed copy when required;
(b) which is secure from loss or unauthorised interference.

Application

3.—(1) These Regulations shall apply—

(a) in Great Britain; and
(b) outside Great Britain as sections 1 to 59 and 80 to 82 of the 1974 Act apply by virtue of the Health and Safety at Work etc. Act 1974 (Application outside Great Britain) Order 2001[4].

(2) The requirements imposed by these Regulations on an employer shall apply in relation to work—

(a) by an employee of his; or
(b) by any other person under his control, to the extent of his control.

(3) The requirements imposed by these Regulations on an employer shall also apply to—

(a) a self-employed person, in relation to work—
   (i) by him; or
   (ii) by a person under his control, to the extent of his control; and

(b) to any person other than a self-employed person, in relation to work by a person under his control, to the extent of his control.

(4) Regulations 4 to 16 of these Regulations shall not apply to or in relation to—

(a) the master and crew of a ship, or to the employer of such persons, in respect of the normal ship-board activities of a ship's crew which—
   (i) are carried out solely by the crew under the direction of the master; and

(ii) are not liable to expose persons at work other than the master and crew to a risk to their safety;

(b) a place specified in regulation 7(6) of the Docks Regulations 1988[5] where persons are engaged in dock operations;

(c) a place specified in regulation 5(3) of the Loading and Unloading of Fishing Vessels Regulations 1988[6] where persons are engaged in fish loading processes; or

(d) the provision of instruction or leadership to one or more persons in connection with their engagement in caving or climbing by way of sport, recreation, team building or similar activities.

(5) Regulation 11 of these Regulations shall not apply to an installation while regulation 12 of the Offshore Installations and Wells (Design and Construction, etc) Regulations 1996[7] apply to it.

(6) In this regulation—

(a) "caving" includes the exploration of parts of mines which are no longer worked;

(b) "climbing" includes traversing, abseiling or scrambling over natural terrain or man-made structures;

(c) "ship" includes every description of vessel used in navigation, other than a ship which forms part of Her Majesty's Navy.

Organisation and planning

4.—(1) Every employer shall ensure that work at height is—

(a) properly planned;

(b) appropriately supervised; and

(c) carried out in a manner which is so far as is reasonably practicable safe,

and that its planning includes the selection of work equipment in accordance with regulation 7.

(2) Reference in paragraph (1) to planning of work includes planning for emergencies and rescue.

(3) Every employer shall ensure that work at height is carried out only when the weather conditions do not jeopardise the health or safety of persons involved in the work.

(4) Paragraph (3) shall not apply where members of the police, fire, ambulance or other emergency services are acting in an emergency.

Competence

5. Every employer shall ensure that no person engages in any activity, including organisation, planning and supervision, in relation to work at height or work equipment for use in such work unless he is competent to do so or, if being trained, is being supervised by a competent person.

Avoidance of risks from work at height

6.—(1) In identifying the measures required by this regulation, every employer shall take account of a risk assessment under regulation 3 of the Management Regulations.

(2) Every employer shall ensure that work is not carried out at height where it is reasonably practicable to carry out the work safely otherwise than at height.

(3) Where work is carried out at height, every employer shall take suitable and sufficient measures to prevent, so far as is reasonably practicable, any person falling a distance liable to cause personal injury.

(4) The measures required by paragraph (3) shall include—

   (a) his ensuring that the work is carried out—
      (i) from an existing place of work; or
      (ii) (in the case of obtaining access or egress) using an existing means,

   which complies with Schedule 1, where it is reasonably practicable to carry it out safely and under appropriate ergonomic conditions; and

   (b) where it is not reasonably practicable for the work to be carried out in accordance with sub-paragraph (a), his providing sufficient work equipment for preventing, so far as is reasonably practicable, a fall occurring.

(5) Where the measures taken under paragraph (4) do not eliminate the risk of a fall occurring, every employer shall—

   (a) so far as is reasonably practicable, provide sufficient work equipment to minimise—
      (i) the distance and consequences; or
      (ii) where it is not reasonably practicable to minimise the distance, the consequences, of a fall; and

   (b) without prejudice to the generality of paragraph (3), provide such additional training and instruction or take other additional suitable and sufficient measures to prevent, so far as is reasonably practicable, any person falling a distance liable to cause personal injury.

Selection of work equipment for work at height

7.—(1) Every employer, in selecting work equipment for use in work at height, shall—

(a) give collective protection measures priority over personal protection measures; and

(b) take account of—

    (i) the working conditions and the risks to the safety of persons at the place where the work equipment is to be used;

    (ii) in the case of work equipment for access and egress, the distance to be negotiated;

    (iii) the distance and consequences of a potential fall;

    (iv) the duration and frequency of use;

    (v) the need for easy and timely evacuation and rescue in an emergency;

    (vi) any additional risk posed by the use, installation or removal of that work equipment or by evacuation and rescue from it; and

    (vii) the other provisions of these Regulations.

(2) An employer shall select work equipment for work at height which—

(a) has characteristics including dimensions which—

    (i) are appropriate to the nature of the work to be performed and the foreseeable loadings; and

    (ii) allow passage without risk; and

(b) is in other respects the most suitable work equipment, having regard in particular to the purposes specified in regulation 6.

Requirements for particular work equipment

8. Every employer shall ensure that, in the case of—

(a) a guard-rail, toe-board, barrier or similar collective means of protection, Schedule 2 is complied with;

(b) a working platform—

    (i) Part 1 of Schedule 3 is complied with; and

    (ii) where scaffolding is provided, Part 2 of Schedule 3 is also complied with;

(c) a net, airbag or other collective safeguard for arresting falls which is not part of a personal fall protection system, Schedule 4 is complied with;

(d) a personal fall protection system, Part 1 of Schedule 5 and—

    (i) in the case of a work positioning system, Part 2 of Schedule 5;

    (ii) in the case of rope access and positioning techniques, Part 3 of Schedule 5;

    (iii) in the case of a fall arrest system, Part 4 of Schedule 5;

    (iv) in the case of a work restraint system, Part 5 of Schedule 5, are complied with; and

(e) a ladder, Schedule 6 is complied with.

Fragile surfaces

9.—(1) Every employer shall ensure that no person at work passes across or near, or works on, from or near, a fragile surface where it is reasonably practicable to carry out work safely and under appropriate ergonomic conditions without his doing so.

(2) Where it is not reasonably practicable to carry out work safely and under appropriate ergonomic conditions without passing across or near, or working on, from or near, a fragile surface, every employer shall—

  (a) ensure, so far as is reasonably practicable, that suitable and sufficient platforms, coverings, guard rails or similar means of support or protection are provided and used so that any foreseeable loading is supported by such supports or borne by such protection;

  (b) where a risk of a person at work falling remains despite the measures taken under the preceding provisions of this regulation, take suitable and sufficient measures to minimise the distances and consequences of his fall.

(3) Where any person at work may pass across or near, or work on, from or near, a fragile surface, every employer shall ensure that—

  (a) promZinent warning notices are so far as is reasonably practicable affixed at the approach to the place where the fragile surface is situated; or

  (b) where that is not reasonably practicable, such persons are made aware of it by other means.

(4) Paragraph (3) shall not apply where members of the police, fire, ambulance or other emergency services are acting in an emergency.

Falling objects

10.—(1) Every employer shall, where necessary to prevent injury to any person, take suitable and sufficient steps to prevent, so far as is reasonably practicable, the fall of any material or object.

(2) Where it is not reasonably practicable to comply with the requirements of paragraph (1), every employer shall take suitable and sufficient steps to prevent any person being struck by any falling material or object which is liable to cause personal injury.

(3) Every employer shall ensure that no material or object is thrown or tipped from height in circumstances where it is liable to cause injury to any person.

(4) Every employer shall ensure that materials and objects are stored in such a way as to prevent risk to any person arising from the collapse, overturning or unintended movement of such materials or objects.

Danger areas

11. Without prejudice to the preceding requirements of these Regulations, every employer shall ensure that—

(a) where a workplace contains an area in which, owing to the nature of the work, there is a risk of any person at work—

(i) falling a distance; or

(ii) being struck by a falling object,

which is liable to cause personal injury, the workplace is so far as is reasonably practicable equipped with devices preventing unauthorised persons from entering such area; and

(b) such area is clearly indicated.

Inspection of work equipment

12.—(1) This regulation applies only to work equipment to which regulation 8 and Schedules 2 to 6 apply.

(2) Every employer shall ensure that, where the safety of work equipment depends on how it is installed or assembled, it is not used after installation or assembly in any position unless it has been inspected in that position.

(3) Every employer shall ensure that work equipment exposed to conditions causing deterioration which is liable to result in dangerous situations is inspected—

(a) at suitable intervals; and

(b) each time that exceptional circumstances which are liable to jeopardise the safety of the work equipment have occurred,

to ensure that health and safety conditions are maintained and that any deterioration can be detected and remedied in good time.

(4) Without prejudice to paragraph (2), every employer shall ensure that a working platform—

(a) used for construction work; and

(b) from which a person could fall 2 metres or more,

is not used in any position unless it has been inspected in that position or, in the case of a mobile working platform, inspected on the site, within the previous 7 days.

(5) Every employer shall ensure that no work equipment, other than lifting equipment to which the requirement in regulation 9(4) of the Lifting Operations and Lifting Equipment Regulations 1998[8] ("LOLER") applies—

(a) leaves his undertaking; or

(b) if obtained from the undertaking of another person, is used in his undertaking,

unless it is accompanied by physical evidence that the last inspection required to be carried out under this regulation has been carried out.

(6) Every employer shall ensure that the result of an inspection under this regulation is recorded and, subject to paragraph (8), kept until the next inspection under this regulation is recorded.

(7) A person carrying out an inspection of work equipment to which paragraph (4) applies shall—

(a) before the end of the working period within which the inspection is completed, prepare a report containing the particulars set out in Schedule 7; and

(b) within 24 hours of completing the inspection, provide the report or a copy thereof to the person on whose behalf the inspection was carried out.

(8) An employer receiving a report or copy under paragraph (7) shall keep the report or a copy thereof—

(a) at the site where the inspection was carried out until the construction work is completed; and

(b) thereafter at an office of his for 3 months.

(9) Where a thorough examination has been made of lifting equipment under regulation 9 of LOLER—

(a) it shall for the purposes of this regulation, other than paragraphs (7) and (8), be treated as an inspection of the lifting equipment; and

(b) the making under regulation 10 of LOLER of a report of such examination shall for the purposes of paragraph (6) of this regulation be treated as the recording of the inspection.

(10) In this regulation"inspection", subject to paragraph (9)—

(a) means such visual or more rigorous inspection by a competent person as is appropriate for safety purposes;

(b) includes any testing appropriate for those purposes,

and "inspected" shall be construed accordingly.

Inspection of places of work at height

13. Every employer shall so far as is reasonably practicable ensure that the surface and every parapet, permanent rail or other such fall protection measure of every place of work at height are checked on each occasion before the place is used.

Duties of persons at work

14.—(1) Every person shall, where working under the control of another person, report to that person any activity or defect relating to work at height which he knows is likely to endanger the safety of himself or another person.

(2) Every person shall use any work equipment or safety device provided to him for work at height by his employer, or by a person under whose control he works, in accordance with—

    (a) any training in the use of the work equipment or device concerned which have been received by him; and

    (b) the instructions respecting that use which have been provided to him by that employer or person in compliance with the requirements and prohibitions imposed upon that employer or person by or under the relevant statutory provisions.

Exemption by the Health and Safety Executive

15.—(1) Subject to paragraph (2), the Health and Safety Executive ("the Executive") may, by a certificate in writing, exempt—

    (a) any person or class of persons;

    (b) any premises or class of premises;

    (c) any work equipment; or

    (d) any work activity,

from the requirements imposed by paragraph 3(a) and (c) of Schedule 2, and any such exemption may be granted subject to conditions and to a limit of time and may be revoked at any time by a certificate in writing.

(2) The Executive shall not grant any such exemption unless, having regard to the circumstances of the case and in particular to—

    (a) the conditions, if any, which it proposes to attach to the exemption; and

    (b) any other requirements imposed by or under any enactments which apply to the case,

it is satisfied that the health and safety of persons who are likely to be affected by the exemption will not be prejudiced in consequence of it.

Exemption for the armed forces

16.—(1) Subject to paragraph (2), the Secretary of State for Defence may, in the interests of national security, by a certificate in writing exempt any person or class of persons from any requirement or prohibition imposed by these Regulations in respect of activities carried out in the interests of national security, and any such exemption may be granted subject to conditions and may be revoked by the Secretary of State by a certificate in writing at any time.

(2) The Secretary of State shall not grant any such exemption unless he is satisfied that the health and safety of the employees concerned are ensured as far as possible in the light of the objectives of these Regulations.

Amendment of the Provision and Use of Work Equipment Regulations 1998

17. There shall be added to regulation 6(5) of the Provision and Use of Work Equipment Regulations 1998[9] the following sub-paragraph—

"(f) work equipment to which regulation 12 of the Work at Height Regulations 2005 applies".

Repeal of section 24 of the Factories Act 1961

18. Section 24 of the Factories Act 1961[10] is repealed.

Revocation of instruments

19. The instruments specified in column 1 of Schedule 8 are revoked to the extent specified in column 3 of that Schedule.

Signed by authority of the Secretary of State

Jane Kennedy

Minister of State,

Department for Work and Pensions

16th March 2005

Regulation 6(4)(a)

Schedule 1 Requirements for existing places of work and means of access or egress at height

Every existing place of work or means of access or egress at height shall—

(a) be stable and of sufficient strength and rigidity for the purpose for which it is intended to be or is being used;
(b) where applicable, rest on a stable, sufficiently strong surface;
(c) be of sufficient dimensions to permit the safe passage of persons and the safe use of any plant or materials required to be used and to provide a safe working area having regard to the work to be carried out there;
(d) possess suitable and sufficient means for preventing a fall;
(e) possess a surface which has no gap—
   (i) through which a person could fall;
   (ii) through which any material or object could fall and injure a person; or
   (iii) giving rise to other risk of injury to any person, unless measures have been taken to protect persons against such risk;

(f) be so constructed and used, and maintained in such condition, as to prevent, so far as is reasonably practicable—
   (i) the risk of slipping or tripping; or
   (ii) any person being caught between it and any adjacent structure;

(g) where it has moving parts, be prevented by appropriate devices from moving inadvertently during work at height.

Regulation 8(A)

Schedule 2 Requirements for guard-rails, toe-boards, barriers and similar collective means of protection

1. Unless the context otherwise requires, any reference in this Schedule to means of protection is to a guard-rail, toe-board, barrier or similar collective means of protection.
2. Means of protection shall—

(a) be of sufficient dimensions, of sufficient strength and rigidity for the purposes for which they are being used, and otherwise suitable;
(b) be so placed, secured and used as to ensure, so far as is reasonably practicable, that they do not become accidentally displaced; and
(c) be so placed as to prevent, so far as is practicable, the fall of any person, or of any material or object, from any place of work.

3. In relation to work at height involved in construction work—

(a) the top guard-rail or other similar means of protection shall be at least 950 millimetres or, in the case of such means of protection already fixed at the coming into force of these Regulations, at least 910 millimetres above the edge from which any person is liable to fall;

(b) toe-boards shall be suitable and sufficient to prevent the fall of any person, or any material or object, from any place of work; and

(c) any intermediate guard-rail or similar means of protection shall be positioned so that any gap between it and other means of protection does not exceed 470 millimetres.

4. Any structure or part of a structure which supports means of protection or to which means of protection are attached shall be of sufficient strength and suitable for the purpose of such support or attachment.

5.—(1) Subject to sub-paragraph (2), there shall not be a lateral opening in means of protection save at a point of access to a ladder or stairway where an opening is necessary.

(2) Means of protection shall be removed only for the time and to the extent necessary to gain access or egress or for the performance of a particular task and shall be replaced as soon as practicable.

(3) The task shall not be performed while means of protection are removed unless effective compensatory safety measures are in place.

Regulation 8(b)

Schedule 3 Requirements for working platforms

Part 1: Requirements for all working platforms

Interpretation

1. In this Schedule, "supporting structure" means any structure used for the purpose of supporting a working platform and includes any plant used for that purpose.

Condition of surfaces

2. Any surface upon which any supporting structure rests shall be stable, of sufficient strength and of suitable composition safely to support the supporting structure, the working platform and any loading intended to be placed on the working platform.

Stability of supporting structure

3. Any supporting structure shall—

(a) be suitable and of sufficient strength and rigidity for the purpose for which it is being used;

(b) in the case of a wheeled structure, be prevented by appropriate devices from moving inadvertently during work at height;

(c) in other cases, be prevented from slipping by secure attachment to the bearing surface or to another structure, provision of an effective anti-slip device or by other means of equivalent effectiveness;

(d) be stable while being erected, used and dismantled; and

(e) when altered or modified, be so altered or modified as to ensure that it remains stable.

Stability of working platforms

4. A working platform shall—

(a) be suitable and of sufficient strength and rigidity for the purpose or purposes for which it is intended to be used or is being used;

(b) be so erected and used as to ensure that its components do not become accidentally displaced so as to endanger any person;

(c) when altered or modified, be so altered or modified as to ensure that it remains stable; and

(d) be dismantled in such a way as to prevent accidental displacement.

Safety on working platforms

5. A working platform shall—

(a) be of sufficient dimensions to permit the safe passage of persons and the safe use of any plant or materials required to be used and to provide a safe working area having regard to the work being carried out there;

(b) possess a suitable surface and, in particular, be so constructed that the surface of the working platform has no gap—
 (i) through which a person could fall;
 (ii) through which any material or object could fall and injure a person; or
 (iii) giving rise to other risk of injury to any person, unless measures have been taken to protect persons against such risk; and

(c) be so erected and used, and maintained in such condition, as to prevent, so far as is reasonably practicable—
 (i) the risk of slipping or tripping; or
 (ii) any person being caught between the working platform and any adjacent structure.

Loading

6. A working platform and any supporting structure shall not be loaded so as to give rise to a risk of collapse or to any deformation which could affect its safe use.

Part 2: Additional requirements for scaffolding

Additional requirements for scaffolding

7. Strength and stability calculations for scaffolding shall be carried out unless—

(a) a note of the calculations, covering the structural arrangements contemplated, is available; or
(b) it is assembled in conformity with a generally recognised standard configuration.

8. Depending on the complexity of the scaffolding selected, an assembly, use and dismantling plan shall be drawn up by a competent person. This may be in the form of a standard plan, supplemented by items relating to specific details of the scaffolding in question.

9. A copy of the plan, including any instructions it may contain, shall be kept available for the use of persons concerned in the assembly, use, dismantling or alteration of scaffolding until it has been dismantled.

10. The dimensions, form and layout of scaffolding decks shall be appropriate to the nature of the work to be performed and suitable for the loads to be carried and permit work and passage in safety.

11. While a scaffold is not available for use, including during its assembly, dismantling or alteration, it shall be marked with general warning signs in accordance with the Health and Safety (Safety Signs and Signals) Regulations 1996[11] and be suitably delineated by physical means preventing access to the danger zone.

12. Scaffolding may be assembled, dismantled or significantly altered only under the supervision of a competent person and by persons who have received appropriate and specific training in the operations envisaged which addresses specific risks which the operations may entail and precautions to be taken, and more particularly in—

(a) understanding of the plan for the assembly, dismantling or alteration of the scaffolding concerned;
(b) safety during the assembly, dismantling or alteration of the scaffolding concerned;
(c) measures to prevent the risk of persons, materials or objects falling;
(d) safety measures in the event of changing weather conditions which could adversely affect the safety of the scaffolding concerned;
(e) permissible loadings;

(f) any other risks which the assembly, dismantling or alteration of the scaffolding may entail.

Regulation 8(c)

Schedule 4 Requirements for collective safeguards for arresting falls

1. Any reference in this Schedule to a safeguard is to a collective safeguard
for arresting falls.
2. A safeguard shall be used only if—

(a) a risk assessment has demonstrated that the work activity can so far as
is reasonably practicable be performed safely while using it and without
affecting its effectiveness;
(b) the use of other, safer work equipment is not reasonably practicable; and
(c) a sufficient number of available persons have received adequate training
specific to the safeguard, including rescue procedures.

3. A safeguard shall be suitable and of sufficient strength to arrest safely the
fall of any person who is liable to fall.
4. A safeguard shall—

(a) in the case of a safeguard which is designed to be attached, be securely
attached to all the required anchors, and the anchors and the means of
attachment thereto shall be suitable and of sufficient strength and stability
for the purpose of safely supporting the foreseeable loading in arresting
any fall and during any subsequent rescue;
(b) in the case of an airbag, landing mat or similar safeguard, be stable; and
(c) in the case of a safeguard which distorts in arresting a fall, afford sufficient clearance.

5. Suitable and sufficient steps shall be taken to ensure, so far as practicable,
that in the event of a fall by any person the safeguard does not itself cause
injury to that person.

Regulation 8(d)

Schedule 5 Requirements for personal fall protection systems

Part 1: Requirements for all personal fall protection systems

1. A personal fall protection system shall be used only if—

(a)   a risk assessment has demonstrated that—
   (i)   the work can so far as is reasonably practicable be performed safely while using that system; and
   (ii)   the use of other, safer work equipment is not reasonably practicable; and

(b)   the user and a sufficient number of available persons have received adequate training specific to the operations envisaged, including rescue procedures.

2. A personal fall protection system shall—

(a)   be suitable and of sufficient strength for the purposes for which it is being used having regard to the work being carried out and any foreseeable loading;
(b)   where necessary, fit the user;
(c)   be correctly fitted;
(d)   be designed to minimise injury to the user and, where necessary, be adjusted to prevent the user falling or slipping from it, should a fall occur; and
(e)   be so designed, installed and used as to prevent unplanned or uncontrolled movement of the user.

3. A personal fall protection system designed for use with an anchor shall be securely attached to at least one anchor, and each anchor and the means of attachment thereto shall be suitable and of sufficient strength and stability for the purpose of supporting any foreseeable loading.

4. Suitable and sufficient steps shall be taken to prevent any person falling or slipping from a personal fall protection system.

Part 2: Additional requirements for work positioning systems

A work positioning system shall be used only if either—

(a)   the system includes a suitable backup system for preventing or arresting a fall; and
(b)   where the system includes a line as a backup system, the user is connected to it; or
(c)   where it is not reasonably practicable to comply with sub-paragraph (a), all practicable measures are taken to ensure that the work positioning system does not fail.

Part 3: Additional requirements for rope access and positioning techniques

1. A rope access or positioning technique shall be used only if—

(a)   subject to paragraph 3, it involves a system comprising at least two separately anchored lines, of which one ("the working line") is used as a means of access, egress and support and the other is the safety line;

(b) the user is provided with a suitable harness and is connected by it to the working line and the safety line;

(c) the working line is equipped with safe means of ascent and descent and has a self-locking system to prevent the user falling should he lose control of his movements; and

(d) the safety line is equipped with a mobile fall protection system which is connected to and travels with the user of the system.

2. Taking the risk assessment into account and depending in particular on the duration of the job and the ergonomic constraints, provision must be made for a seat with appropriate accessories.

3. The system may comprise a single rope where—

(a) a risk assessment has demonstrated that the use of a second line would entail higher risk to persons; and

(b) appropriate measures have been taken to ensure safety.

Part 4: Additional requirements for fall arrest systems

1. A fall arrest system shall incorporate a suitable means of absorbing energy and limiting the forces applied to the user's body.

2. A fall arrest system shall not be used in a manner—

(a) which involves the risk of a line being cut;

(b) where its safe use requires a clear zone (allowing for any pendulum effect), which does not afford such zone; or

(c) which otherwise inhibits its performance or renders its use unsafe.

Part 5: Additional requirements for work restraint systems

A work restraint system shall—

(a) be so designed that, if used correctly, it prevents the user from getting into a position in which a fall can occur; and

(b) be used correctly.

Regulation 8(e)

Schedule 6 Requirements for ladders

1. Every employer shall ensure that a ladder is used for work at height only if a risk assessment under regulation 3 of the Management Regulations has demonstrated that the use of more suitable work equipment is not justified because of the low risk and—

(a) the short duration of use; or

(b) existing features on site which he cannot alter.

2. Any surface upon which a ladder rests shall be stable, firm, of sufficient strength and of suitable composition safely to support the ladder so that its rungs or steps remain horizontal, and any loading intended to be placed on it.

3. A ladder shall be so positioned as to ensure its stability during use.

4. A suspended ladder shall be attached in a secure manner and so that, with the exception of a flexible ladder, it cannot be displaced and swinging is prevented.

5. A portable ladder shall be prevented from slipping during use by—

(a) securing the stiles at or near their upper or lower ends;
(b) an effective anti-slip or other effective stability device; or
(c) any other arrangement of equivalent effectiveness.

6. A ladder used for access shall be long enough to protrude sufficiently above the place of landing to which it provides access, unless other measures have been taken to ensure a firm handhold.

7. No interlocking or extension ladder shall be used unless its sections are prevented from moving relative to each other while in use.

8. A mobile ladder shall be prevented from moving before it is stepped on.

9. Where a ladder or run of ladders rises a vertical distance of 9 metres or more above its base, there shall, where reasonably practicable, be provided at suitable intervals sufficient safe landing areas or rest platforms.

10. Every ladder shall be used in such a way that—

(a) a secure handhold and secure support are always available to the user; and
(b) the user can maintain a safe handhold when carrying a load unless, in the case of a step ladder, the maintenance of a handhold is not practicable when a load is carried, and a risk assessment under regulation 3 of the Management Regulations has demonstrated that the use of a stepladder is justified because of—
  (i) the low risk; and
  (ii) the short duration of use.

Regulation 12(7)

Schedule 7 Particulars to be included in a report of inspection

1. The name and address of the person for whom the inspection was carried out.

2. The location of the work equipment inspected.

3. A description of the work equipment inspected.

4. The date and time of the inspection.

5. Details of any matter identified that could give rise to a risk to the health or safety of any person.

6. Details of any action taken as a result of any matter identified in paragraph 5.

7. Details of any further action considered necessary.

8. The name and position of the person making the report.

Regulation 19

Schedule 8 Revocation of instruments

(1)	(2)	(3)
Description of instrument	*Reference*	*Extent of revocation*
The Shipbuilding and Ship-repairing Regulations 1960	S.I. 1960/1932, amended by S.I. 1983/644 and 1998/2307	Regulations 7 to 10 and 12 to 30
The Docks, Shipbuilding etc. (Metrication) Regulations 1983	S.I. 1983/644	In the Schedule the entries relating to regulations 9(1)(a) to 26(1) of the Shipbuilding and Ship-repairing Regulations 1960
The Docks Regulations 1988	S.I. 1988/1655	Regulation 7(4) and (5); in regulation 7(6) the words "and (c) any other place not being a quay or jetty where any person working or passing might fall a distance of more than 2 metres"
The Loading and Unloading of Fishing Vessels Regulations 1988	S.I. 1988/1656	In regulation 5(3) the words "and (c) any other place not being a quay where any person working or passing might fall a distance of more than two metres"
The Workplace (Health, Safety and Welfare) Regulations 1992	S.I. 1992/3004	Regulation 13(1) to (4)
The Construction (Health, Safety and Welfare) Regulations 1996	S.I.1996/1592	In regulation 2(1), the definitions of "fragile material", "personal suspension equipment" and "working platform"; regulations 6 to 8; in regulation 29(2) the word "scaffold" in both instances; regulation 30(5) and (6)(a); Schedules 1 to 5; and the entry first mentioned in columns 1 and 2 of Schedule 7

Index